T0134994

Web-Scale Data Management for the Cloud

Wolfgang Lehner • Kai-Uwe Sattler

Web-Scale Data Management for the Cloud

 Springer

Wolfgang Lehner
Dresden University of Technology
Dresden, Germany

Kai-Uwe Sattler
Ilmenau University of Technology
Ilmenau, Germany

ISBN 978-1-4899-9771-5   ISBN 978-1-4614-6856-1 (eBook)
DOI 10.1007/978-1-4614-6856-1
Springer New York Heidelberg Dordrecht London

© Springer Science+Business Media New York 2013
Softcover re-print of the Hardcover 1st edition 2013
This work is subject to copyright. All rights are reserved by the Publisher, whether the whole or part of the material is concerned, specifically the rights of translation, reprinting, reuse of illustrations, recitation, broadcasting, reproduction on microfilms or in any other physical way, and transmission or information storage and retrieval, electronic adaptation, computer software, or by similar or dissimilar methodology now known or hereafter developed. Exempted from this legal reservation are brief excerpts in connection with reviews or scholarly analysis or material supplied specifically for the purpose of being entered and executed on a computer system, for exclusive use by the purchaser of the work. Duplication of this publication or parts thereof is permitted only under the provisions of the Copyright Law of the Publisher's location, in its current version, and permission for use must always be obtained from Springer. Permissions for use may be obtained through RightsLink at the Copyright Clearance Center. Violations are liable to prosecution under the respective Copyright Law.
The use of general descriptive names, registered names, trademarks, service marks, etc. in this publication does not imply, even in the absence of a specific statement, that such names are exempt from the relevant protective laws and regulations and therefore free for general use.
While the advice and information in this book are believed to be true and accurate at the date of publication, neither the authors nor the editors nor the publisher can accept any legal responsibility for any errors or omissions that may be made. The publisher makes no warranty, express or implied, with respect to the material contained herein.

Printed on acid-free paper

Springer is part of Springer Science+Business Media (www.springer.com)

This book is dedicated to our families – this book would not have been possible without their constant and comprehensive support.

Preface

The efficient management of data is a core asset of almost every organization. Data is collected, stored, manipulated, and analysed to drive the business and derive support for the decision making process. Establishing and running the data management platform within a larger organization is a complex, time- and budget-intensive tasks. Not only do data management systems have to be installed, deployed, and populated with different sets of data. The data management platform of an organization has to constantly maintained on a technical as well as on a content level. Changing applications and business requirements have to be reflected within the technical setup, new software versions have to be installed, hardware has to be exchanged etc. Although the benefit of an efficient data management platform can be enormous not only in terms of a direct controlling of the business or a competitive advantage but also in terms of strategic advantages, the technical challenges are enormous to keep a data management machinery running.

In the age of "Everything-as-a-Service" using cloud-based solutions, it is fair enough to question on-premise data management installations and consider "Software-as-a-Service" an alternative or complementary concept for system platforms to run (parts of) a larger data management solution. Within this book, we tackle this question to give answers to some of the huge number of different facets, which have to be considered in this context. We will therefore review the general concept of the "Everything-as-a-Service" paradigm and discuss situations where this concept may fit perfectly or where the concept is only well-suited for specific scenarios. The book will also review the general relationship between cloud computing on the one hand and data management on the other hand. We will also outline the impact of being able to perform data management on a web-scale as one of the key challenges and also requirements for future commercial data management platforms.

In order to provide a comprehensive understanding of data management services in the large, we will introduce the notion of virtualization as one of the key techniques to establish the "Everything-as-a-Service"-paradigm. Virtualization can be exploited on a physical and logical layer to abstract from specific hardware software environments providing an additional indirection layer which can be used to differentiate between services or components running remotely in cloud environments or locally within a totally controlled system and administration setup. Chapter 2 will therefore discuss different techniques ranging from low-level machine virtualization to application-aware virtualization techniques on schema and application level.

In the following two chapters, we dive into detail while discussing different methods and technologies to run web-scale data management services with special emphasis on operational or analytical workloads. Operational workload on the one hand usually consists of highly concurrent accesses to the same database with conflict potential resulting in a requirement of transactional behavior of the data management service. Analytical workloads on the other hand usually touch hundreds of million of rows within a single query feeding complex statistical models or produce the raw material for sophisticated cockpit applications within larger Business Intelligence environments. Due to the completely different nature of using a data management system, we take a detailed look with respect to the individual scenarios. The first part (Chap. 3) addressing challenges and solutions for transactional workload patterns focuses on consistency models, data fragmentation, and data replication schemes for large web-scale data management scenarios. The second part (Chap. 4) outlines the major techniques and challenges to efficiently handle analytics in big data scenarios by discussing pros and cons of the MapReduce data processing paradigm and presenting different query languages to directly interact with the data management platform.

Cloud-based services do not only offer an efficient data processing framework by providing a specific degree of consistency but also comprise non-functional services like considering quality of service agreements or adhere to certain security and privacy constraints. In Chap. 5, we will outline the core requirements and provide insights into some already existing approaches. In a final step, the book gives the reader a state-of-the-art overview of currently available "everything-as-a-service"-implementations or commercial services with respect to infrastructural services, platform services or within the context of software as a service.

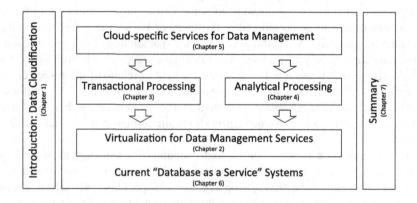

The book closes with an outlook on challenges and open research questions in the context of providing a data management solution following the "as-a-service"-paradigm. Within this discussion, we reflect the different discussion points and outline future directions for a wide and open field of research potential and commercial opportunities.

The overall structure of the book is reflected in the accompanying figure. Since the individual sections are – with the exception of the general introduction – independent of each other, readers are encouraged to jump into the middle of the book or use a different path to capture the presented material. After having read the book, the readers should have a deep understanding of the requirements and existing solutions to establish and operate an efficient data management platform following the "as-a-service"-paradigm.

Dresden, Germany   Wolfgang Lehner
Ilmenau, Germany   Kai-Uwe Sattler

Acknowledgements

Like every book written in addition to the regular life as university professor, this manuscript would not have been possible without the help of quite a few members of the active research community. We highly appreciate the effort and would like to thank all of them!

- Volker Markl and Felix Naumann helped us to start the adventure of writing such a book. We highly appreciate their comments on the general outline and their continuing support.
- Florian Kerschbaum who authored the section on security in outsourced data management environments (Sect. 5.3). Thanks for tackling this especially for commercial applications highly relevant topic. We are very grateful.
- The thanks to Maik Thiele goes for authoring significant parts of the introductory chapter of this book. Maik did a wonderful job in spanning the global context and providing a comprehensive and well-structured overview. He also authored the section on Open Data as an example of "Data-as-a-Service" in Sect. 6.3.
- Tim Kiefer and Hannes Voigt covered major parts of the virtualization section. While Tim was responsible for the virtualization stack (Sect. 2.2) and partially for the section on hardware virtualization (Sect. 2.3), Hannes was in charge for the material describing the core concepts for logical virtualization (Sect. 2.4).
- Daniel Warneke contributed the sections on "Infrastructure-as-a-Service" and "Platform-as-a-service" in Chap. 6; Thanks for this very good overview!
- The section on "Web-Scale Analytics" (Chap. 4) was mainly authored by Stephan Ewen and Alexander Alexandrov. Stephan contributed the foundations and the description of the core principles of MapReduce. Alexander gave the overview on declarative query languages. A big Thank You goes to those colleagues!

Last but definitely not at least goes our largest "THANK YOU" to our families. Every minute spent on this book is a loss of family time! We promise compensation.

Acknowledgements

Contents

Chapter 1
Data Cloudification

Although we already live in a world of data, we just see the tip of an iceberg. Data is everywhere and decisions based on large data sets are driving not only business related but more and more personal decisions. The challenges are enormous and range from technical questions on how to setup and run an efficient and cost-effective data management platform to security and privacy concerns to prevent the loss of personal self-determination. Within this section, we present the general setup of the "-as-a-Service"-paradigm and discuss certain facets of data management solutions to cope with the existing and upcoming challenges.

1.1 Big Data, Big Problems

Over the last years the world collected an astonishing amount of digital information. This particularly applies to data collected and generated within modern web applications which leads to unprecedented challenges in data and information management. Search engines such as Google, Bing or Yahoo! collect and store billions of web documents and click trails of their users in order to improve the search results. For example, in 2008 Google alone processed 20 PB of data every day. Auctions on eBay, blogs at Wordpress, postings or pictures shared on Facebook, media content on YouTube or Flickr, all these modern social web applications generate an enormous amount of data day by day. Each minute, 15 h of video are uploaded to YouTube, eBay collects 50 TB/day of user data and 40 billion photos are hosted by Facebook. Additionally, the way people communicate about social media such as blogs, videos or photos creates even more data which is extremely valuable for statistical analyses like sentiment analysis procedures, user profiling for highly focused advertisement placements etc.

However, web-scale data management is not just about high-volume datasets; the respective workloads are very challenging in terms of response time, throughput, peak load, and concurrent data access: the web analytics company Quantcast

W. Lehner and K.-U. Sattler, *Web-Scale Data Management for the Cloud*,
DOI 10.1007/978-1-4614-6856-1_1, © Springer Science+Business Media New York 2013

estimated between 100 and 200 million monthly unique U.S. visitors in June 2012[1] for each of the "Big five" web companies Google, Facebook, YouTube, Yahoo, and Twitter. Amazon with the corresponding world-wide e-commerce platform serves millions of customers with thousands of servers located in many data centers around the world. As an e-commerce company, Amazon is exposed to extreme changes in load especially before holidays like Christmas or when offering promotions. Amazon's shopping cart service served tens of millions requests that resulted in over three million checkouts within a single day. The service managing session states handled hundreds of thousands of concurrently active sessions [9]. Bad response times or even loss of availability are absolutely not acceptable for such web services because of the direct impact on customers' trust and the companie's revenue. Tests at Amazon revealed that every 100 ms increase in response time of their e-commerce platform decreased sales by 1% [14]. Google discovered that a change from 400 ms to load a page with 10 search results to 900 ms to load a page with 30 result entries decreased ad revenues by 20% [17]. A change at Google Maps decreased the transfer volume from 100 to 70–80 KB with an increase in traffic by 10% in the first week and an additional 25% in the following 3 weeks [10].

As all these examples show, that modern web applications are subject to very strict operational requirements in terms of availability, performance, reliability, and efficiency. Regarding the Amazon example, customers should be able to view and add items to their shopping cart even if disks are failing, network routes are flapping, or data centers are being destroyed by natural disasters [9]. In addition, web-scale data management systems must be designed to support continuous growth which calls for highly scalable architectures. At the same time, we have to avoid an over-provisioning with resources and an underutilization of hardware assets.

These operational aspects of web-scale data management reflect only one side of the medal (Fig. 1.1). The other side of the medal addresses web-scale data analytics in order to get full value out of the massive amounts of data already collected by web companies. Good examples for such "data-centric economies" are Facebook or Twitter where the business models completely rely on social content processing and analytics. Another famous example is Google Search which covered about 47 billion web pages in July 2012.[2] These pages need to be analyzed regarding term frequencies, inbound and outbound links as well as number of visits which are somehow integrated into the final search index. Performing data analysis at such high volume web data in a timely fashion demands a high degree of parallelism. For example, reading a Terabyte of compressed data from secondary storage in 1 s would require more than 10,000 commodity disks [20]. Similarly, compute-intensive calculations may need to run on thousands of processors to complete in a timely manner. In order to cope with such data-intensive and compute-intensive problems, web companies started to build shared clusters of commodity machines around the world. On top of these clusters they implemented file systems like GFS

---

[1]http://www.quantcast.com/top-sites/US/.

[2]http://www.worldwidewebsize.com/.

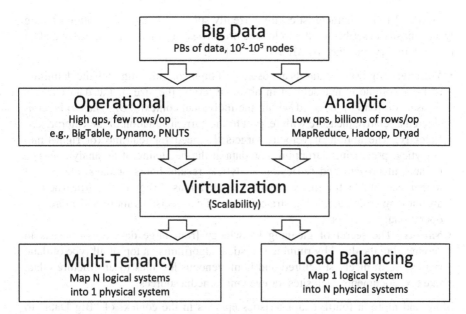

Fig. 1.1 Web-scale data management – overview [19]

(Google File System) or HDFS (Hadoop File System) to efficiently partition the data as well as compute frameworks like MapReduce or Hadoop to massively distribute the computation (see Chap. 4). Since the introduction of the MapReduce programming model at Google in 2003 more than 10,000 distinct programs have been implemented using MapReduce at Google, including algorithms for large-scale graph processing, text processing, machine learning, and statistical machine translation [8].

Designing and operating such web-scale data management systems used by millions of people around the world provides some very unique and difficult challenges. All of them are very data-intensive and have to deal with massive amounts of data up to several Petabytes which will continue to rise. The data processing itself can be distinguished into an operational and an analytical mode, both with different implications. The operational data management requires to concurrently query and manipulate data while ensuring properties such as atomicity and consistency. The number of queries in such scenarios is very high (hundreds of thousands of concurrent sessions) whereas the data touched by these queries is very small (point queries). In the opposite, the number of queries in the analytical scenarios is comparatively low and concurrent updates are the exception. Instead, analytical queries tend to be very data- and compute-intensive. The design of both types of data management systems has to consider unforeseen access patterns and peak loads which call for highly scalable and elastic architectures. To make things even more complicated, the design has to anticipate the heterogeneous, error-prone, and distributed hardware platform consisting of thousands of commodity server nodes. We will elaborate on this aspect in more detail in the following sections.

Some of those characteristics are currently subsumed under the notion of "Big Data", mostly described by the following properties, originally introduced in a 2001 research report published by META Group [16]:

- **Volume:** "Big Data"-datasets are usually of high volume. Although the definition of high volume is not defined in absolute terms, the size of the data exceeds datasets currently processed within the individual context. "Big" has to be considered a relative measure with respect to the current situation of the enterprise.
- **Velocity:** The notion of velocity targets the need for realtime (or right-time) analytical processing. Dropping raw data at the beginning of an analytical data refinement process and retrieving analytical results hours or days later is not longer acceptable for many business applications. "Big data" infrastructures are moving from supporting strategic or tactical decisions more and more into operational processes.
- **Variety:** The secret of gleaning knowledge from large databases consists in "connecting the dots" by running statistical algorithms on top of all type of data, starting from nicely structured and homogeneous log files to unstructured data like text documents, web sites, or even multimedia sources.

More and more, a fourth characteristics appears in the context of "Big Data" to comprise the core requirements of classical data-warehouse environments:

- **Veracity:** The property of veracity within the "Big Data" discussion addresses the need to establish a "Big Data" infrastructure as the central information hub of an enterprise. The "Big Data" datastore represents the single version of truth and requires substantial governance and quality controls. The discussion to support "veracity" clearly shows that – especially in commercial enterprise environments – "Big Data" infrastructure are making inroads into core operations systems and processes.

To put it into a nutshell, the design of operational and analytical web-scale data management systems requires to make complex tradeoffs in a number of dimensions, e.g. number of queries, response latency, update frequency, availability, reliability, consistency, error probability, and many more. In the remainder of the section, we will provide additional context for understanding these dimensions as well as their mutual dependencies and will give profound knowledge in order to build such systems.

1.2   Classic Database Solutions as an Alternative

In the previous section we briefly outlined the challenges in building large-scale data management systems in the context of web applications. However, we still have to answer the following question: Why not just use a given commercial database solution (DBMS) in order to build web-scale data management systems? Obviously there are many "right" answers going into different directions. One of the usually provided answers is that the scale required in web applications scenarios is too large for most relational databases, designed from an implementation and conceptual point of view to store and process only a low number of Terabytes. Classical database architectures are not able to scale to hundreds or thousands of loosely coupled machines. The answers continue. For example, the cost for building and operating a large-scale database system with thousands of nodes would be just too high. Paying software licence costs, installing different servers, administrating the individual database instances for each of the million server nodes running at Google would be an unthinkable effort. Furthermore, many data web services, e.g. Amazon's shopping cart example, only need simple primary-key access instead of a full-fledged query processing model. The overhead of using a traditional relational database for such cases would be a limiting factor in terms of scale and availability. Therefore, the big web companies started to implement their own file systems (GFS or HDFS), distributed storage systems (Google Bigtable [6]), distributed programming frameworks (MapReduce or Hadoop), and even distributed data management systems (Amazon Dynamo [9] or Apache Cassandra [15]). These different, license-free systems can be applied easily across many different web-scale data management projects for very low incremental cost. Additionally low-level storage optimizations are much easier to implement compared to traditional database systems.

Obviously, different directions of database research and development already tackle the indicated problems of classical DBMS. Multiple approaches exist to implement a best-of-bread-approach by reusing existing DBMS technology and combining it with additional layers on top in an attempt to achieve scalability. HadoopDB [1] for example is such an approach providing a hybrid engine between PostgreSQL and Hadoop.

Looking especially at web-scale data analytics there is another difference between traditional DBMS and the new programming models like MapReduce (Sect. 4.1.2). Many developers coming from the web community are entrenched procedural programmers who find the declarative SQL style to be unnatural [22] but feel very comfortable with MapReduce-like procedural languages. Nevertheless, the MapReduce paradigm is often too low-level and rigid which makes it hard to optimize, to maintain, and to reuse. To get the best of both worlds, there are some projects which provide a higher-level language and a compiler that takes this higher-level specifications and translates them into MapReduce jobs. Section 4.3 reviews some popular projects going in that direction.

The demand for highly scalable architectures led to clusters build upon low-end commodity hardware nodes which have many advantages compared to high-end shared memory systems. First, they are significantly more cost-efficient, since low-end server platforms share many key components with the high-volume PC market and therefore benefit more substantially from the principle of economy of scale [12]. Second, it is very convenient to scale-out the capacity of a web-scale data management application by easily adding more servers. Scaling up a high-end shared memory system is much more difficult and cost-intensive depending on the resource bottleneck (CPU, memory or storage throughput). Third, a cluster of commodity hardware nodes already facilitates all aspects of automation and simplifies the failure handling. If a server looks suspicious, it can be swapped out and only few users are affected.

Alongside these benefits, scale-out architectures also suffer from some serious problems. Frequent load balancing and capacity adjustments are required to achieve good utilization in order to avoid hardware over-provisioning and to handle temporary load peaks. Large data sets managed by a scale-out architecture have to be distributed across multiple servers which could lead to inefficiencies during query processing. Therefore, data needs to be carefully fragmented (Sect. 3.3) and partitioned (Sect. 3.4) in order to avoid shuffling around large amounts of data and to minimize inter-server communication. Guaranteeing ACID properties in highly distributed environments faced with update queries would require distributed synchronization protocols with all their disadvantages such as blocking, tight coupling of nodes, and additional processing overhead. It can be shown that for certain web data management applications, a certain amount of inconsistency can be tolerated in order to speed up updates and to ensure availability (Sect. 3.2). The limitations of scale-out architectures regarding different design criteria like consistency, availability, and partition-tolerance are considered by the CAP theorem which will be discussed in detail in Sect. 3.1.2.

The use of error-prone commodity hardware at a very large scale is not without difficulties. At any point in time there are failing server and network components, which should be exemplified by the following error log taken from a typical first year of a new cluster [7]:

- $\sim$0.5 overheating (power down most machines in <5 min, $\sim$1–2 days to recover)
- $\sim$1 PDU failure ($\sim$500–1,000 machines suddenly disappear, $\sim$6 h)
- $\sim$1 rack-move (plenty of warning, $\sim$500–1,000 machines powered down, $\sim$6 h)
- $\sim$1 network rewiring (rolling $\sim$5% of machines down over 2-day span)
- $\sim$5 racks go wonky (40–80 machines see 50% packetloss)
- $\sim$1,000 individual machine failures
- $\sim$thousands of hard drive failures slow disks, bad memory, misconfigured machines

Dealing with such failure rates in web-scale data management systems consisting of tens of thousands components is a very challenging task. Theses systems have to be designed in a manner that treats failure handling as a default case without impacting any service level agreements (Sect. 5.1). A pragmatic approach dealing with unreliable hardware, frequently used in real-live scenarios, is to heavily rely on replication (Sects. 3.4 and 4.1.3).

Given that highly scalable architecture build by companies like Google, Amazon or Facebook offering in-house services in order to retrieve, store, and process data, it is a natural step to open up this platform and make them accessible to everyone. The technical implications of such a platform will be discussed in the following section.

1.3   Cloud Computing

Web-scale data management systems described in the previous sections are based on the concept of "Cloud Computing" representing on-demand access to external and virtualized IT resources shared by many consumers. More precisely, cloud computing is a model for enabling ubiquitous, convenient, on-demand network access to a shared pool of configurable computing resources (e.g., networks, servers, storage, applications, and services) that can be rapidly provisioned and released with minimal management effort or service provider interaction [23]. Looking at the server landscapes in large companies there is an increasing trend in outsourcing locally installed and maintained hardware and applications to the cloud, i.e. going from so-called software on-premise to software on-demand.

The trend is generally being fueled by the chance to lower the spendings for IT services. On the one hand, capital expenditures (CapEx) can be avoided because there is no need to provide data centers on premise anymore. Instead, the outsourced IT resources fall into ongoing operating expenditures (OpEx). On the other hand, there is a real reduction of costs because large, centralized cloud data centers can be operated much more cost-efficiently compared to a small enterprise data center. The servers, networking equipment, data storage, power, floor space etc. can result in a enormous start-up costs especially for smaller companies. Additionally, operating a data center is a difficult job and needs skilled IT staff, which demands further investments. Cloud computing infrastructure is shared across many projects and customers, providing economies of scale at all involved resources. Since real world estimates of average server utilization in data centers range from 5 to 20% [3], cloud infrastructure represent an important step forward. For example, Amazon as one of the first players in the cloud computing market found that they used only 10% of their capacity at certain points in time which led to launch of Amazon Web Service (AWS) in 2006.

Looking at the most common definitions of cloud computing provided by literature [23, 24, 27] we can identify the following key characteristics:

- **On-demand access:** Consumers' demand for computing resources can be fulfilled instantly and automatically without human intervention.
- **Resource pooling:** The cloud computing resources, e.g. CPU, storage, processing capacity, are pooled to several customers using hardware virtualization (Sect. 2.3) and multi-tenancy (Sect. 2.4).
- **Network accessibility:** All computing resources are available over the network that allows data exchange between customers and resources and the resources itself.
- **Abstracted infrastructure:** All resources of a cloud system provide an abstract service interface. The exact location or details about the underlying hardware resource are hidden from the user. Instead, the cloud computing platform provides transparency using performance metrics (the notion of cloud SLA's is covered by Sect. 5.1).

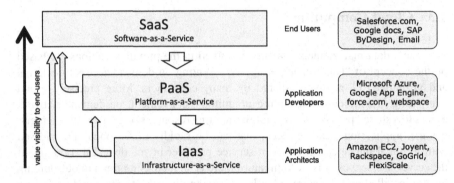

Fig. 1.2 Three cloud service models

- **Elasticity:** Computing capabilities are provided on-demand when needed and immediately released when the work has finished. This characteristics of scaling up and down also demands virtualization.
- **Pay-per-use pricing model:** Cloud resource charges are based on the quantity used (Sect. 5.2 for economic models of cloud systems).

The types of cloud services provided to the customer can be distinguished into mainly three deployment models, whereas each model addresses a specific business need (Fig. 1.2): Infrastructure-as-a-Service (IaaS), Platform-as-a-Service (PaaS) and Software-as-a-Service (SaaS).

The concept of "Infrastructure-as-a-Service" delivers computing infrastructure as a service which is used by the customer to deploy and operate arbitrary operating systems and software. IaaS is widely used for hosting websites or to outsource complex data transformations and analytics. Amazon with it's Elastic Compute Cloud (EC2) is the largest IaaS provider. However, there are also other IaaS companies like Joyent (hosting many Facebook applications), Rackspace, GoGrid, and FlexiScale. Platform-as-a-Service reflects a combination of an infrastructure and development platform delivered in an on-demand fashion. It enables the consumers to develop their own applications without managing and operating the respective hardware and software. Examples of PaaS include Microsoft's Azure and Google's App Engine. Software-as-a-Service finally describes software which is running on a cloud infrastructure and that is deployed over the Internet. The software is accessible through standard web browser and is billed per usage. Examples include Salesforce.com, SAP ByDesign, Google Docs or Google Mail.

We will discuss specific IaaS, PaaS, and SaaS systems in Chap. 6 and compare them according their offered services, pricing models, performance characteristics, and interoperability.

Orthogonal to the main characteristics of cloud computing outlined above, there are different types of a cloud infrastructures with respect to their sphere of control or sphere of administration. The so-called *public cloud*, which is conform to the above definition, is open for everybody and owned by an organization selling cloud

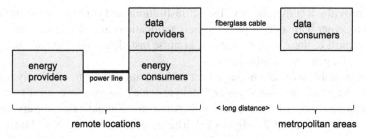

Fig. 1.3 Energy savings by building data centers near to power plants

services, e.g. Amazon EC2. This type of infrastructure offers the greatest level of resource sharing and is thus very cost-efficient. However, they are also more vulnerable than *private clouds*, which are operated solely for one company in an on-premise or off-premise manner. *Hybrid clouds* combine the best of both worlds consisting of two or more private or public clouds which are coupled by a common interface that allows data and application portability. The private cloud is intended for applications which demand security and reliability whereas the public cloud has to absorb peaks by providing "infinite" computation resources.

Beside the cost savings associated with the principle of economy of scale there is another big advantage of having centralized cloud data centers. Since the location of data centers can be more or less arbitrary, they can be moved into cold regions to save energy for cooling (e.g. Google runs data centers in Finland [21]) or close to the energy production. In case of the last option, it is far more cheaper to move photons over the fiberoptic backbone of the Internet than transmitting electrons over the power grid [4] (Fig. 1.3). Therefore energy providers and energy consumers are co-located usually in remote regions providing computing power to the data consumers sitting in metropolitan areas.

1.4 Data Management and Cloud Computing

The concept of cloud computing with its properties such on-demand access, scalability, elasticity, and pay-per-use pricing is very powerful and fills some everlasting needs within IT management. In this section we discuss whether the same principles can be applied to the field of data management which is faced with very similar problems from a 10,000 feet perspective. With applications becoming more and more data-intensive, there is an increasing demand to outsource data and to use cloud resources for complex data processing and analysis. Google, for example, is using the MapReduce programming model for distributed grep, web link-graph reversal, document clustering, and statistical machine translation [13].

Apache provides a comprehensive list[3] of institutions and companies that are using Hadoop together with a description of their applications and cluster configurations. However, most of these examples are on-premise installations that avoid most of the problems of a genuine cloud solution.

The first problem of data management in the cloud is: how to efficiently transfer data into the cloud at a Terabyte or Petabyte scale? Suppose we want to copy a 10 TB data set from a business server to Amazon's Simple Storage Service (S3) with an average speed of 20 Mbits/s [3]. The transfer of this file would take about 4 million seconds or more than 45 days and would cost about $1,000 (with $100 to $150 per TB). Therefore, already Jim Gray argued that the cheapest and in most cases even the fasted way to send high volume data is to ship whole disks [2]. This problem was already recognized by the industry offering cloud data import and export services based on portable storage devices.[4] Yet one problem remains: if an application needs to migrate data between different cloud providers they have to be very careful in terms of data placement and traffic in order to minimize transfer times and costs. Another issue in this context is the problem of data lock-in. Since every cloud provider has its proprietary storage API, it is very hard to extract and transfer data from one site to another. Therefore, the need for standardized APIs allowing to share or replicate data across several cloud providers so that a failure of a specific company does not affect the overall system is obvious. Such standards would be also very useful in order to build consistent hybrid cloud systems which need to combine different clouds. Open-source re-implementations of existing proprietary APIs, such as OpenStack, Eucalyptus or DeltaCloud, are a very first step into this direction.

The biggest concern about cloud computing which prevents many companies to go into this direction is control of ownership, security, and data privacy. The first subject refers to questions like: are you able to delete your data from a cloud storage after a job was done and what happens with your data if you fail to pay your bill [11]? The second topic, cloud security along with data privacy, also reflects one of the most complex problems and has to be addressed by a set of techniques involving different parties (cloud users, cloud vendors and third-party software vendors). Securing a cloud infrastructure from outside threats is very similar to those problems already addressed by data centers. For example, internal protection mechanisms against tenants which share the same resources are needed in a public cloud environment. In practice this is solved by virtualization techniques shielding the user from each other. However, not all resources in a database hardware and software stack can be virtualized in the same way and there are trade-offs between the degree of consolidation, performance, and privacy at each level. Virtualization on a database schema level is also referred to as multi-tenancy which is described in detail in Sect. 2.4. The most difficult issue in terms of security is the protection of the data against the cloud provider itself. When the service provider cannot be

---

[3]http://wiki.apache.org/hadoop/PoweredBy.

[4]http://aws.amazon.com/de/importexport/.

trusted, data needs to be encrypted while ensuring that this encrypted data can be queried. Therefore querying over encrypted data is challenging and requires to maintain additional content information on the consumer and the server side (Sect. 5.3 for further details). A second security issue on the provider side is the private information retrieval which should allow the customer to retrieve a data item from a cloud provider without revealing which data is retrieved. This is like buying in a store without the seller knowing what you buy and generally represents a really hard problem. Possible solutions for that will also be discussed in Sect. 5.3.

1.5 Summary

Data management is facing a new wave of relevance with extremely challenging requirements. On the one hand, "Big Data" is not only commonplace in large companies but can be generated and consumed by almost every organization using web information or sensors to record real world events in a very detailed manner. Analytical applications crawling through those massive amounts of data are of statistical nature and require significant compute power to create or evaluate analytical models. On the other hand, data management is the backbone of large application platforms to run classical business applications for hundreds or even thousands of different users following a multi-tenancy principle with strict or – in some dimensions – relaxed transactional guarantees. Large scale cluster systems with sophisticated fragmentation and replication schemes are required to cope with requirements coming from that direction.

Throughout the book, we will dive into detail with respect to the requirements and characteristics sketched in this introductory chapter. An excellent overview of cloud services in general can be found in [27] and [25]. From a more business oriented perspective, [28] is a good source for further reading. Looking more into the data management aspect of cloud solutions, [18] and [5] are definitely worth reading. Within [5], the core concepts of data services as software components to provide a simple but powerful access method to distributed data stores is outlined and might be considered a design guideline for future application development. Last but not at least, we would like to point the interested reader to [26] very nicely describing the integration of crowd computing into application environments using web infrastructures as the underlying enabling technology.

References

1. Abouzeid, A., Bajda-Pawlikowski, K., Abadi, D., Silberschatz, A., Rasin, A.: Hadoopdb: an architectural hybrid of mapreduce and dbms technologies for analytical workloads. VLDB **2**, 922–933 (2009)
2. A Conversation with Jim Gray. ACM Queue **1**(4), 8–17 (2003)

3. Armbrust, M., Fox, A., Griffith, R., Joseph, A.D., Katz, R., Konwinski, A., Lee, G., Patterson, D., Rabkin, A., Stoica, I., Zaharia, M.: A view of cloud computing. Communications of the ACM **53**, 50–58 (2010)

4. Brynjolfsson, E., Hofmann, P., Jordan, J.: Cloud computing and electricity: beyond the utility model. Communications of the ACM **53**(5), 32–34 (2010)

5. Carey, M.J., Onose, N., Petropoulos, M.: Data services. Communications of the ACM **55**(6), 86–97 (2012)

6. Chang, F., Dean, J., Ghemawat, S., Hsieh, W.C., Wallach, D.A., Burrows, M., Chandra, T., Fikes, A., Gruber, R.E.: Bigtable: a distributed storage system for structured data. In: OSDI, pp. 205–218 (2006)

7. Dean, J.: Designs, lessons and advice from building large distributed systems (2009). LADIS keynote, http://www.cs.cornell.edu/projects/ladis2009/talks/deankeynote-ladis2009.pdf

8. Dean, J., Ghemawat, S.: Mapreduce: a flexible data processing tool. Communications of the ACM **53**, 72–77 (2010)

9. DeCandia, G., Hastorun, D., Jampani, M., Kakulapati, G., Lakshman, A., Pilchin, A., Sivasubramanian, S., Vosshall, P., Vogels, W.: Dynamo: amazon's highly available key-value store. In: SOSP, pp. 205–220 (2007)

10. Farber, D.: Google's marissa mayer: Speed wins (2006). http://www.zdnet.com/blog/btl/googles-marissa-mayer-speed-wins/3925

11. Hayes, B.: Cloud computing. Communications of the ACM **51**(7), 9–11 (2008)

12. Hoelzle, U., Barroso, L.A.: The Datacenter as a Computer: An Introduction to the Design of Warehouse-Scale Machines. Morgan and Claypool Publishers (2009)

13. Jeff Dean, S.G.: Mapreduce: Simplified data processing on large clusters. http://labs.google.com/papers/mapreduce-osdi04-slides/index-auto-0005.html

14. Kohavi, R., Longbotham, R.: Online experiments: Lessons learned. Computer **40**(9), 103–105 (2007)

15. Lakshman, A., Malik, P.: Cassandra: a decentralized structured storage system. SIGOPS **44**, 35–40 (2010)

16. Laney, D.: 3D Data Management: Controlling Data Volume, Velocity, and Variety. Meta Group (2001)

17. Linden, G.: Marissa mayer at web 2.0 (2006). Geeking with Greg, http://glinden.blogspot.com/2006/11/marissa-mayer-at-web-20.html

18. Meijer, E.: All your database are belong to us. Communications of the ACM **55**(9), 54–60 (2012)

19. Melnik, S.: The frontiers of data programmability. In: BTW, pp. 5–6 (2009)

20. Melnik, S., Gubarev, A., Long, J.J., Romer, G., Shivakumar, S., Tolton, M., Vassilakis, T.: Dremel: interactive analysis of web-scale datasets. Communications of the ACM **54**, 114–123 (2011)

21. Miller, R.: Sea-cooled data center heats homes in helsinki (2011). http://www.datacenterknowledge.com/archives/2011/09/06/sea-cooled-data-center-heats-homes-in-helsinki/

22. Olston, C., Reed, B., Srivastava, U., Kumar, R., Tomkins, A.: Pig latin: a not-so-foreign language for data processing. In: Proceedings of the ACM International Conference on Management of Data (SIGMOD), pp. 1099–1110 (2008)

23. Peter Mell, T.G.: The nist definition of cloud computing (2011). National Institute of Science and Technology, http://csrc.nist.gov/publications/drafts/800-145/Draft-SP-800-145_cloud-definition.pdf

24. Rajkumar Buyya James Broberg, A.M.G.: Cloud Computing: Principles and Paradigms. John Wiley and Sons (2011)

25. Rosenberg, J., Mateos, A.: The Cloud at Your Service. Manning Publications Co. (2010)

26. Savage, N.: Gaining wisdom from crowds. Communications of the ACM **55**(3), 13–15 (2012)

27. Sosinsky, B.: Cloud Computing Bible. John Wiley and Sons (2011)

28. Weinman, J.: Cloudonomics: The Business Value of Cloud Computing. Wiley Publishing (2012)

Chapter 2
Virtualization for Data Management Services

Virtualization is the key concept to provide a scalable and flexible computing environment in general. In this chapter, we focus on virtualization concepts in the context of data management tasks. We review existing concepts and technologies spanning multiple software layers. We first start outlining the general principles of virtualization in the context of Database-as-a-Service by looking at the different layers in the software and hardware stack. Thereafter, we will dive into detail by walking through the software stack and discuss different techniques to provide virtualization at different layers. Overall, the chapter provides a comprehensive introduction and overview of virtualization concepts for data management services in large scale scenarios.

2.1 Core Concepts of Virtualization

The concept of virtualization is one of the conceptual and system architectural pillars of computer science and computer infrastructures. Virtualization in general provides a layer of indirection to build an abstract view in order to hide the specific implementation of computing resources. Creating such an indirection step between the resources and the access to the resources provides a huge variety of advantages. The decoupling hides the implementation details to the using component. It also adds flexibility and agility to the computing infrastructure to reduce capital expenditures as well as operational expenditures as already discussed in the introductory chapter. In general, the concept of virtualization can be used to solve many problems related to provisioning, manageability, security etc. by pooling and sharing computing resources, simplifying administrative and management tasks and improving fault tolerance with regard to a complex software stack. Already in

W. Lehner and K.-U. Sattler, *Web-Scale Data Management for the Cloud*,
DOI 10.1007/978-1-4614-6856-1_2, © Springer Science+Business Media New York 2013

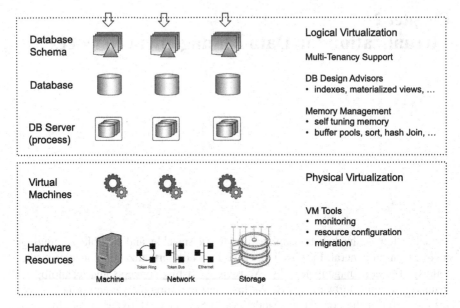

Fig. 2.1 Physical and logical virtualization in a data management service software stack

2010, IDC forecasted that "Enterprise Server Virtualization Market to Reach $19.3 Billion by 2014".[1]

While virtualization is a general concept for computing infrastructure, we will focus on data management specific views within this section. To enable data management services, we distinguish between physical and logical virtualization within the complete system stack. As shown in Fig. 2.1, we can clearly identify two different layers of physical and logical virtualization.

Physical virtualization comprises the abstract view with regard to physical devices such as computing nodes on the one side and storage systems on the other side. At the same time, all infrastructural devices like switches, routers etc., are subsumed by the virtual view of computing resources. More specifically, physical virtualization abstracts from

- **CPU:** The variety of different types of CPU, multi cores or heterogenous processors like GPU or FPGA for special purpose computing tasks are hidden by a virtual CPU.
- **Memory:** The running application does no longer see the real memory of the hardware but – similar to classical virtual memory concept of operating systems – will see only the fraction of (virtual) memory which is explicitly assigned to the

---

[1] http://www.information-management.com/news/IDC_predicts_virtualization_growth-10019216-1.html.

virtual resource. Additionally, the software does no longer have access to features like DMA (direct memory access) or memory of a graphic card.

- **Network:** The physical virtualization concept abstracts from specific network infrastructures and topologies. Load balancing at a lower level (e.g. HTTP request for web server farms) happens "behind the scenes" and therefore transparently for the application running in a virtualized computing environment.
- **Storage:** Most important for the application area of data management services, physical virtualization can also provide an abstract view of specific storage environments, e.g., to transparently perform data replication between different sites/systems or integrate heterogenous types of storage (SAN versus NAS; SSDs versus HD drives; fast versus slow devices; . . .). We will detail this kind of virtualization when considering different use cases in the remainder of this chapter.

Logical virtualization in our context addresses the abstraction on a data management level. The scope of logical virtualization comprises the following concepts:

- **Database Server:** The level of a database server provides a runtime for database services and acts as host for multiple databases with individual schemas, users, and potentially physical setups. A database may be placed at a server without any knowledge about the specific characteristics of the underlying software and (when running in a physically virtualized environment) hardware setup.
- **Database Schema and Databases:** Although not in the focus of a traditional database design process, there are many applications with multiple users (or user groups) having a slightly different view on a database schema. The concept of multi-tenancy recently addressed this issue as a modeling and system design problem. This level abstracts from having multiple tenants in the same database schema (with common and private data sets) or maintaining individual databases for different user groups. Section 2.4 will discuss the different options and alternative implementations in depth.

Since the specifics of the physical devices or the database systems are hidden from the application layer, the properties of the devices and software components have to be published in the form of Service Level Agreements (SLAs) to enable an efficient and cost-effective software stack. SLAs can be considered contracts between different layers which can be (dynamically) negotiated and monitored during runtime. The core concept of SLAs will be discussed in great detail in Sect. 5.1.

Moreover, it is important to point out that the different layers shown in Fig. 2.1 reflect the possible points of virtualization. Every layer or component within a layer can be virtualized in a specific setup; there is no must to apply virtualization for every piece in the stack. For example, hosting multiple applications within the same database running on one single database system, directly on bare hardware is a valid setup for data management services. The same holds for the other extreme of creating a separate database for every application running in an isolated database server on a virtualized node. The great challenge in the context is therefore to determine an "optimal" or "well-balanced" setup based on an end-to-end design.

2.1.1   Limits of Virtualization

Having listed most of the benefits of virtualization in general, we also have to pinpoint some of the limits. We already mentioned the loss of direct access of the computing resources by introducing the indirection step of virtualization. Specific features of the underlying mechanisms have to be explicitly modeled in form of some service description and SLAs have to be potentially determined. Hiding the details of physical resources however turns out to be extremely unfortunate for applications making some of their behavioral decisions based on assumptions about the physical layout. This of course is true for database systems in terms of node configurations. For example, the size of a buffer pool may have an impact on the choice of a specific physical plan operator (hash versus nested loop join). Another example with respect to storage systems is the alternative of an index scan compared to a table scan; the optimizer usually bases the decision on a cost model which is supposed to directly reflect the physical representation.

In addition to the abstraction of features, virtualization always causes some degree of performance penalty by the overhead introduced through the virtual machine, virtual storage, virtual schemas in the context of a shared database for multiple applications. The performance issue can only be reduced by better virtualization support, e.g. native support of multi-tenant database or hardware support when applying virtualization at the node level.

2.1.2   Use Cases for Virtualization

In order to achieve a better understanding, we outline three typical use cases for virtualization in the context of data management services: server consolidation, migration and load balancing, and high availability.

- **Server consolidation:** One of the driving forces to exploit some form of virtualization is based on the observation that typical server systems are grossly underutilized. For multiple reasons, ranging from organizational to security or fault tolerance reasons, we can observe a single server system per application. Not only applications but also database servers (sometimes in combination with web servers) are placed onto a single system. Without virtualization, provisioning is usually performed to cope with potential peak load requirements leading to usually underutilized computing resources. Figure 2.2 illustrates the situation.

  Running multiple applications in virtual machine environments opens up the potential to share the same physical machine and saving hardware energy costs

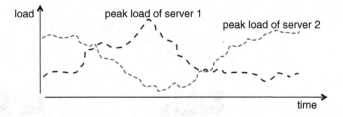

Fig. 2.2 Time dependent peak load provisioning as motivation for server consolidation

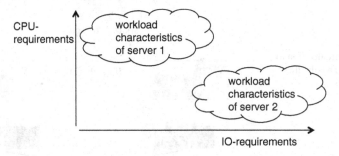

Fig. 2.3 Time invariant workload characteristics as hint for server consolidation

and reducing administration overheads. The major challenge however is to cluster applications with "compatible" applications and deploy them on the same component. In the context of physical virtualization, such a component is either the computing node or some storage system. For logical virtualization, database systems may hold multiple databases or applications may share a common database schema (multi-tenancy) to achieve the goal of peak leveling. In all scenarios, applications with contrary SLA requirements or contrary resource requirements should share the same underlying component. For example, as illustrated in Fig. 2.3, database workloads with IO-intensive queries should be "paired" with workloads exhibiting a more CPU intensive query load.

- **Migration and Load Balancing:** Usually ranked second behind the server consolidation scheme, virtualization can substantially help in load balancing or support of maintenance task. Exploiting the indirection layer introduced by the virtualization scheme enables to migrate the current state of an application to a different "location", i.e. either physical node or database server at the data management application level. The application within a virtual machine or the virtual machine itself can be suspended; the image can be shipped either directly or via a shared storage to another resource; afterwards, the application (or the computing node) can be resumed. Figure 2.4 shows the basic principle of this migration scheme which is very popular in enterprise-scale setups.

   The triggering event of a migration procedure can be either caused by administrative tasks, i.e. reconfiguration of the "source" systems or driven by load balancing actions. As soon as the infrastructure detects SLA violations at

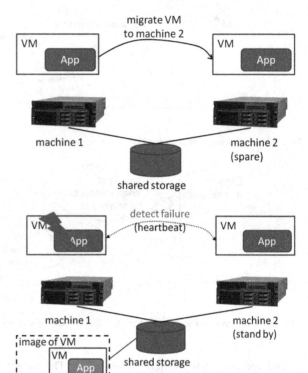

Fig. 2.4 Virtualization to support server/service migration

Fig. 2.5 Virtualization to support high availability requirements

certain levels, a migration of specific applications or computing nodes happens to less utilized nodes.

- **High Availability:** In analogy to the server migration use case, virtualization helps to achieve some basic level of high availability. Although the same principles apply, the triggering event is implicitly caused by the failure of the "home system". As illustrated in Fig. 2.5, a failure will be detected at a stand-by system by a missing heartbeat of the original system. The stand-by system may then start up an image of the virtual machine and continue to deliver the required service.

  Achieving high availability using only the image of a virtual machine is obviously restricted to stateless services like for example web servers. If a physical node fails, another system may load the image, start the system and provide access to the web site. For stateful applications especially for databases with transactional guarantees, this simple setup has to be extended with additional recovery procedures at the database server level to protect against data loss or inconsistent database states.

In order to achieve high or permanent availability at a database level, usually a stand-by database is maintained receiving logical or physical log information from the primary database system. For example IBM HADR[2] provides a mechanism to propagate data changes (DML operations) and structural changes, e.g. DDL statements, operations on table spaces and buffer pools, and reorganization operations to the stand-by system. In order to mirror the behavior of the primary system at the stand-by system, even meta-data of user-defined functions and database procedures are reflected at the stand-by system allowing a different implementation to reflect the procedural semantics if applied at the secondary system. Some systems, e.g, Oracle Data Guard,[3] provide the choice of propagating physical log structure to the stand-by system providing a binary compatible system, i.e. usually exactly the same system, as target for logical log. This option is based on SQL statements which are sent to the secondary system and applied like coming from any other application. This functionality provides the benefit to mix high availability with techniques to implement information integration scenarios by propagating state changes of a database to systems requiring the data from a business perspective.

Keeping a stand-by system running causes obviously extra costs; in some enterprise-scale data management infrastructures, such systems are either running in smaller virtual machines or are used for read-only applications. Especially decision-support application may benefit from having a separate database instance next to the operational system.[4] For example Oracle Data Guard or IBM DB2 explicitly have an option to provide read-consistent views on the secondary system for read-only applications.

Obviously, deploying virtualization schemes in large enterprise IT infrastructures offers even more scenarios with significant benefit for the use of virtualization techniques. Also, all illustrated use cases are valid on the physical section as well as on the logical section of the complete software stack. For example, migration may be performed on a virtual machine layer or on the database layer. In this case, replication techniques are usually used to propagate data from one database system to the other; as soon as the complete database has been moved to a different system, the corresponding connections to the dependent applications are either rerouted to the new system or explicitly disconnected – a re-connect, triggered by the application, then connects the application to the new target system.

---

[2]http://publib.boulder.ibm.com/infocenter/db2luw/v9r7/topic/com.ibm.db2.luw.admin.ha.doc/doc/c0011267.html.

[3]http://www.oracle.com/technetwork/database/availability/index.html.

[4]This typical separation of transactional mode and analytical mode is also reflected within the structure of the book (see next two chapters); Although there is a clear trend in bringing both world closer together in order to provide real-time analytics, the methods and techniques used to implement and optimize transactional systems or platforms for large-scale data analytics are worth to be considered separately.

2.1.3 Summary

To summarize, there exists a huge variety of use cases exploiting the concept of virtualization; virtualization may be implemented at different layers – ranging from a physical device layer to abstract from the real implementation and physical characteristics to the concept of schema sharing where multiple (obviously similar) applications share the same database schema. In the following section, we will detail the concepts and techniques of virtualization at the physical and at the database system level.

2.2 Virtualization Stack

Having the data management service software stack in Fig. 2.1, there are several layers that can possibly be virtualized. We assume that only one layer is virtualized at a time – merely for simplicity reasons. It is of course possible to virtualize at several layers in a singe setup, although such configurations shall be beneficial only in rare cases. As shown in Fig. 2.6, this assumptions results in four distinct classes of data management service configurations [25]:

- Class 1: PRIVATE OPERATING SYSTEM (PRIVATE OS)
- Class 2: PRIVATE PROCESS/PRIVATE DATABASE
- Class 3: PRIVATE SCHEMA
- Class 4: SHARED TABLES

A brief overview of these classes will be given shortly, followed by a comparison of the important characteristics. Details about Classes 1 and 4 will be provided in the following sections (while these classes have experienced great attention in the research community, Classes 2 and 3 are only about to be explored in detail and hence have not been researched to that extend.)

Class 1: PRIVATE OPERATING SYSTEM

In Class 1 (PRIVATE OS), physical virtualization occurs on the level of hardware resources (CPU, memory, network). Virtual machine monitors, e.g., VMware, XEN, or KVM, can be used to realize the virtualization. Access to the physical storage is usually virtualized independently of the computing resources (in order to allow for light-weight migration without moving large amounts of data).

Each application in a Class 1 data management architecture owns a separate operating system as well as a database server and databases. Consequently, isolation between different applications with respect to security, performance, and availability is the strongest among all classes. At the same time, resource usage per application is very high which leads to poor utilization of the underlying hardware. Given

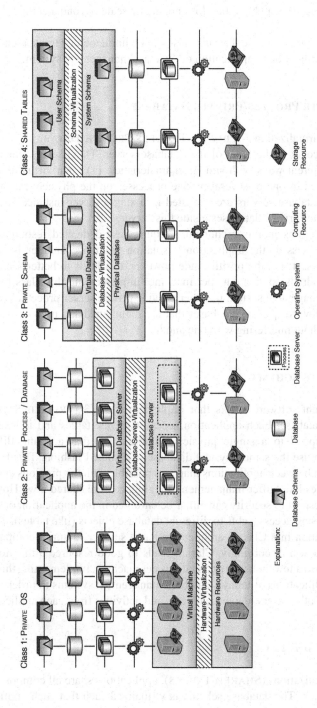

Fig. 2.6 Different classes for data management virtualization

todays hardware, only a few tens of different applications can be hosted on a single machine and hence this architecture does not easily scale beyond a certain number of applications.

Also, it is important to note that this class can be implemented transparently and without any modification to application or database management system.

Class 2: PRIVATE PROCESS/PRIVATE DATABASE

With Class 2 virtualization – PRIVATE PROCESS/PRIVATE DATABASE – logical virtualization occurs at the level of the database server. This can be achieved in two slightly different ways with similar characteristics: (1) Each virtual database server is executed in one or several private processes on the physical machine or (2) all virtual database servers are executed in a single server instance and each application creates private databases inside this server.

While applications in this architecture require less dedicated resources than applications in Class 1, the applications' isolation from one another is weaker compared to Class 1. On the positive side however, this leads to better scalability up to a few hundreds applications per machine. Implementing this class requires the database management system to either provide private server processes (e.g. as instances) or allow for private databases that are maintained and used by different applications without interfering with one another.

Class 3: PRIVATE SCHEMA

Data management software stacks that implement Class 3 (PRIVATE SCHEMA) virtualize the database. Each application accesses private tables and indexes that are in turn mapped to a single physical database. On that account, different applications can use the same physical database in a shared fashion. This leads to weaker isolation between applications than was possible with the previous classes – database facilities like buffer management, logging, etc. are shared now. However, isolation with respect to security can either be enforced in the application or on the database level using access rights to different database objects (like tables).

Each application in a Class 3 architecture has a smaller footprint compared to the previous classes. Accordingly, Class 3 leads to good resource utilization and scalability of up to a few thousand applications per machine. Implementing this class can lead to modifications of today's database management systems in order to hide the existence of other users' database objects and activities from each application.

Class 4: SHARED TABLES

In Class 4 virtualizations (SHARED TABLES), applications share all components in the software stack. The database schema is virtualized such that each application sees a private schema. However, all private schemas are mapped to a single system schema. This class is best suited for Software-as-a-Service infrastructures where tenants (applications) use the same or a very similar database schema. The databases are then often referred to as "Multi-Tenant-Databases" [3, 4, 23]. Applications that do not share common ground cannot easily be implemented with this class. Although there are means for generic schemas that allow for storing arbitrary relational data – e.g., pivot tables that mimic key-value-stores or universal tables with a number of string columns that all data are mapped to – these implementations have disadvantages with respect to, for example, poor performance or the loss of strong typing.

This class offers the least isolation between applications. Security can be enforced on application level or with row-level-authorization in the database system, but with respect to performance or availability there is almost no isolation. Losing the natural separation of different applications leads to high complexity in the database management system – e.g., the query optimizer needs to be aware of the intermingled data – and complicates maintenance tasks like, e.g., backup, restore or migration of single tenants. The latter operations require costly queries to the operational system.

Particularly advantageous in using this class is the extreme scalability. Because each application requires a minimal amount of dedicated resources, such setups can scale to up to several thousands of applications per single machine.

Although it is possible to implement a Class 4 setup with today's database management systems without major modifications, the system should be aware of the multi-tenancy (and particularly support it) in order to provide fundamental isolation and good performance.

Comparison of all Classes

Table 2.1 summarizes the high-level characteristics of all four classes. Details about all classes will be provided in the following sections and the comparison will be further detailed in the summary of this chapter. The classes differ greatly with respect to different characteristics and the application of any of the classes is highly dependent on the particular application, its requirements, and desired system properties.

An evaluation of the basic properties is not straightforward, as the following example shall demonstrate. Take for example the "isolation" of applications which is obviously strong in Class 1 and decreases stepwise all the way to Class 4 where it is the weakest. While a strong isolation may be beneficial with respect to security or performance, this strong isolation may prevent, e.g. access to shared data. On the one hand, applications being isolated on a low level implies that single tenants can be backed up, restored, and migrated individually and with little overhead on the remaining tenants. On the other hand, when tenants are hosted in individual operating systems or database servers, strong isolation leads to increased complexity

Table 2.1 Comparison of Classes 1 (PRIVATE OS), 2 (PRIVATE PRO-
CESS/PRIVATE DATABASE), 3 (PRIVATE TABLE) and 4 (SHARED TABLES)
with evaluations ranging from "particularly advantageous" (++) to "particularly disadvantageous" (– –)

	Class 1	Class 2	Class 3	Class 4
Resources per application (costs)	– –	o	++	++
Resource utilization/scalability	– –	–	+	++
Provisioning time and costs	– –	–	++	++
Maintainability (updates/patches)	– –	–	+	+
Isolation (performance)	+	+	o	–
Application independence	++	+	+	–
Isolation (security)	++	++	+	o
Maintainability (Backup/Restore)	+	+	o	– –

and costs of other maintenance tasks like applying updated or patches to the system
(which is simple in a single database like it is given in Classes 3 and 4).

The comparison in Table 2.1 furthermore shows that the scalability of the
architectures increases steadily from Classes 1 to 4. This relates to the circumstance
that a single application requires a decreasing amount of dedicated resources and
hence has a smaller footprint in Class 4 as compared to, e.g., Class 1. A smaller
footprint also leads to lower provisioning costs for new applications which in turn
leads to faster provisioning times.

Finally, Table 2.1 shows that all classes are not equally independent from the
applications they host. While Class 1 setup can host any application (as long as
it provides the necessary performance), Class 4 setups require applications with a
common core and similar database schemas to be beneficial.

2.3   Hardware Virtualization

As mentioned in Sect. 2.2, the software stack provides different options to introduce
virtualization concepts or specific techniques. In the following, we will focus on the
opportunities and existing techniques to implement physical virtualization shielding
the specific hardware setup. Following the basic scheme of discussing the relationship of the different layers in the overall software stack, we call this hardware
virtualization scenario the **Class 1 Virtualization Scheme (PRIVATE OS)**.

As shown in Fig. 2.7, this class preserves the classic "application software
stack" by simulating individual machines, storage devices, and network infrastructures. While the software stack remains basically intact by providing a private
operating system environment, hardware resources are shared. Referring to the
different classes of "as-a-Service"-models, this setup pictures a "Infrastructure-as-
a-Service"-model. The virtual machines and virtual disks are playing the role of
the infrastructures which can be used by the application software stack without any

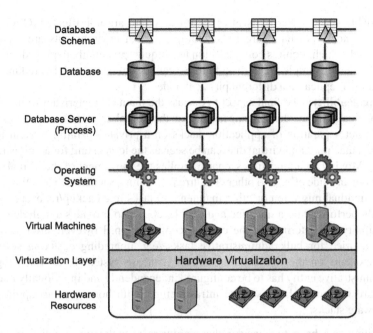

Fig. 2.7 Class 1 Virtualization scheme (PRIVATE OS) – hardware virtualization

detailed knowledge about the technical setup. The overall properties of this scheme can be best illustrated by looking at the notion of "isolation" from different angles:

- **Security:** Since the system resources are accessible only within a private operating system environment, low-level techniques of the virtual machines with the help of native hardware support provide the highest degree of isolation. Software failures or explicit security attacks in a VM container do not affect other concurrently running operating systems with their individual applications. This holds for activating code as well as for accessing data, be it in (virtual) main memory or explicitly stored on virtual disk storage. The downside of this property can be seen in the fact that access to shared data has to be implemented on the application side, i.e. the strict isolation of the virtual environment conceptually does not enable shortcuts for virtual machines running on the same system. Classical remote access techniques have to be used.
- **Performance:** Since virtual machine or disk environments allow to limit the usage of physically available resources, overload on one application system does not affect other applications running in another virtual machine. For example, a VM can be allowed to use only 50 % of the available CPU power. Due to this strict isolation, there is no starvation of other virtual environments.
- **Failure:** Strong isolation also shows the benefit in case of system failures. The failure of one application stack including the private operating systems does not influence other virtual environments. This holds on the machine level as well as on the disk level. If a partition of a virtual disk "fails", e.g. by running out of

available space, other parts of the storage system are not affected. Obviously, if the underlying hardware fails, multiple virtual environments are typically affected, which requires compensation techniques, potentially deployed on other layers. For example, real disk failures can be compensated by redundantly holding a replica on a different physical node.

- **Manageability:** The final aspect to discuss the main characteristics of hardware virtualization considers manageability of the complete infrastructures. Due to the strict separation of application stacks on a private operating system level, virtual machines and virtual disk can be seen as the logical unit for administrative jobs. Moving an application scenario implies the movement of the virtual disks without any side effects to other concurrently running scenarios. Therefore, tasks of individual migration or other maintenance tasks like backup/recovery can be easily performed on a machine and disk level. It also provides a high degree of flexibility for determining the optimal configuration. However, strict isolation has a price for bulk administrative tasks, e.g. upgrading or fixing software components on the operating system or database system level. Each logical administrative entity has to be configured independently and individually making it hard to operate large service infrastructures with homogeneous application software stacks.

In addition, we have to consider that hardware virtualization on the one hand exhibits a significant footprint with respect to resources, because every instance of a working unit requires a separate OS installation, separate software stack etc. On the other hand, hardware virtualization allows to run heterogeneous application stacks within the same computing environments, for example to support different applications or even different versions of applications requiring different versions/configurations of the underlying operating system. The strong isolation also allows to provide a very scalable infrastructure, because different virtual machine environments are totally independent of each other. From an overall resource perspective however, a price has to be paid for the strong isolation guarantees. Since no software can be shared, the footprint is typically larger compared to other schemes.

As already shown in Fig. 2.1, hardware virtualization comprises the three types of components machines, storage, and network infrastructures. While virtual network infrastructures are highly specific to the concrete physical environment and not of primary interest for data management services, we will focus on machine and storage virtualization in the following two subsections.

2.3.1 Machine Virtualization

Machine virtualization has a long history going back to 1972, when IBM offered the concept of hypervisors for the S/370 under the label of "Virtual Machine Facility/370". As of now, there are a huge variety of different machine virtualization

Fig. 2.8 Classical stack of hardware, operating system, and applications

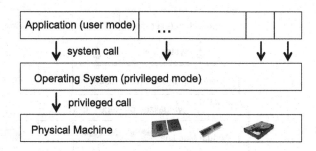

techniques as open source as well as commercially available. Although the different techniques cover a wide spectrum of technical properties in terms of their usage scenario, they all share the same architectural concepts of hypervisors. In order to get the basic idea of machine virtualization, Fig. 2.8 shows the classical setup of hardware, operating system, and applications. An application sitting on top of an operating system issues a system call to get access to the resources of the underlying machine. The operating system schedules the physical accesses and coordinates the privileged access to the hardware. Specific hardware characteristics are shielded by the operating system.

In an environment with virtual machines, a hypervisor basically decouples the pure hardware from the operating system level. Applications interact with the operating system in the same way as in the native stack. However, an operating system is now running in user mode. System calls issued by the application are propagated to the hardware by the operating system. Since the operating system is running in user mode, the hardware intercepts the call and propagates the request to the hypervisor running in privileged mode. The hypervisor is handling the request coming from the operating system and maps it to the existing hardware. In order to be able to run on different hardware configurations, virtual machine hypervisors are providing only a restricted set of virtual hardware components. Since this set of hardware components is fixed and implemented by hypervisors running on a variety of different hardware platforms, virtual machines can be easily moved from one hardware to another. Figure 2.9 illustrates the revised system stack with the additional layer of a hypervisor. The figure also intuitively shows that based on hypervisors, it is now possible to run multiple virtual machines on a single physical box.

As a final comment, we would like to point out two variants of the classical virtualization principle. First of all, para-virtualization comprises the fact that a hypervisor is semi-transparent, i.e., some real hardware components are directly visible and accessible by the guest operating systems. Para-virtualization is used in situations when either specific hardware has to be exploited by the application (e.g. license dongles) or the performance penalty coming with the virtualization layer is not acceptable (e.g. graphic cards). However, para-virtualization requires the guest operating system to be virtualization-aware. To run in a para-virtualized setup, the guest operating system has to be modified in order to implement the modified interface that is provided by the hypervisor. Secondly, virtualization on

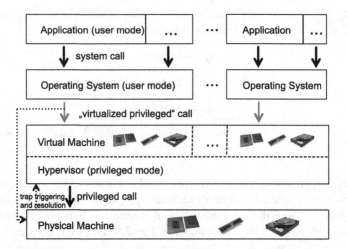

Fig. 2.9 System stack using virtual machines

the machine layer should not be mixed with the concept of emulation. In this setup, an intermediate layer has to simulate the complete hardware allowing applications with an underlying operating system to be run for different machines architectures especially for different types of CPUs. The Bochs IA-32 Emulator Project[5] is a famous example to provide an x86 hardware architecture for multiple platforms. Recently, Fabrice Bellard demonstrated an emulator of an x-86 architecture running linux completely written in JavaScript and running inside a regular Web browser.[6] Finally, some operating systems provide virtualization techniques on its own. In such a setup, guest and host operating system are using the same kernel. Examples are the Solaris Container concept[7] or the Parallels Virtuozzo Container concept.[8] While typically having a significantly lower overhead, such a container concept provides only a homogeneous operating system environment by exhibiting different views of the same system.

2.3.2 Virtual Storage

Virtual storage follows the same ideas and principles as other virtualized hardware components like CPUs or memory. However, storage takes a prominent role in data management architectures because it hosts the actual persistent data and often is

---

[5]http://bochs.sourceforge.net/.

[6]http://bellard.org/jslinux/.

[7]http://www.oracle.com/technetwork/server-storage/solaris/containers-169727.html.

[8]http://www.parallels.com/ptn/documentation/virtuozzo/.

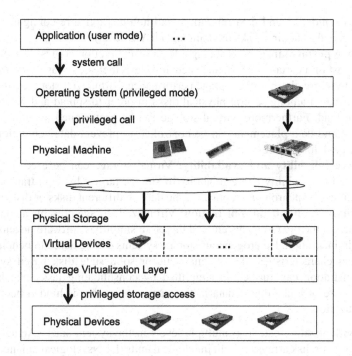

Fig. 2.10 System stack using virtual storage

the bottleneck in data-intensive applications. When moving to flexible, service-oriented architectures, storage requires even more attention because the ability to provision resources or migrate workloads on demand depends heavily on the storage system's flexibility. Storage virtualization introduces a layer of indirection that allows the definition of virtual storage devices (see Fig. 2.10). Whenever an application accesses a storage device, the appropriate driver or the operating system catches the call and redirects it either to the correct partition on a local disk or to the network where it is sent to an external storage device, e.g., a disk array. Here we concentrate on storage that is outside and hence not part of the machine that is running the software (disks that are part of the system are covered by virtual machines, described in the previous section).

The benefits of storage virtualization are manifold and stem from the layer of indirection that is introduced. Motivations to introduce storage virtualization can be as divers as:

- **Minimize/avoid downtime:** Managing virtual storage devices can be done on demand and while the system is running. Otherwise disruptive operations like changing the RAID level of a disk array or higher level operations like resizing a file system can be performed without the need to take down the system. More precisely, storage virtualization allows for non-disruptive creation, expansion and deletion of virtual storage targets (logical units), non-disruptive data consolidation and data migration, and non-disruptive re-configuration (as fundamental as adding disks or changing a RAID level).

- **Improve performance:** Introducing a level of indirection comes – by nature – at the cost of a certain performance penalty. Nevertheless, storage virtualization can help to greatly improve storage performance. Virtualized storage can easily be distributed among several physical disks in order to spread and balance the storage load. Furthermore, virtual storage can be provisioned dynamically, on demand and data placement can be controlled to prevent data contention even during peak load phases.
- **Improve reliability and availability:** Virtual storage can be used to greatly improve the reliability and availability of storage targets by, e.g., transparently maintaining (synchronous) replicas of the data on different disks or disk arrays.
- **Simplify/consolidate administration:** Virtualized storage presents a consistent interface to the operating system and therefore simplifies software development and administration. Heterogeneous storage systems can be tiered to benefit from different characteristics of, e.g., magnetic or solid state disk based systems. Administration can further be simplified by consolidating tasks like backup and restore or archiving of data in the storage layer that is hidden behind the virtualization.

Storage virtualization can span multiple levels in the system stack. Actual disks, RAID groups or disk arrays are split into logical units (LUNs – logical unit numbers) and presented as regular storage targets to the operating system. There, a logical volume manager (LVM) further divides storage targets or spans logical volumes over several targets. Hence, there can be arbitrary and flexible mappings from raw disks to actual file systems. Basic operations that are supported by virtualized storage devices are:

- **create/destroy:** Logical volumes can be created or destroyed even without taking down the system.
- **grow/shrink:** Logical volumes can be resized on demand to overcome changes in storage requirements.
- **add/remove bandwidth:** Basic properties of logical storage devices can be changed as needed, for example to increase the bandwidth to a certain target or to add additional disks as needed.
- **increase/decrease reliability:** Adding and removing disks can also be used to change, e.g., RAID levels transparently to the user and hence increase the reliability of a certain storage target.

Technical Realization of Storage Virtualization

While significant work has be conducted to provide an abstract model for CPUs, virtualizing disks and describing the performance behavior for virtual storage did not receive much attention. Pioneering work was done by Kaldewey et al. [24] providing an abstract model and an infrastructure to implement admission control

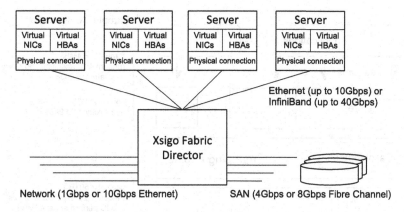

Fig. 2.11 Xsigo systems storage virtualization solution

for different types of access, i.e. sequential versus random access. Within [24], the authors show that disk time utilization (similar to utilization of CPU in the context of CPU scheduling) provides a significantly more efficient use of the underlying disk resources.

To provide an even deeper insight on how commercially available storage virtualization can be realized, an example setup is presented. A sophisticated solution to the problem is provided by a company named Xsigo systems[9] recently acquired by Oracle.[10] The solution's architecture is shown in Fig. 2.11. Each machine in a server rack is connected to a central I/O director that handles the virtualization of storage devices and network connections. To connect the server to the machine, either existing Ethernet ports with up to 10 Gbps or faster InfiniBand ports with up to 40 Gbps can be used. All requests can be served by a single connection, though a redundant second connection can be added for availability.

The I/O director switches all machines' requests and forwards them to the appropriate networks or storage devices. It is therefore connected to the network or SANs via Ethernet or to disk arrays directly via fibre channel.

The virtualization of storage and network is transparent to the operating system, where special drivers help to access virtual host base adapters (vHBAs) as well as virtual network interface controllers (vNICs). Virtual interfaces can be moved, created or dropped, and modified in the running system. The interfaces are even consistent when the (virtual) machine itself is moved, MAC addresses stay the same. It is hence possible to migrate virtual machines without affecting the storage system at all and without any need to propagate the changes to connected software applications. In order to control the service quality of virtualized storage and network, QoS parameters can be configured in the I/O director, e.g., to allow for a certain bandwidth.

---

[9]http://www.xsigo.com/.

[10]http://www.oracle.com/us/corporate/acquisitions/xsigo/index.html.

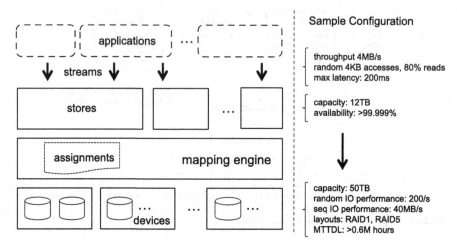

Fig. 2.12 The mapping problem for an attribute-managed storage system [42]

Storage System Organization and Configuration

When storage is separated from the actual machines and consolidated in large disk array systems, the question of how to manage such beasts quickly arises. This includes questions like how to build LUNs (on which disk, what size, ...) or how to choose RAID subsystems and the appropriate RAID levels. Hewlett Packard's Storage System Program (SSP)[11] tackled many of these questions in the last two decades (partly related to data management workloads, partly agnostic to the specific workload). A recent work by John Wilkes [42] provides a good overview of the different concepts and components that have been developed in the SSP.

The mapping problem, that is fundamental to storage management, is shown in Fig. 2.12. On a very abstract level, applications that run in the system generate I/O load – dubbed streams – that is directed to virtual storage containers, called stores. These containers on the other hand are mapped to actual devices like disks or disk arrays. The challenge is to find a mapping that satisfies all applications' I/O needs and at the same time fulfills certain optimality criteria like minimizing the number of disks needed and hence reducing costs.

One key concept is to annotate streams, stores, and devices with their characteristic attributes and requirements. Attributes associated with a stream capture, e.g., the dynamic aspects of the workload like the rate at which data is accessed or whether data is read or written. Furthermore, the I/O workload that builds a stream may be associated with attributes like the average request size and whether requests are random or sequential in nature. Attributes associated with stores capture

---

[11]http://www.hpl.hp.com/research/ssp/.

```
{ store store1 {                              # a 100GB store
  { capacity 100e9 }                          # mapped to a logical unit
  { boundTo array4.lu_3 }                     #   on an array (not shown)
}}

{ stream stream1 {                            # a stream
  { boundTo store1 }                          #  bound to that store
  { source  host_A1}                          # originating at this host
  { interArrivalTimeOpen {                    # inverse of request rate
      { datamodelNormal best {                # normal fit
          { mean 0.83e-3 }{ stddev 0.6e-3 }   # mean = 1200/sec
          { chiSquare 0.7 }                   # goodness of fit metric
      }}
      { datamodelExponential poor {           # exponential fit
          { mean 0.83e-3 } { chiSquare 0.2 }  # 1200/sec, less-good fit
      }}
  }}
  { requestSize {                             # a simple behavior
      { datamodelUniform {                    # uniform size in 4-12KiB,
          { mean 8192 }                       #   on 1024-byte boundaries
          { lbound 4096 } { ubound 12288 } { granularity 1024 }
      }}
  { responseTime {datamodelExponential {mean 50e-3}}} # a goal
  { stream read {                             # just the read requests
      { filteredBy { opType read }}
      { interArrivalTimeOpen 1e-3 }           # 1000/sec
      { requestSize 9216 }                    # larger requests on avg.
  }}
  { stream write {
      { filteredBy { opType write }}
      { interArrivalTimeOpen 5e-3 }           # 200/sec
      { requestSize 4096 }
  }}
  { stream degraded {                         # something not right
      { filteredBy {{ outageDuration 3600 }   # 1 hour at a time
                    { outageFraction 0.002 }}} # 17 hours/year
      { interArrivalTimeOpen 1.67e-3 } # 600/sec
      { stream write {
          { filteredBy { opType write }}
          { interArrivalTimeOpen 0.1 } # 10/sec
      }}
  }}
  { stream broken {                           # completely stopped
      { filteredBy {{ outageDuration 300 }    # 5 min at a time
                    { outageFraction 0.00001 }}} # 5 min/year
      { interArrivalTimeOpen inf }            # nothing: 0/sec
  }}
}}
```

Fig. 2.13 A (much simplified) sample workload specification example [41]

the requirements of these virtual containers, such as how much capacity they must provide, and their desired availability. Finally, devices, i.e., the actual disks, have attributes that capture their capabilities – capacity, performance, reliability, or cache behavior. Figure 2.13 shows a sample workload specification, i.e., annotations for stores and streams. One store is accessed by one stream. In normal mode, it receives 1,200 requests/s; in "degraded" mode, it can limp along for an hour at a time at half that rate; and it can be "broken" (non-accessible) no more than 5 min a year ("five nines availability"). For simplicity, most of the data models shown are simple numeric values; in practice, distributions would normally be used.

In order to solve the mapping problem and to guarantee performance and availability of the data access, a mapping engine needs to take care of the following aspects: map stores to (possibly redundant) devices (or groups of devices) and configure devices with the appropriate RAID level. Different orthogonal questions (or demands) may be asked during the optimization process like: "How many devices are needed to support this load?" or "How much load can this set of devices support?". Hence, once implemented, the mapping engine can be used to achieve different optimization goals.

The possible solution space for a mapping from stores to devices is huge and as such prohibits searching it exhaustively for the optimal solution (the problem is actually a variant of the multi-dimensional, multi-knapsack problem and as such NP-complete [42]). Solvers that intend to solve the constraint-based optimization problem apply greedy search, advanced heuristics, or speculative exploration in order to find near-optimal configurations after a reasonable amount of time.

2.4   Schema Virtualization

While hardware virtualization offers techniques for the lower part of the virtualization stack, this section focuses on the virtualization techniques for the upper part of the stack. Usually, "Software-as-a-Service"-providers host the same type of application for many users or tenants. For example, a webmail service such as Google Mail or Yahoo Mail provides the same email application to millions of users. Although managing their private emails isolated from each other, all webmail users manage the same type data, i.e. data of similar structure. As a consequence on the database layer, many tenants in "Software-as-a-Service"-infrastructures use the same or a very similar database structures or database schemas. Besides similar metadata, many tenant-specific applications partially work on shared data, stored once and used in multiple applications. In webmail services, for instance, users, especially from the same social group, may have overlapping address books. Other typical cases of common data are currencies, currency conversion rates or topographical entities such as nations or cities. Therefore, it is important for the data management layer that many of the tenants' entities (or tables in a classical relational context) may exhibit not only a similar structure but also same sort of overlapping content.

The promise of "as-a-Service" is to lower the total cost of ownership for each tenant compared to an on-premise installation operating the computing infrastructure individually and locally at a customer's site. Within the database, the noticeable overlap of data and metadata of tenants offers the opportunity to lower the cost of data management by keeping only one copy with different views for the specific applications. Depending on the scenario, a multi-tenant database may therefore be significantly smaller than the sum of single tenant databases [23]. However,

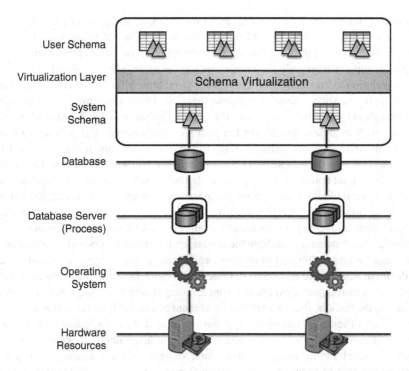

Fig. 2.14 Class 4 Virtualization scheme (SHARED TABLES) – schema virtualization

consolidating the shared data and metadata of multiple tenants into one single database requires a virtualization layer that offers each tenant a private and isolated view of their respected data. Through this virtualization layer, a tenant sees the shared database like a private database. As the actual database schema becomes transparent to the tenant, such a virtualization is called SCHEMA VIRTUALIZATION.

Following the basic scheme of the virtualization stack, schema virtualization is the Class 4 Virtualization Scheme (SHARED TABLES). Within this section, we further detail on the overall properties of schema virtualization and present existing techniques to implement virtualized schemas.

As illustrated in Fig. 2.14, this class simulates individual database schemas. While the external view of the database remains unchanged, the complete database stack is shared, including the database, the database server, the operating system, and the hardware resources. This scheme corresponds to a "Database-as-a-Service"-model. Each simulated individual database schema plays the role of a database which can be used by applications without any detailed knowledge about the specific setup. Again, looking at the different aspects of isolation provides the best summary of the overall properties of this virtualization scheme.

- **Security:** Generally, schema virtualization provides a very low level of isolation. Disasters or security attacks to the database affect all tenants equally. Once an attacker has gained access privileges for the database, the attacker may also have access to data of all tenants. More specifically, sharing metadata, i.e., sharing a table structure requires the management of isolation on tuple level. A corrupted private tuple affects only the tenant owning the tuple. Sharing also data reduces the isolation to transactions. A corrupted shared tuple affects all tenants that share the tuple. In such a case, the transactional isolation determines how quickly transactions see a tuple after its corruption. The same holds for shared access data, such as index entries. On the positive side however, the general cost for security and safety are shared among all tenants: an average tenant puts its data into a system with more security features managed on a highly professional level than the tenant could afford on premise. In the same way, all security updates are to the benefit of all tenants in a single operation. However, with respect to explicit security attacks, the effective security may not increase, because a system with many thousand tenants is much more worth to attack than a system serving only a single user. Hosted serves draw the attention of more attackers and – very often – these attackers are willing to invest more in order to gain access to the database.

- **Performance:** Since all tenants operate on the same database, they influence each others performance. Besides the simple competition for computing resources among the tenants, the performance of a tenant can suffer because of transactional isolation of tenants. The number of transactions of different tenants influencing each other depends on the transactional isolation level and the degree of sharing on the level of metadata, payload data, or index data. Because the tenants share the cost of the system, they run either on a more powerful system which they would afford on their own or the system is running in an environment where performance bottlenecks can be reduced by moving tenants to different systems. Depending on the specific virtualization scheme, query processing for a single user may also touch irrelevant data, whenever queries are implemented by database scans. If the data is not clustered by tenants, each tenant loses data locality and has to pay the price for the "as-a-Service"-paradigm. Obviously, a table scan over the data of thousands of tenants is unacceptable costly for a single tenant. Therefore, data structures, especially access paths such as B-trees, scaling logarithmically with the number of entries are absolutely essential to achieve reasonable performance. Further, data statistics are less accurate for a single tenant because they represent the mean of all tenants. A "Database-as-a-Service"-provider may take special measures to limit and control the mutual performance influence among tenants. That way, the provider is able to offer different Service Level Agreements to the various tenants. For example, if a system holds some large tenants and a huge number of smaller tenants, the query optimizer may decide to use an index access for a specific query pattern, because the average tenant is small. Unfortunately, if the same query plan is executed for a large tenant, the query might end up in an enormous number of index accesses and an suboptimal plan.
- **Failure:** If a tenant's application accidentally corrupts any metadata, payload data or access data that is shared, the failure affects all tenants. Failures that result in corrupted private data are not visible to other tenants. To prevent the impact of

a single tenant's failure on other tenants, a provider usually grants restricted rights on any shared data. For instance, tenants cannot simply drop a table, delete or update a shared tuple or remove an index. Obviously, if the underlying database stack fails, all tenants are affected. Since tenants share the costs, more failures prevention and compensation mechanism become affordable. The reliability of the hardware and database stack increases.

- **Manageability:** Since almost the complete database stack is shared, most administrative tasks, e.g., backup, recovery, tenant migration, user management or database software updates can be easily done for all tenants at once. Performing these tasks for single tenants, however, is difficult or impossible. For instance, most database systems support only backup and recovery of the complete database or tables as a whole. To back up a shared table for a single tenant, the backup process has to query the operational system to extract the tenant's specific data from the shared tables. If the used database system offers no explicit multi-tenancy support, management tasks of the individual tenants have to be implemented on top of the database system on application level. The same observation holds for constraints. Typically, a database system enforces a set of user-defined constraints to maintain data quality, integrity, and consistency. Without explicit multi-tenancy support, the database system can enforce only global constraints that hold for all tenants. Tenant-specific constraints have to be enforced on application level.

2.4.1 Sharing

Using schema virtualization, the data of many tenants is stored in a single database schema. On top of the database schema the virtualization layer simulates private schemas for every tenant. These private schemas exists only virtually. Regarding to scope of shared content of the tenants, we may distinguish four schema virtualization patterns with an increasing order of amount of shared data:

- **Common Metadata:** In the case of shared metadata, tenants share the definition of a table, but not the content of a table. Each tenant has access to multiple tuples in the shared table. Each tuple, however, is accessed only by a single tenant.
- **Locally Shared Data:** The next level of locally shared data allows that tenants share the definition of a table and partially the content of a table. Each tenant has access to multiple tuples and some of these tuples can be also accessed by other tenants. Nevertheless, tuples are not shared among all tenants.
- **Globally Shared Data:** For globally shared data, tenants share the definition of a table and partially the content of a table. Each tenant has access to multiple tuples. Some tuples can be accessed by all tenants equally.
- **Common Data:** Tenants share the definition of a table and the complete content of a table. All tenants have access to all tuples.

Table 2.2 Schema
virtualization patterns

Tenant	Tuple	Pattern
1	n	Common Metadata
m	n	Locally Shared Data
*	n	Globally Shared Data
*	*	Common Data

Table 2.2 lists the four patterns with the cardinality of the relationship between tenants and tuples for each pattern. In the following, we discuss the four patterns in more detail.

In the **Common Metadata** pattern, tenants share the definition of a table. The content of the same tenant tables are stored in a single system table, while the tenants interact only with their virtual tables. If a tenant inserts data into a virtual table, the tuples are associated with the tenant and inserted into the corresponding system table. In the system table, each tuple is associated with a single tenant. The tenant references the entries via the primary key of the virtual table as part of a composite primary key of the system table. If a tenant queries its private data, the virtualization layer rewrites the query. Each reference to a virtual table in a query is replaced with the corresponding system table. Additionally, the virtualization layer adds a selection of the tuples associated with the specific tenant, such that the each tenant only sees its own data. Figure 2.15a illustrates the process for the Product table of an online shop service and three tenants. Similarly, the virtualization layer masks every update and delete operation triggered by a tenant.

In the **Locally Shared Data** pattern, tenants additionally share tuples. Shared tuples are not only accessed by a single tenant, but by groups of tenants. For each locally shared table, the system manages the system table that contains the data and a access table consisting of tenant id and primary key of the shared table. The content of the access table determines which tenant is allowed to access which tuple in the system table. Joining the access table and the corresponding system table allows selecting the tuple associated with a tenant. For each tenant query, the virtualization layer rewrites virtual table references accordingly. Figure 2.15b illustrates the process for the online shop service scenario. Rewriting update and delete operation is more complicated. Before the actually update or delete operation on the system table happens, the virtualization layer has to poll the access table for the list of tuples the tenants is allowed to access. In a second step, the virtualization layer rewrites the selection predicate of the update or delete operation. The primary key of the requested data entries has to be in the list of accessible tuples. For a list L of accessible tuples, a given predicate p and a primary key k, the virtualization layer rewrites p to $p \wedge k \in L$. The pattern can be easily extended to more access control. With another column in the access table, the virtualization layer can manage different access privileges of the tenants. The Locally Shared Data pattern is the most general pattern; it can represent all four patterns at once. On the downside, locally shared data in combination with the access table induces the most management overhead.

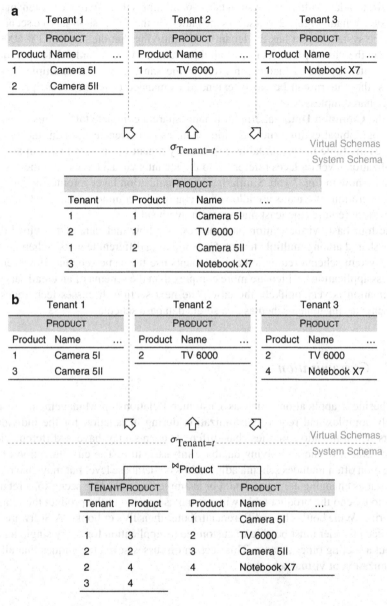

Fig. 2.15 Schema virtualization patterns detailed. (**a**) Common metadata. (**b**) Locally shared data

In the **Globally Shared Data** pattern, shared tuples are always shared among all tenants. Similar to the Common Metadata pattern, each tuple in the system table is associated with a single tenant, who has access to the tuple. All globally shared tuples reference a special system tenant. If a tenant queries its virtual table, the virtualization layer filters the system table for all tuples that reference the tenant and the system tenant. Figure 2.16a shows the pattern in the online shop service scenario. Here, the system tenant has the tenant id *G*, implying that the product TV 6000 is visible in the virtual product table of all three tenants. Update and delete operations are rewritten by the virtualization layer in the same way. With multiple system tenants, the pattern can be easily extended to manage different access privileges for the shared tuples.

In the **Common Data** pattern, all tenants share a complete table. This is useful for topographical entities such as cities, nations or currencies. Again, the system manages the tuple in system table. Since every tenant has access to all tuples, the virtualization layer replaces references to the tenant's virtual tables with the system tables as show in Fig. 2.16b. Similarly, the virtualization layer reroutes update and delete operations if tenants are allowed to change the common data. The Common Data pattern requires the least management overhead.

The four basic virtualization patterns describe how metadata and payload data can be shared among multiple tenant. Consolidating different tenants' schemas in a single system schema requires that the tenants use the same schema. However, in business applications, which are more complex than the schema of an email service, this situation is very unlikely the case. The next section discusses techniques to represent varying tenant schemas in a single database schema.

2.4.2   Customization

Real business applications such as Customer Relationship Management are extremely complex and require customization during installation for the individual tenants. Customization implies that different tenants may have a different view on the content of the underlying database infrastructure. The customization of an application often includes schema adjustments on database level but may also reach as far out as changing common data. For example in a web shop scenario, a retailer wants to extend the product table with attributes specific to the product the retailer is offering: Wine bottles have different attributes then TVs or books. A Software-as-a-Service provider must be able to customize its application for every single tenant without affecting other tenants. This section discusses seven techniques that allow customization of virtual schemas.

Extension Table

A big part of customization can be carried out in modules, extensions, or add-ons. Such extensions add well-defined functionality to the service and are offered by the service provider. Tenants can book extensions to adapt the service to their needs. Since the service provider is in full control of the offered extension, the provider can model the system tables of the database accordingly. Decomposing the system tables

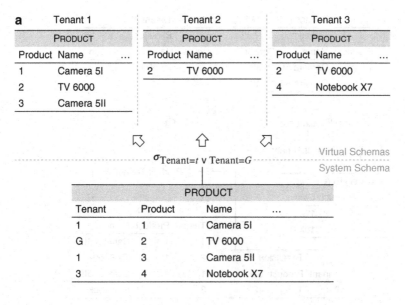

a

Tenant 1	
PRODUCT	
Product	Name ...
1	Camera 5I
2	TV 6000
3	Camera 5II

Tenant 2	
PRODUCT	
Product	Name ...
2	TV 6000

Tenant 3	
PRODUCT	
Product	Name ...
2	TV 6000
4	Notebook X7

σTenant=t ∨ Tenant=G

Virtual Schemas
System Schema

PRODUCT			
Tenant	Product	Name	...
1	1	Camera 5I	
G	2	TV 6000	
1	3	Camera 5II	
3	4	Notebook X7	

b

Tenant 1		
PRODUCT		
Product	Name	...
1	Camera 5I	
2	TV 6000	
3	Camera 5II	
4	Notebook X7	

Tenant 2		
PRODUCT		
Product	Name	...
1	Camera 5I	1
2	TV 6000	2
3	Camera 5II	3
4	Notebook X7	4

Tenant 3		
PRODUCT		
Product	Name	...
1	Camera 5I	1
2	TV 6000	2
3	Camera 5II	3
4	Notebook X7	4

Virtual Schemas
System Schema

PRODUCT		
Product	Name	...
1	Camera 5I	
2	TV 6000	
3	Camera 5II	
4	Notebook X7	

Fig. 2.16 Schema virtualization patterns detailed (cont.). (**a**) Globally shared data. (**b**) Common data

avoids NULL values in the extension columns [12]. The base table encompasses the columns every tenant needs. The columns of an extension are combined in an extension table. Each tuple in the extension table references its corresponding tuple in the base table. If a tenant has not booked an extension, no tuple in the corresponding extension table belong to the tenant.

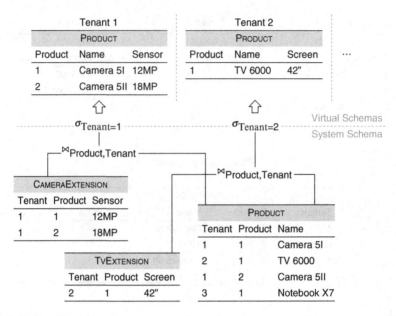

Fig. 2.17 Extension tables

The virtual table of a tenant exhibits the column of the base table and the column of all extensions the tenant has booked. If the tenant queries its virtual table, the virtualization layer selects the tenant's tuples from the base table and joins them with all booked extension tables. This way, the tenant sees its data including all booked extensions without seeing empty columns of not booked extensions. Figure 2.17 illustrates the querying procedure. Note that the example shown in the figure assumes the Common Metadata pattern. Insert, update, and delete operations have to occur on the base table and all booked extensions. Insert operations can be simply routed to all involved tables by decomposing the inserted tuples into base columns and extensions. Update and delete operations with a predicate require the virtualization layer to determine which tuples the operation affects. Therefore, the virtualization layer probes all involved tables with the applying parts of the given predicate. Depending on the predicate, the virtualization layer combines or intersects resulting lists of tuples into a single list. Finally, the operation is routed to all involved tables.

With extension tables, the data resides in a well modeled system schema. Hence, most features of the database system such as constraints, indexes, or aggregation are usable on the level of the system table without any modifications. The additional joins required to answer queries impose overhead for the virtualization layer. If the number of extensions per table and tenant are small, this overhead remains moderate. On the downside, extension tables allow customization only in relatively coarse-grained, predefined modules. Fine-grained extensions strongly decompose the system tables to tables with a single payload column in the extreme

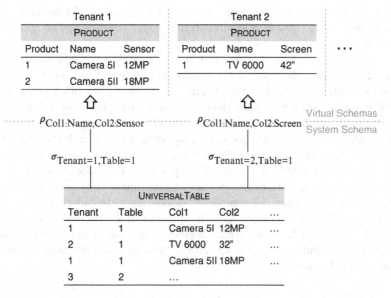

Fig. 2.18 Universal table

case. Although tenants can easily add new extensions without any change of the system schema, offering new extension requires changing the system schema. New extensions add new system tables. If many extensions are only booked by a single tenant, the consolidations effects decline. The extension table approach also has been used to map object-oriented inheritance to the relational model [8, 36].

Universal Table

A generic system schema allows consolidating arbitrary virtual schemas. The universal table is one possible generic system schema. Here, the system schema contains a single table consisting of a fixed number of generic byte string or char string columns [26]. Each tuple of the universal table corresponds to one tuple in a virtual table of a tenant. The system associates each tuple with the tenant and the virtual table it belongs to. Furthermore, the system relates the columns of each virtual table to the generic columns in the universal table while the virtual table is created. The mapping between virtual tables and universal table is stored in the system catalog. Whenever a tenant inserts a tuple into a virtual table, the virtualization layer maps each value to the corresponding generic column. Note that the values have to be cast to the technical type of the columns of the universal table.

If a tenant queries a virtual table, the virtualization layer rewrites the query to the universal table. Each table reference is replaced with the universal table and all column references are replaced with their corresponding generic column. Additionally, the virtualization layer has to wrap each column reference with a cast operation to map the values back to their original technical type. Figure 2.18

exemplarily shows the query rewrite procedure for the universal table (except the value casting). Analogously, the virtualization layer rewrites update and delete operations.

Since a generic schema does not reflect any application-specific data schema, it provides the most flexibility for customization. A tenant can adapt its virtual schema without affecting the system schema. The query rewriting procedure is simple and does not impose additional joins on a query. However, the necessary cast operations introduce a considerable overhead to the query processing. Further, the generically typed columns prevent direct constraints and index support; both have to be implemented on top. To mitigate the overhead, the universal table approach can be changed to technically typed columns. Instead of generically typed columns the universal table provides a fixed number of columns for each technical type. In any case, the number of columns has to be sufficiently high to fit every tuple in the whole system. As result, the universal table contains very wide rows with many NULL values, which imposes additional overhead. As reported, Salesforce successfully uses some variation of the universal table approach within its Force.com platform [40].

Pivot Table

The pivot table represents another generic system schema. The pivot table, also known as vertical schema, is the relational version of a triple store. It consists of five columns and contains a tuple for each value in all virtual tables. A single generically typed column contains the values; the other four columns reference the tenant, the virtual table, the virtual column, and the virtual tuple the value belongs to [2, 14]. Table names and column names can be stored directly in the pivot table, which, however, produces a heavy redundancy of these names. Hence, table names and column names are usually normalized into additional catalog tables.

If a tenant inserts a new tuple with n values into a virtual table, the virtualization layer inserts n new tuples into the pivot table. When tuples are queried, the virtualization layer has to reconstruct the originally inserted tuples. For every virtual column of a virtual table reference in a query, the virtualization layer queries the pivot table and joins the results by tenant, table, and reference to the virtual tuple. Figure 2.19 illustrates the process. Predicates on a single virtual column can be evaluated before the join; more complex predicate have to be evaluated after the join. An alternative way of reconstructing tuples is a conditional projection with grouping. Here, the virtualization layer projects every value to its virtual column and groups the fanned out tuples by tenant, table, and reference to the virtual tuple. Each group represents one virtual tuple and contains a single value in each of the value columns; the remains are NULL values. During grouping, the virtualization layer aggregates each column to the single value it contains. Update and delete operations follow the two stage model, again. First, the virtualization layer determines which virtual tuples need to be updated or deleted. Second, it performs to actual operation.

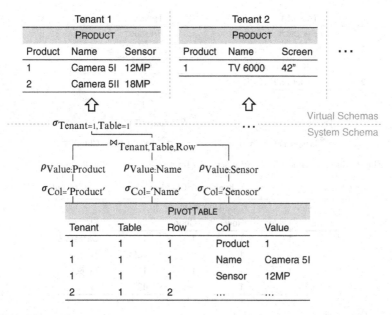

Fig. 2.19 Pivot table

In both querying rewriting schemes, however, the values have to be cast to the respective technical type (not shown in Fig. 2.19). Updates on a virtual table require one update of the pivot table per updated virtual tuple and updated virtual column. Delete operations require one delete in the pivot table per deleted virtual tuple and column in the virtual table.

Like the universal table, the pivot table allows tenants to customize their virtual schema without affecting the system schema. The pivot table avoids NULL values, to the price of considerable processing overhead. Querying a virtual table with n column requires $n - 1$ self-joins on the system table. The generically typed columns prevent direct constraints and index support. Similar to the universal table, this can be mitigated by partitioning the pivot table by technical type. Here, the system schema encompasses a pivot table for every technical type. This avoids casts and allows indexing. Pivot tables are also used successfully in clinical systems, e.g., to store the multifarious and varying examination data collected for a patient during consultation and surgery [20]. Another application of the concept maps XML to a pivot table for fast evaluation of XPath queries [21].

Chunk Table

The chunk table approach combines the universal table with the pivot table. While the number of different virtual columns is very high, the number of technical types is low and not higher than in a single tenant system. With only a small number of

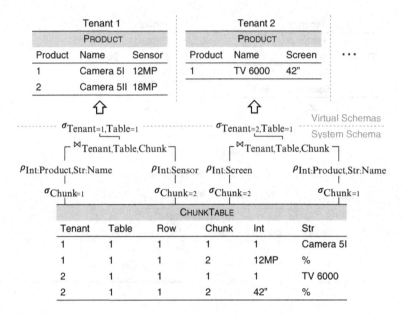

Tenant 1				Tenant 2		
PRODUCT				PRODUCT		
Product	Name	Sensor		Product	Name	Screen
1	Camera 5I	12MP		1	TV 6000	42"
2	Camera 5II	18MP				

Virtual Schemas
System Schema

$\sigma_{\text{Tenant}=1,\text{Table}=1}$ $\sigma_{\text{Tenant}=2,\text{Table}=1}$

$\bowtie_{\text{Tenant,Table,Chunk}}$ $\bowtie_{\text{Tenant,Table,Chunk}}$

$\rho_{\text{Int:Product,Str:Name}}$ $\rho_{\text{Int:Sensor}}$ $\rho_{\text{Int:Screen}}$ $\rho_{\text{Int:Product,Str:Name}}$

$\sigma_{\text{Chunk}=1}$ $\sigma_{\text{Chunk}=2}$ $\sigma_{\text{Chunk}=2}$ $\sigma_{\text{Chunk}=1}$

CHUNKTABLE					
Tenant	Table	Row	Chunk	Int	Str
1	1	1	1	1	Camera 5I
1	1	1	2	12MP	%
2	1	1	1	1	TV 6000
2	1	1	2	42"	%

Fig. 2.20 Chunk table

technical types, certain combinations of technical types can be found across many virtual tables. Many tuples may consist of, e.g., integer – string pairs or string triples. Chunk tables decompose the tenant data into chunks of these frequent technical type combinations. The system schema contains for each frequent combination a chunk table. It contains the respective chunks from tenant tuples accompanied by a chunk number and references to the tenant, the virtual tables, and the virtual tuple. A tenant tuple can be spread across different chunk tables and multiple chunk in the same chunk table. The system maintains a mapping for each virtual table. Each column is mapped to a defined chunk table and chunk number. This allows reconstructing the tenant tuples from the chunk tables [3].

If a tenant queries its data, the virtualization layer rewrites the query to the chunk tables. The rewriting process is a mixture of the rewriting for the universal table and the rewriting for the pivot table. As for the universal table, the virtualization layer has to replace a reference to virtual columns with the corresponding column in a chunk table. Similar to the pivot table, the system has to self-join a chunk table if it contains multiple chunks of the same virtual table. Each branch of the self-join selects chunks with a specific chunk number. If the queried virtual table spreads across multiple chunk tables, these have to be joined to. All chunk table access branches are joined by the tenant, the virtual table, and the virtual tuple reference. Similar to other approaches, the virtualization layer also adds filters for tenant and virtual table. Figure 2.20 illustrates the rewriting process. For clarity, the virtual product tables in the figure are mapped to a single chunk table only. The rewrite process for update and delete operations is analogous to the pivot table.

The virtualization identifies the affected chunks and then routes the operation to every chunk table. Since all value columns are technically typed, neither queries nor manipulation operations require casting.

Chunk tables form a semi-generic system schema. Tenants cannot change their virtual schema arbitrarily, though. Any virtual table has to fit on the available chunk tables. Nevertheless, this approach provides considerably more flexibility than extension tables. For full flexibility, the system requires a strategy how to handle the cutoff chunks that do not fit any of the existing chunk tables. Two strategies are reasonable. First, the system can store cutoff chunks in a full-generic table structure such as a universal table or a pivot tables to the price of a twice as complex virtualization layer. Second, the system maps cutoff chunks to the most similar of the available chunk tables to the price of NULL values (as shown in Fig. 2.20). The crucial point is the design of the chunk tables. With well selected chunk tables, the approach achieves full flexibility and technically typed values with a bearable number of required joins and a negligible small need for NULL values. The technical typed columns avoid expensive casts and allow index support. Because different virtual columns are consolidated into one system column, constraints have to be implemented on top, however.

Interpreted Column

If customization concentrates on augmenting a well-modeled database schema with a moderate number of additional columns, the interpreted column approach offers an easy solution. The system schema matches the common core schema, except that each extendable table contains an additional text column. Without any customization the column remains empty. If a tenant adds columns to a virtual table, the virtualization layer serializes the data in these columns to text and stores it in the text column. For each tuple, the serialization contains the values of the custom columns plus a reference to the column definition [1, 19]. The specific process of serialization of the data is independent of the principles of the approach as long as all accesses use the same technique. Usually, other data models with a defined text serialization, such as XML [38], JSON [13] or CSV [30], serve the purpose.

If a tenant queries data, the virtualization layer rewrites the query to the system tables according to the used sharing pattern. Before handing the result to the tenant, the system de-serializes the text column and projects the contained values to their respective virtual columns. Figure 2.21 illustrates the basic process in case of XML. In the example, the XPath expression [37] applied to the XML column marks the de-serialization. On a pure relational database system, predicates on the custom columns have to be evaluated by the virtualization layer. However, some database systems offer direct query support for complex values in columns typed by a secondary data model. For instance, IBM DB2 supports XML columns [9, 28], which can be directly queried with XQuery [39]. In such a case, the supported data model is strongly preferable, because the virtualization layer can rewrite predicates on the custom columns to the specific query capabilities pushing the evaluation

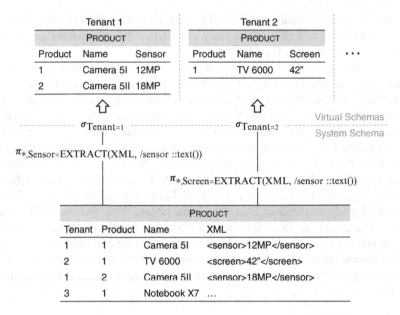

Fig. 2.21 Interpreted column

of these predicates down to the data. Similarly, the database system performs update and delete operations on custom columns directly if it offers the necessary capabilities. On a pure relational database system, the virtualization layer helps out. Following the two stage model, the virtualization layer queries the affected tuples and then executes the operation on the base table. For update operations, the first stage is necessary if the tenant updates values in custom columns, because the virtualization layer has to de-serialize the text column value to perform these updates. Before the virtualization layer writes the tuples back to the system table, it serializes the custom columns again. For update and delete operation the first stage is also required if the tenant specifies the affected tuples with predicates on custom columns.

The interpreted column approach is appealing, because it provides flexibility to add custom columns without sacrificing capabilities of the database system for the common part of the database schema. If the database system supports complex values such as XML including query and update capabilities, the virtualization layer remains very lean and the only overhead arises from the serialization and de-serialization. Without database system support, the necessary serialization and de-serialization within the virtualization layer imposes additional overhead in shape of extra data movement between database system and virtualization layer. The same holds for constraints and indexing. If constraints or indexing is not supported by the database system but required on custom columns, it must be implemented on top in the virtualization layer.

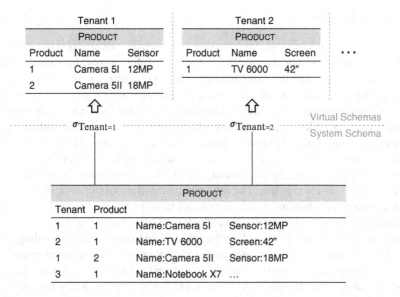

Fig. 2.22 Interpreted record

Interpreted Record

The interpreted record concept implements support for flexible structured tuples in a relational database system without the detour of a secondary database model. Instead of storing only the values of a tuple in its record, an interpreted record explicitly marks every value with a column reference. The interpreted record omits NULL values as representation of not instantiated columns and stores sparse tuples efficiently. Further, the user can add new columns to an interpreted record table easily. None of the tuples existing in the table needs to be touched. The database system adds the new column only to the system catalog, that new tuples or updated tuples can reference the column [6, 10].

With interpreted record support in the database system, the virtualization layer only realizes the sharing pattern. The flexibility required for customization is directly provided by the system tables. If a tenant adds a custom column to a virtual table, the virtualization merely routes this operation to the system table. If a tenant drops a column, the virtualization has to check if other tenants use the column before it drops the column on the system table. Queries, inserts, updates, and deletes are handled by the virtualization layer according to the used sharing pattern; no additional processing is required, as illustrated in Fig. 2.22.

The interpreted record concept convinces with no extra overhead in the virtualization layer and full support for constraints and indexing. In disk-bound database systems the additional expense of interpreting every record individually is negligible. The gained flexibility is limited to customization of the table structure, i.e., adding and dropping tables. The concept does not allow the consolidation of complete individual tenant schemas, as universal table and pivot table do.

Polymorphic Table

All approaches discussed so far consider only schema customization, which is
perfectly suitable for metadata sharing. However, if the tenants share data, tenants
may want to customize the shared data as well. Polymorphic tables [5] combine
sharing and customization of metadata and data in a single concept. Generally,
customization is the process of deriving a specialized table from a base table offered
by the service provider. The tenant may add columns and may add or update tuples.
Customization is similar to object inheritance (or specialization) [17]. The custom
table of a tenant inherits structure and data of the table it customizes. Tenants
derive their virtual tables, by customizing base tables or specialized extension tables
offered by the service provider. The multiple customizations of the same base table
form an inheritance hierarchy. A polymorphic table represents such an inheritance
hierarchy. The system database is the collection of all polymorphic tables.

Each tenant table is a leave node in the inheritance tree of its corresponding polymorphic table and has an inheritance path to the base table. The inheritance path of a
table segments the table into the stages of its customization. Metadata customization
slices the table vertically into base schema, extension schemas, and tenant schema.
Data customization slices the tables horizontally into shared base data, shared
extension data, and private tenant data. The table header decomposes into fragments;
the table body decomposes into segments. Each segment schematically complies
with a specific fragment. Beside the columns defined by its fragments, the segment
contains the primary key columns of the polymorphic table. The polymorphic table
manages all fragments and segments in the inheritance hierarchy of the customized
tables.

If a tenant accesses a virtual table, the virtualization layer traverses the inheritance hierarchy of the polymorphic table from the node that represents the
queried table up to the root node. While traversing the hierarchy, the virtualization
layer collects the fragment information and the segment references. All collected
fragments are concatenated to the schema of the virtual table. The segments form
the content of the table. The virtualization layer reads every segment and unites
the tuples of all segments from the same fragment. Finally, the unions of all
fragments are joined by the primary key to form the virtual table. Figure 2.23
illustrates the basic process for one polymorphic tables with one extension and two
tenants. Remember that segments of similar structure, for instance `ProductBase`,
`ProductBaseTenant1`, and `ProductBaseTenant2`, share their metadata by
referencing the same fragment. Polymorphic tables are meant to be implemented
within the database system. Nevertheless, the concept can also be realized on top of a
database system. Then, segments of the same fragment reside in a dedicated system
table or share a system table. Figure 2.23 shown the first case. Here, fragments
with multiple segments are stored redundantly in the metadata of multiple tables. In
the second case, the system table storing multiple segments requires an additional
column to distinguish the segments.

A polymorphic table allows comprehensive customization of shared data beyond
the addition of attributes. In such a case, the updated version of a shared tuple is

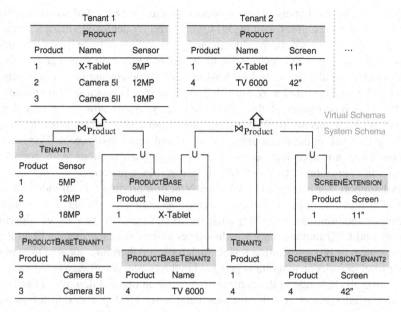

Fig. 2.23 Polymorphic table

placed in the lower segment that represents the customization step. During query processing, the virtualization layer additionally probes every tuple of a segment against the lower segments that belongs to the same fragment. The probing step is a left anti-semi-join of the higher segment with the lower segment on the primary key.

The polymorphic table concept covers multiple sharing patterns in one strike. Segments are the granularity of sharing. Base segments are shared globally among all tenants, extension segments are shared locally among a subset of tenants, and tenant segments are private to each tenant. The approach consolidates metadata and data as much as possible, while allowing very flexible customization of a table and its data. The processing overhead depends on the degree of customization. The deeper the inheritance tree of customizations gets, the more joins the processing requires. Similar to extension tables, the data resides in a well modeled system schema. Constraints, indexes, or aggregation operators are usable in a polymorphic table without any modification.

2.5 Configuring the Virtualization

Running an infrastructure based on virtual machines raises the issues of virtual machine *allocation* and *configuration*. Allocation addresses the issue of mapping a set of virtual machines to a set of given (potentially heterogeneous) hardware machines. Configuration focuses on the parameterization of the individual virtual machines. Since the hypervisor is in control of the hardware and the scheduling of the computing resources with regard to the currently deployed virtual machines instances, the administrator is able to assign limits usually in terms of main memory and overall CPU ratio. Allocation and configuration goes hand in hand and is usually a rather static and (at least initially) time-consuming administrative activity. The goal is to find a "reasonable" good balance between system utilization and the SLA-based goals of throughput and delay. As of now, most virtualized system environments are performing allocation and configuration tasks manually resulting in a sub-optimal resource utilization and static assignment. Very often, administrators are applying heuristics by grouping applications with complete behaviorally opposites in terms of CPU or storage usage patterns.

Tool support, for example the VMware Vmotion product[12] is provided on the layer of virtual machines without considering application knowledge. For example, hypervisor monitors are proposing changes to the infrastructure by considering memory and CPU requirements plus low-level system-oriented metrics like reference counters or process waiting times. Such tools are therefore not able to exploit higher level knowledge potentially provided by higher-level software components.

The overall challenge in the context of creating an optimal deployment scheme for virtualized services is – on the one hand – to develop a design advisor to capture the dynamic behavior. A monitoring component should signal situations of a re-configuration or re-allocation based on high-level utilization characteristics specified within the SLA contracts. On the other hand a design advisor component is supposed to compile knowledge of the running applications into design recommendations. For example, if a design advisor has knowledge about the temporal access behavior, it should allocate services for peak loads at different times within the same computing environment (depending on the virtualization class). In the literature, the topic of optimizing the deployment scenario gained some attention as well. For example [29] outlined a techniques of feedback-controlled virtual machines in the context of HPC infrastructures to precisely predict the resource consumption and runtime-behavior evaluated on five widely-used HPC applications. Other approaches tackling this challenge from a more database-centric perspective. For example the NIMO project at Duke [31] learns application performance models based in active learning methods and subsequently uses this models to adjust the deployment of virtual resources. The database-specific properties stem from the fact that NIMO exhibits a special data profiler which is used to feed what-if analysis procedures to provide performance estimates for potential scenarios like performance improvements when doubling the memory bound for the database system.

---

[12]http://www.vmware.com/products/vmotion/overview.html.

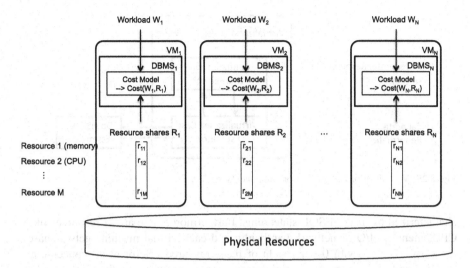

Fig. 2.24 Overview of the virtualization design advisor components

Virtualization Design Advisor for Database Services

One way to tackle the problem of incorporating application knowledge in a virtualization design advisor was proposed by Soror et al. in [33] and later more detailed in [34]. Since this is the first and most detailed work in this field, some of the main concepts are presented here to convey the basic idea and show how application knowledge is used to find and improve VM configurations.

The idea is to optimize Class 1 Virtualization Schemes by analyzing the anticipated workloads of all DBMSs, estimating the costs that occur from executing these workloads, and allocating resources to the virtual machines accordingly. The knowledge about the workload that is to be expected in the different virtual machines helps to, e.g., distinguish CPU intensive from I/O intensive workloads, and allows for optimal configurations. Treating the DBMS as a privileged application instead of a black box (with a simple performance model) enables the proposed virtualization design advisor to utilize the database management system's internal optimizer, especially its cost model, in a what-if mode to predict a configuration's performance with little overhead. Comparable to classical database advisors, specific configurations do not have to be implemented and tested in a time consuming experimental phase, but instead can be evaluated quickly. In contrast to classical database design advisors, the virtualization design advisor recommends the VM configuration instead of the DBMS configuration.

The general *virtualization design problem* that is introduced and solved by Soror et al. is formalized as follows (all components are shown in Fig. 2.24). Assume there are N virtual machines, running independent – possibly heterogeneous – database management systems, competing for a pool of shared physical resources on a single machine. Each workload W_i that is presented to the different virtual machines is

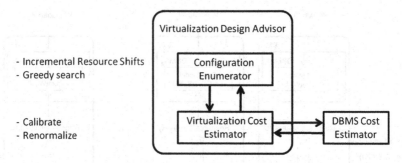

Fig. 2.25 Virtualization design advisor components

characterized by a set of SQL statements. Furthermore, there are M resources like CPU, memory, I/O or network bandwidth and each virtual machine gets a share $R_i = [r_{i1}, \ldots, r_{iM}]$ (with $0 \leq r_{ij} \leq 1$) of these resources. Soror et al. concentrate on CPU and main memory as primary resources to provision as these two can be configured in all available virtual machine monitors. Having formalized workloads and configurations, one can denote $Cost(W_i, R_i)$ as the cost of workload W_i under resource allocation R_i. The virtualization design problem is then given as choosing r_{ij} ($\leq i \leq N, 1 \leq j \leq M$) such that

$$\sum_{i=1}^{N} Cost(W_i, R_i)$$

is minimized, subject to $r_{ij} \geq 0$ for all i, j and $\sum_{i=1}^{N} r_{ij} = 1$.

The rather general formulation of the problem can further be refined, e.g., by introducing the notion of degradation and limiting this degradation in order to prevent certain workloads from being discriminated too much or by adding weights to the costs of each virtual machine to prioritize certain workloads over others.

The proposed virtualization design problem is solved by the virtualization design advisor in two major components as is shown in Fig. 2.25: (1) a configuration enumerator that searches the solution space and (2) a cost estimator that predicts the cost for each configuration.

The configuration enumerator assumes a smooth and concave objective function (which is reasonable as is shown in several experiments) and applies a greedy search in the search space. The search is accomplished by starting with a fair share of all resources among all virtual machines and increasing or decreasing shares in increments of, e.g., 5 %. Each new configuration is evaluated and the best is chosen as the starting point for a new search. The search ends when no better configuration can be found.

The cost estimation component of the virtualization design advisor is illustrated in Fig. 2.26. It wraps the two methods *calibrate* and *renormalize* around the DBMS cost estimator as the key component that subsumes deep knowledge about the

Fig. 2.26 Cost estimation for
virtualization design [34]

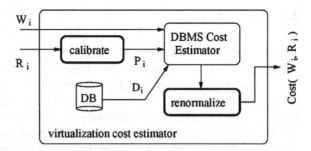

database management system's specific characteristics, methods, and behavior. Wrapping the cost estimator is required because the cost model cannot directly be applied to the given resource shares – which requires the calibrate method – and the cost model's results cannot easily be compared among different database management systems, which calls for the renormalization. Given that both methods require deep knowledge about the internals of the database management system, they need to be implemented (once) by an expert.

The calibration method takes the given resource shares R_i and maps them to a number of DBMS configuration parameters P_i. These parameters can either be *descriptive*, i.e., they describe the underlying system such that the DBMS understands its performance (e.g., cpu_tuple_cost or random_page_cost in PostgreSQL). Or parameters can be *prescriptive*, i.e., they define the configuration of the DBMS itself and thereby mimic rules or policies of the configuration (e.g., shared_buffers or work_mem in PostgreSQL). Both sets of parameters can be obtained by either applying policies and rules-of-thumb or by carefully running calibration queries and building simple models. Once obtained, the parameters can be applied and the DBMS's optimizer can be invoked with the expected workload on the database D_i in question. The database contains necessary statistics about the data and their distribution.

Because the costs that are estimated by DBMS optimizers are intended to compare different plans for the same query they do not need to be meaningful outside the DBMS. Hence, they are usually formulated in abstract units and cannot easily be compared among different database management systems. In order to compare them, they need to be normalized to a common unit like, e.g., consumed resources of a certain type or elapsed time.

In summary, the outlined technique presents a first step into the direction of automatically optimizing the deployment scenarios in Database-as-a-Service environments. Unfortunately, a comprehensive virtualization advisor requires to be aware not only of the characteristics and behavior of the individual layers but also has to incorporate the relationships and dependencies between the different layers. The core concept of layering software environments by shielding the working behavior from each other comes into a critical situation if a global optimization is required. Cross-cutting optimizations are still a hot topic for research projects with a certainly significant commercial relevance.

2.6   Summary

The principle of economy of scale demands to have multiple database users of tenants deployed on a shared system. The concept of virtualization plays a key role in this discussion. By definition, virtualization comprises the technique to hide physical or logical properties of computing devices by providing a virtual version of such a device (or computing entity). Unfortunately, virtualization also has two faces. On the one hand, clearly layering software stacks by means of abstracting from physical entities provides clear interfaces and makes the software stack easier to control and manage. On the other hand, finding cross-cutting optimizations for defining allocation and configuration schemes is extremely hard, if only the functional behavior of the underlying software layer is known. Within this section, we position the notion of virtualization as the key concept in order to provide "Database-as-a-Service"-functionality. We therefore introduced and discussed different classes with respect to the application of virtualization in a software stack, clearly distinguishing physical and logical virtualization. We also intensively described different techniques to achieve different requirements for "Data-Management-as-a-Service"-environments. For example, isolation of different users (or tenants) is highest, if virtualization is performed on a physical level. Alternatively, the overall system is flexible for a huge number of tenants, if database schemas or even some parts of the database content are shared. Having the notion of virtualization in mind, we may now dive into details on providing transactional or large-scale analytical data management services.

Additional related material can be found in various recent publications. Clark et al. [11] and Elmore et al. [18] investigate the problem of virtual machine migration and how migration can be used to implement shared nothing databases. Other publications concentrate on storage virtualization [32] as well as workload characterization [22] and resource allocation [35] for virtualized storage. FlurryDB, a dynamically scalable relational database that builds on virtual machine cloning, is described by Mior et al. [27]. The Relational Cloud project is a research prototype at MIT proposing scale-in, scale-out, and security for a private database virtualization – the project is driven by Curino et al. [15, 16]. Finally, Bernstein et al. report on Microsoft's approach to adapt the SQL Server for cloud computing [7].

References

1. Acharya, S., Carlin, P., Galindo-Legaria, C.A., Kozielczyk, K., Terlecki, P., Zabback, P.: Relational support for flexible schema scenarios. VLDBJ **1**(2), 1289–1300 (2008)
2. Agrawal, R., Somani, A., Xu, Y.: Storage and querying of e-commerce data. In: VLDB, pp. 149–158 (2001)
3. Aulbach, S., Grust, T., Jacobs, D., Kemper, A., Rittinger, J.: Multi-tenant databases for software as a service: schema-mapping techniques. In: SIGMOD, pp. 1195–1206 (2008)

4. Aulbach, S., Jacobs, D., Kemper, A., Seibold, M.: A comparison of flexible schemas for software as a service. In: SIGMOD, pp. 881–888 (2009)
5. Aulbach, S., Seibold, M., Jacobs, D., Kemper, A.: Extensibility and data sharing in evolving multi-tenant databases. In: ICDE, pp. 99–110 (2011)
6. Beckmann, J.L., Halverson, A., Krishnamurthy, R., Naughton, J.F.: Extending rdbmss to support sparse datasets using an interpreted attribute storage format. In: ICDE, p. 58 (2006)
7. Bernstein, P.A., Cseri, I., Dani, N., Ellis, N., Kalhan, A., Kakivaya, G., Lomet, D.B., Manne, R., Novik, L., Talius, T.: Adapting Microsoft SQL Server for Cloud Computing. In: ICDE conference, pp. 1255–1263 (2011)
8. Cabibbo, L., Carosi, A.: Managing inheritance hierarchies in object/relational mapping tools. In: CAiSE, *Lecture Notes in Computer Science*, vol. 3520, pp. 135–150. Springer (2005)
9. Cheng, J.M., Xu, J.: Xml and db2. In: ICDE, pp. 569–573 (2000)
10. Chu, E., Beckmann, J.L., Naughton, J.F.: The case for a wide-table approach to manage sparse relational data sets. In: SIGMOD, pp. 821–832 (2007)
11. Clark, C., Fraser, K., Hand, S.M., Hansen, J.G., Jul, E., Limpach, C., Pratt, I., Warfield, A.: Live migration of virtual machines. In: NSDI, pp. 273–286 (2005)
12. Copeland, G.P., Khoshafian, S.: A decomposition storage model. In: SIGMOD, pp. 268–279 (1985)
13. Crockford, D.: The application/json media type for javascript object notation (json), rfc 4627. http://tools.ietf.org/html/rfc4627 (2006)
14. Cunningham, C., Graefe, G., Galindo-Legaria, C.A.: Pivot and unpivot: Optimization and execution strategies in an rdbms. In: VLDB, pp. 998–1009 (2004)
15. Curino, C., Jones, E.P., Madden, S., Balakrishnan, H.: Workload-Aware Database Monitoring and Consolidation. In: SIGMOD conference, pp. 313–324 (2011)
16. Curino, C., Jones, E.P.C., Popa, R.A., Malviya, N., Wu, E., Madden, S., Balakrishnan, H., Zeldovich, N.: Relational Cloud: A Database-as-a-Service for the Cloud. In: CIDR (2011). URL http://dspace.mit.edu/handle/1721.1/62241
17. Currim, F., Ram, S.: When entities are types: Effectively modeling type-instantiation relationships. In: ERW, *Lecture Notes in Computer Science*, vol. 6413. Springer (2010)
18. Elmore, A.J., Das, S., Agrawal, D., El Abbadi, A.: Zephyr: live migration in shared nothing databases for elastic cloud platforms. In: SIGMOD conference, pp. 301–312 (2011). URL http://cs.ucsb.edu/~sudipto/papers/zephyr.pdf
19. Foping, F.S., Dokas, I.M., Feehan, J., Imran, S.: A new hybrid schema-sharing technique for multitenant applications. In: ICDIM, pp. 211–216 (2009)
20. Friedman, C., Hripcsak, G., Johnson, S.B., Cimino, J.J., Clayton, P.D.: A generalized relational schema for an integrated clinical patient database. In: SCAMC, pp. 335–339 (1990)
21. Grust, T., van Keulen, M., Teubner, J.: Accelerating xpath evaluation in any rdbms. ACM Transactions on Database Systems **29**(1), 91–131 (2004)
22. Gulati, A., Kumar, C., Ahmad, I.: Storage Workload Characterization and Consolidation in Virtualized Environments. In: VPACT (2009)
23. Jacobs, D., Aulbach, S.: Ruminations on multi-tenant databases. In: BTW, *LNI*, vol. 103, pp. 514–521 (2007)
24. Kaldewey, T., Wong, T.M., Golding, R.A., Povzner, A., Brandt, S.A., Maltzahn, C.: Virtualizing disk performance. In: RTAS, pp. 319–330 (2008)
25. Kiefer, T., Lehner, W.: Private table database virtualization for dbaas. In: UCC, pp. 328–329 (2011)
26. Maier, D., Ullman, J.D.: Maximal objects and the semantics of universal relation databases. ACM Transactions on Database Systems **8**(1), 1–14 (1983)
27. Mior, M.J., Lara, E.D.: FlurryDB: A Dynamically Scalable Relational Database with Virtual Machine Cloning. In: SYSTOR conference. Haifa, Israel (2011)
28. Nicola, M., der Linden, B.V.: Native xml support in db2 universal database. In: VLDB, pp. 1164–1174 (2005)
29. Park, S.M., Humphrey, M.: Self-tuning virtual machines for predictable escience. In: CCGrid, pp. 356–363 (2009)

30. Shafranovich, Y.: Common format and mime type for comma-separated values (csv) files, rfc 4180 (2005)
31. Shivam, P., Babu, S., Chase, J.S.: Learning application models for utility resource planning. In: Proc. of the 3rd Int. Conf. on Autonomic Computing (ICAC) 2006, Dublin, Ireland, pp. 255–264 (2006)
32. Singh, A., Korupolu, M., Mohapatra, D.: Server-storage virtualization: integration and load balancing in data centers. In: Super Computing Conference, p. 53 (2008)
33. Soror, A.A., Minhas, U.F., Aboulnaga, A., Salem, K., Kokosielis, P., Kamath, S.: Automatic Virtual Machine Configuration for Database - SIGMOD. In: SIGMOD (2008)
34. Soror, A.A., Minhas, U.F., Aboulnaga, A., Salem, K., Kokosielis, P., Kamath, S.: Automatic Virtual Machine Configuration for Database Workloads. ACM Transactions on Database Systems **35**(1), 1–47 (2010)
35. Soundararajan, G., Lupei, D., Ghanbari, S., Popescu, A.D., Chen, J., Amza, C.: Dynamic Resource Allocation for Database Servers Running on Virtual Storage. In: FAST, pp. 71–84 (2009)
36. Sun: JSR 220: Enterprise JavaBeans^{TM} 3.0 (persistence) (2006)
37. W3C: XML Path Language (XPath) 2.0. http://www.w3.org/TR/2007/REC-xpath20-20070123/ (2007)
38. W3C: Extensible Markup Language (XML) 1.0 (Fifth Edition). http://www.w3.org/TR/2008/REC-xml-20081126/ (2008)
39. W3C: XQuery 1.0: An XML Query Language (Second Edition). http://www.w3.org/TR/2010/REC-xquery-20101214/ (2010)
40. Weissman, C.D., Bobrowski, S.: The design of the force.com multitenant internet application development platform. In: SIGMOD, pp. 889–896 (2009)
41. Wilkes, J.: Traveling to Rome: QoS specifications for automated storage system management. In: IWQoS (2001)
42. Wilkes, J.: Traveling to Rome: a retrospective on the journey. In: SIGOPS (2009)

Chapter 3
Transactional Data Management Services for the Cloud

Since the early years of database applications, transactional processing has been one of the main use cases of database systems. Applications like booking, billing, fund transfer in banking, and order processing – usually known as *Online Transactional Processing (OLTP)* applications – require not only to manipulate data but also to ensure atomicity and consistency even in case of concurrent updates. When moving database functionality into the Cloud by offering database services, supporting this kind of transactional processing is evident for many applications especially in the eBusiness domain. In this chapter, we describe techniques and approaches to realize scalable database services for operational processing. After a brief introduction of foundations we discuss different consistency models, fundamental techniques for fragmented data organization and replication as well as protocols for achieving consensus which are needed for distributed commit protocols.

3.1 Foundations

In this section we give a brief review of the notions and core concepts of transactional systems. Furthermore, we discuss properties of distributed data management systems such as the CAP theorem as well as their consequences for transactional processing. Basic knowledge about these models and concepts is fundamental for understanding techniques and properties of Cloud-based data management solutions. Readers familiar with these concepts can skip this material and proceed with Sect. 3.2.

3.1.1 Transaction Processing

The concept of transactions was originally developed in the context of database systems to cope with failures and with concurrent accesses to shared data. It provides an abstraction which frees developers from the burden of writing code to deal with these problems.

A *transaction* represents a sequence of database operations (insert, update, delete, select) for which the system guarantees four properties also known as ACID [20]:

- **Atomicity:** A transaction is executed completely or not at all thus exhibiting the characteristics of atomicity. As a consequence, all changes to the data made by this transaction become visible only if the transaction reaches commit successfully. Otherwise, if the transaction was terminated abnormally before reaching a commit, the original state of the data from the beginning is restored.
- **Consistency:** The property of consistency guarantees that all defined integrity or consistency constraints are preserved at the end of a transaction, i.e., a transaction always moves the database from one consistent state to another consistent state. This has two consequences: In case a consistency constraint is violated, the transaction may be abnormally terminated and secondly, constraints can be temporarily violated during transaction execution but must be preserved upon the commit.
- **Isolation:** A transaction behaves as if it runs alone on the database without any concurrent operations. Furthermore, it only sees effects from previously committed transactions.
- **Durability:** When a transaction reaches the commit, it is guaranteed that all changes made by this transaction will survive subsequent system and disk failures.

In order to specify the boundaries of a transaction in an application program, two classes of commands are needed:

- *Begin-of-Transaction (BOT)* denotes the beginning of the operation sequence – in some systems (e.g. in SQL database systems) this command is implicitly performed after the end of the previous transaction.
- *Commit* and *rollback* denote the end of the transaction. Commit is the successful end and requires that all updates must be made permanent while rollback is for aborting the entire sequence, i.e. undoing all effects.

The ACID properties are usually implemented by different components of a data management solution.

Maintaining *isolation* of transactions is achieved by a concurrency control component implementing the concept of serializibility. *Atomicity* and *durability* are guaranteed by providing recovery strategies coping with possible failures. Finally, *consistency* is either explicitly supported by checking integrity rules or only implicitly by allowing rollbacks of transactions.

Concurrency control is based on two observations: First, if each transaction alone guarantees consistent data, then consistency is also guaranteed while these transactions are executed serially. Second, if all transactions are executed serially, then each transaction sees only the results of all transactions which have been committed before. However, insisting on a strict serial execution is impractical in

Fig. 3.1 Example of the lost
update problem

T_1	T_2	balance of account o
$X := read(o)$		\$100
	$Y := read(o)$	\$100
$X := X + 50$		\$100
	$Y := Y + 70$	\$100
$write(o, X)$		\$150
	$write(o, Y)$	\$170

most cases. Thus, transactions should be executed concurrently, but produce the
same result (i.e., database state) as in a serial execution order. We denote a given
execution order of possibly concurrent transactions a schedule; a schedule that is
equivalent to a serial schedule, is called *serializable* [5]. Unfortunately, not all
possible schedules are serializable – problems such as non-repeatable reads, dirty
reads (a transaction reads data modified by a second transaction which has not yet
committed and still can be aborted), lost updates (an update of a transaction gets lost
because it is overwritten by an update of a concurrently running transaction), and
the phantom problem can occur. In Fig. 3.1 the lost update problem is illustrated:
two transactions T_1 and T_2 try to deposit money to the account o by first reading the
current balance followed by writing back the updated balance. Unfortunately, the
update of T_1 is overwritten by the update of T_2.

Pessimistic Concurrency Control

In order to ensure serializability, different protocols can be used which are classified into pessimistic and optimistic strategies. Pessimistic protocols prevent
non-serializable schedules by synchronizing concurrent accesses to data objects
while the transactions are executed. One possible solution is to require that these
accesses must be done in a mutually exclusive manner. This is achieved by allowing
a transaction to access a data object only if it is holds a lock on that object. Here,
two types of locks are distinguished: shared or real locks allowing other transactions
to read the same object but forbidding that other transactions can write to the locked
object, and exclusive or write locks prohibiting other transactions from reading or
writing to the data object. In order to ensure serializibility, locks are acquired and
released according to the two-phase locking protocol:

1. Within the growing phase, a transaction acquires shared and exclusive locks but
   must not release any lock.
2. In the shrinking phase, the transaction may release all locks, but is not allowed
   to obtain any new lock.

If all transactions follow this protocol, serializability of the schedule is guaranteed without any further tests. A variant of this protocol is the strict two-phase
locking protocol where all locks are released at the end of a transaction, preventing
dirty reads (Fig. 3.2).

Fig. 3.2 Two-phase locking
protocol

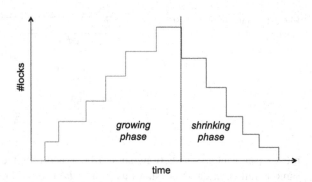

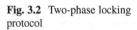

growing
phase

shrinking
phase

time

An alternative synchronization technique is based on timestamp ordering. Here, a serialization order is chosen a priori by assigning a unique timestamp $ts(T_i)$ to each transaction T_i. Timestamps are generated by a transaction manager and are monotonously increasing. During execution, the transactions are forced to process their conflicting operations in the order of the timestamps. Two operations are in conflict if both transactions access the same data object and at least one is a write operation. Timestamp ordering is achieved by enforcing the following rule: Given two conflicting operations p_i of transaction T_i and q_j of transaction T_j, then p_i is executed before q_j if and only if $ts(T_i) < ts(T_j)$.

A basic timestamp ordering strategy can be implemented by checking whether operations come too late. In order to determine this situation, the latest timestamp of a read operation's transaction (denoted by $ts_R(o)$) and of a write operation's transaction (denoted by $ts_W(o)$) for each object o are recorded by the data management component. Whenever $p_i(o)$ of T_i arrives, the timestamps of the object for the conflicting operations are checked, e.g. if p_i is a write operation we check both $ts_R(o)$ and $ts_W(o)$. If $ts(T_i) < ts_R(o)$ or $ts(T_i) < ts_W(o)$ the $p_i(o)$ comes too late and T_i is aborted. Otherwise, p_i is processed and the respective timestamps – in this case $ts_W(o)$ – are updated to $max\{ts(T_i), ts_W(o)\}$. An aborted transaction is restarted and is assigned a new and therefore larger timestamp.

A special optimization is the *Thomas write rule* which can be used for write/write conflicts: when T_i wants to perform a $w_i(o)$ but is too late (i.e., $ts(T_i) < ts_W(o)$) then $w_i(o)$ can be simply ignored instead of rejecting it and aborting T_i. This is because ignoring $w_i(o)$ has the same effect as writing o in timestamp order: the transaction with timestamp $ts_W(o)$ (let us call this transaction T_j) would come after T_i since $ts(T_i) < ts_W(o) = ts(T_j)$. Thus, using timestamp order, $w_i(o)$ would be overwritten by the later write operation in T_j.

Optimistic Concurrency Control

A second class of concurrency control techniques is formed by so-called optimistic protocols. These methods are based on the assumption that conflicts are rather rare: transactions are simply processed without any synchronization effort (particularly

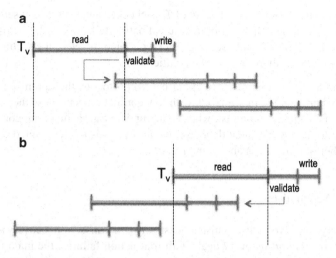

Fig. 3.3 (a) FOCC versus (b) BOCC

without locking), but must be checked before committing to determine whether the resulting schedule is serializable. In order to achieve this, a transaction is divided into three phases:

- **Read phase:** Within a read phase, the transaction reads data but writes only to local copies of the data.
- **Validation phase:** Within a validation phase, the concurrency control component checks the schedule for correctness (serializability).
- **Write phase:** The final write phase is entered only when the validation was successful. Within the write phase, the local copies of the modified data objects are written back to the global database.

If the validation fails, the transaction is aborted and should be restarted. In the simplest case, both the validation phase and the subsequent write phase are placed into a critical section and are indivisible. Alternative approaches introduces some forms of locking during the write phase. Two different approaches exist for the validation (Fig. 3.3):

- **Backward-oriented concurrency control (BOCC):** Within BOCC, a transaction T_v to be validated is checked against all transactions T_i which are already committed but whose commit occurred after T_v started, i.e. while T_v was running. Particularly, it is checked whether the read set RS of T_v (i.e., the set of all objects read by T_v) was "polluted" by the write set WS of any of T_i (the set of objects written by a transaction), i.e. if $RS(T_V) \cap WS(T_i) \neq \emptyset$. In this case, the validation fails and T_v is aborted.
- **Forward-oriented concurrency control (FOCC):** Under FOCC, a transaction T_v is validated against all concurrently running transactions T_j which are still in

their read phase. Here, the write set of T_v is checked against the read sets of these transactions at the validation time. The validation fails, if $WS(T_v) \cap RS(T_j) \neq \emptyset$. In opposite to BOCC, this scheme offers a choice to select the victim, i.e. the transaction to be aborted: T_v or the conflicting T_j.

Compared to the pessimistic (locking-based) protocols, the optimistic methods are usually better suited in scenarios with low conflict rates because they avoid the overhead of locking. In contrast, when many update transactions run concurrently and trying to access the same data, optimistic protocols are less suited due to the high number of transaction aborts and restarts.

Recovery Mechanisms

For recovery, we have to distinguish at least between transaction recovery and crash recovery. *Transaction recovery* deals with transaction failures: the main task is to undo effects of an aborted transaction in the presence of concurrent transactions. This can be achieved by following a strict commit protocol ensuring that each transaction holds its write locks until the end of the transaction. An alternative approach is based on deferred commits and cascading aborts where a transaction which reads data written by an aborted transaction has to be also aborted and – if possible – restarted.

Crash recovery deals with failures which bring the database server down, therefore providing fault-tolerance. This can be achieved using two base strategies: fail-stop and fail-over. *Fail-stop* immediately brings down the server and performs appropriate recovery strategies, e.g. logging. On the other hand, in a *fail-over* strategy the processing is forwarded to another processor – an approach that is typically chosen in high-availability scenarios.

Logging is based on the idea of being able to move between an old and a new database state by using history information written to a stable log. Figure 3.4 illustrates this idea: while executing any update (DO – moving to a new database state) a log entry is written. This information can be used to replay this update (REDO) or to restore the old state by undoing the effects of this operation (UNDO). In the latter case, a so-called compensation log entry is written to the log that is needed to ensure idempotence in case of failures during recovery.

A log consists of totally ordered entries describing the sequence of recent database actions, i.e. begin and end of transactions as well as all write operations to database objects resulting from insert, update, and delete operations. When and how these entries are written is defined by three logging rules [37]:

- **Redo logging rule:** The redo logging rule says that for every transaction in the history which has performed a commit, all data actions of this transaction have to be in the stable database or the stable log. This requires that redo information are written to the log when the transaction commits.

Fig. 3.4 Principle of logging

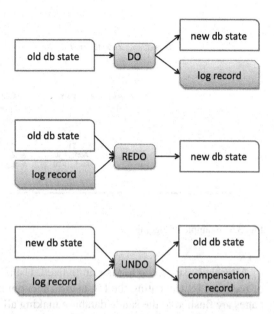

- **Undo logging rule:** The undo logging rule requires that for every action of a transaction without a commit or abort in the history that when this action is present in the database (e.g. the modified objects are written to disk) there must be an entry for this action in the log. This means that undo information has to be written to the log before a page of an uncommitted transaction is flushed to disk.
- **Garbage collection rule:** The garbage collection rule defines when log entries can be removed from the log: A log entry describing a data action can be removed only if this action is already in the stable database and the history of the transaction contains a commit.

Figure 3.5 shows an example of two transactions in a failure scenario. Both transactions try to update an account, but a system failure occurs before the second transaction is able to commit. The log contains records describing the old state (the before image $Acc1_{old}$) as well as new state (the after image $Acc1_{new}$). Furthermore, for transaction T_1 a commit record is logged.

When the system restarts after the failure, the log is analyzed in chronological order and the following steps are performed:

1. All transactions for which a BOT was found are classified into two groups: winner transactions for which a commit record exists and loser transactions without such a record.
2. Next, in order to ensure that all updates are kept in the stable database, a redo of all winner transactions found in the log is performed by writing the after images again to the database.
3. Finally, the effects of all loser transactions are removed by undoing their logged operations (e.g. writing back the before image) in a reverse order.

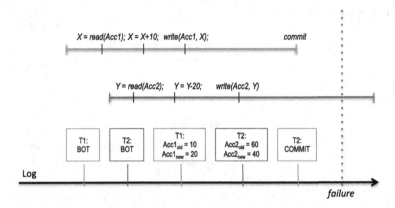

Fig. 3.5 Example of logging

After these steps, the log is reinitialized. Usually, real systems reduce the effort of recovery by truncating the log using checkpoints. During a checkpoint all dirty pages are flushed to the stable database making all previous log entries obsolete.

A second important issue is the idempotence of redo and undo: because a failure may also occur while the database is recovering, the system has to guarantee that repeated redos and undos do not result in an inconsistent state. For redo this can be achieved for instance by keeping information about which log entry has modified a page on disk, while for undo so-called compensation records are written to the log.

3.1.2 Brewer's CAP Theorem and the BASE Principle

In the previous section we briefly discussed techniques for achieving ACID properties in a database system. However, applying these techniques in large-scale scenarios such as data services in the Cloud leads to scalability problems: the amount of data to be stored and processed and the transaction and query load to be managed is usually too large to run the database services on a single machine. To overcome this data storage bottleneck, the database must be stored on multiple nodes, for which horizontal scaling is the typically chosen approach. The database is partitioned across the different nodes: either table-wise or by fragmenting the tables also known as sharding (Sect. 3.3.2). Both cases result in a distributed system for which Eric Brewer has formulated the famous CAP theorem which characterizes three of the main properties of such a system [7]:

- **Consistency:** All clients have the same view, even in the case of updates. For multi-site transactions this requires all-or-nothing semantics. For replicated data, this implies that all replicas have always consistent states.

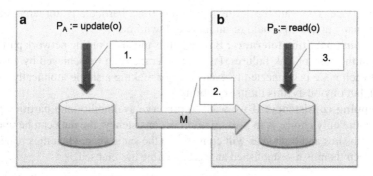

Fig. 3.6 Example scenario for CAP

- **Availability:** Availability implies that all clients always find a replica of data even in the presence of failures.
- **Partition-tolerance:** In the case of network failures which split the nodes into groups (partitions), the system is still able to continue the processing.

The CAP theorem further states that in a distributed, shared-data system these three properties cannot be achieved simultaneously in the presence of failures. In order to understand the implications we have to consider possible failures. We assume the scenario depicted in Fig. 3.6: For scalability reasons the database is running on two sites A and B sharing a data object o, e.g. a flight booking record. This data sharing should be transparent to client applications, i.e. an application P_A connected to site A and P_B accessing the database via site B. Both clients should always see the same state of o even in the presence of an update. Hence, in order to ensure a consistent view, any update performed for instance by P_A and changing o to a new state o' has to be propagated by sending a message m to update o at B so P_B reads o'.

To understand why the CAP theorem holds, we consider the scenario where the network connecting A and B fails, resulting in a network partitioning and whether all three properties can be simultaneously fulfilled. In this situation, M cannot be delivered resulting in an inconsistent (outdated) value of o at site B. If we want to avoid this to ensure consistency, M has to be sent synchronously, i.e. in an atomic operation with the updates. However, this procedure sacrifices the availability property: if M cannot be delivered, the update on node A cannot be performed. However, sending M asynchronously does not solve the problem because then A does not know when B receives the message. Hence, any approach trying to achieve a strong consistent view such as locking, centralized management etc. would either violate availability or partition tolerance. A detailed proof of the CAP theorem was given by Gilbert and Lynch in [17].

In order to address these restrictions imposed by CAP, the system designer has to choose one of the three properties to drop:

- **Dropping availability:** Availability is given up by simply waiting when a partition event occurs until the nodes come back and the data is consistent again.

The service is unavailable during the waiting time. Particularly, for large settings with many nodes this could result in long downtimes.

- **Dropping partition tolerance:** Basically this means avoiding network partitioning in the case of link failures. Partition tolerance can be achieved by ensuring that each node is connected to each other or making a single atomically-failing unit, but obviously, this limits scalability.
- **Dropping consistency:** If we want to preserve availability and partition tolerance, the only choice is to give up or relax consistency: the data can be updated on both sites and both sites will converge to the same state when the connection between them is re-established an a certain time has elapsed.

Classic database systems focus on guaranteeing the ACID properties and, therefore, favor consistency over partition tolerance and availability. This is achieved by employing techniques like distributed locking and two-phase commit protocols. However, giving up availability is often not an option in Web business where users expect an always-on operation. Moreover, techniques for guaranteeing strong consistency in large distributed systems limit scalability and results in latency issues (Sect. 1.1).

To cope with these problems, BASE was proposed as an alternative to ACID. BASE stands for *Basically Available, Soft state, Eventual consistency* [15] and follows an optimistic approach accepting stale data and approximate answers while favoring availability. Some ways to achieve this are by supporting partial failures without total system failures, decoupling updates on different tables (i.e. relaxing consistency), and itempotent operations which can be applied multiple times with the same result [30]. In this sense, BASE describes more a spectrum of architectural styles than a single model. In the following sections we will discuss several techniques for implementing services following the BASE principle.

3.2   Consistency Models

As discussed in the previous section, any distributed data-sharing system that wants to provide availability and partition tolerance has to give up consistency. It should be noted that this refers to a slightly different notion of consistency than the one introduced with ACID. For ACID consistency, at the end of a transaction the database is in a consistent state where all integrity constraints are satisfied again. In contrast, consistency in the CAP theorem focuses on the view of a user or client program in a distributed databases as illustrated in Fig. 3.6. Under *strong consistency* any update by P_A on o leading to a new version o' would be immediately reflected by a read of P_B – P_B reads version o'. Note that P_A and P_B could be the same program which alternatively connects to A or B.

By giving up consistency the system is not able to guarantee that any subsequent access at B will return the updated version o'. There is always an inconsistency window between the update at A and the point in time when the system can guarantee that any access like P_B returns the updated value. This kind of consistency is called *weak consistency*.

A special form of weak consistency is *eventual consistency* [36]. This means the system guarantees that if no new updates are performed, all subsequent accesses will *eventually* return the updated value. Particularly, the maximum size of the inconsistency window can be determined by certain system parameters as long as no failures occur.

In [34, 36] several variations of the eventual consistency model are described:

- **Causal consistency:** If P_A notifies P_B about the update on o, it is guaranteed that a subsequent access to this object will return the updated value. However, this holds only for processes with a causal relationship, i.e. processes which are notified by P_A.
- **Read-your-writes consistency:** This model guarantees that P_A always reads the new value o' after it has updated it, but never reads an outdated value – even if the read request is answered by B. This ensures that a process always sees its own updates.
- **Session consistency:** Read-your-writes consistency is guaranteed only for a session. That means that any access to the system has to be performed in the context of a session and the guarantees do not span multiple sessions.
- **Monotonic read consistency:** In this model a process which has already seen a particular version o' of an object will never read any previous version in all subsequent accesses.
- **Monotonic write consistency:** This is a very important model – basically a write operation is always completed before any subsequent write of the same process.

Further models are, for example:

- **Read-after-writes consistency:** This consistency modes guarantees that all clients see an object immediately after it is newly created.
- **Read-after-updates consistency:** A stronger version of this model guaranteeing that is also the case for updates on objects.

Some of these models can be combined, for example in order to provide a certain consistency model is guaranteed for a session. A simple approach to achieve this is to ensure that a process always accesses the same node during a session. Moreover, different consistency models can be implemented for different operations. For instance, Amazon S3 supports read-after-writes consistency for writing new objects and a weaker eventual consistency model for overwriting objects (which means that read-after-updates is not guaranteed).

3.3 Data Fragmentation

As discussed in Sect. 3.1.2, large-scale data management solutions require partitioning of data to be able to handle huge data volumes and query loads. Partitioning always opens up the great challenge to define the "optimal" partitions. The theory and technique is subsumed under the technical term of fragmentation. A fragmentation scheme is therefore synonym to a partitioning scheme. Fragmentation strategies have a major impact on communication costs when data processing requires access to remote nodes. The fragmentation scheme also has great impact on the capability of load balancing, e.g. by allowing distributed and therefore parallel access on multiple nodes. Finally fragmentation is also crucial for availability, if the failures of a node results in data loss or can be compensated by redundantly stored data. Core techniques and different strategies applicable for large data-management solutions in Cloud environments are outlined below.

3.3.1   Classification of Fragmentation Strategies

The first challenge of fragmentation is to determine the "optimal" *granularity* at which data is distributed over different nodes. One possible approach is to always store entire objects (e.g. a relation) at a single node. This allows single-site operations and simplifies, among other things, integrity checks. However, this scheme makes load balancing difficult when some relations are accessed more frequently than others. An alternative approach is to split an object into fragments or partitions and store each partition on a separate node. In this way, the load can be better balanced among different nodes. Furthermore, inherent parallelism and access locality can be exploited and processing costs reduced if search operations can be restricted to some partitions.

3.3.2   Horizontal Versus Vertical Fragmentation

Fragmentation strategies can be further classified according to the units which are assigned to the individual partitions. In *horizontal fragmentation* a set of tuples from a global table, e.g. specified by selection criterion P_i, forms a partition. As an example consider a customer table which is fragmented by the customer's region:

CustomerEurope $:= \sigma_{Region=Europe}$(Customer)
CustomerNorthAmerica $:= \sigma_{Region=NorthAmerica}$(Customer)
CustomerAsia $:= \sigma_{Region=Asia}$(Customer)

A special case is the horizontally derived fragmentation scheme, where the fragmentation criteria for a table is derived from another table. For example, if the customer table is horizontally fragmented by country, then the orders which are assigned to customers via a foreign key relationship should be fragmented in the same way. This can be achieved by a semijoin of both tables:

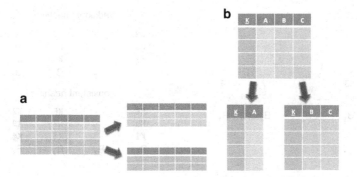

Fig. 3.7 Fragmentation strategies. (**a**) Horizontal. (**b**) Vertical

$$\text{OrdersEurope} \qquad := \text{Orders} \bowtie \left(\sigma_{Region=Europe}(\text{Customer})\right)$$
$$\text{OrdersNorthAmerica} := \text{Orders} \bowtie \left(\sigma_{Region=NorthAmerica}(\text{Customer})\right)$$
$$\text{OrdersAsia} \qquad := \text{Orders} \bowtie \left(\sigma_{Region=Asia}(\text{Customer})\right)$$

This guarantees that order tuples can be stored on the same nodes as their corresponding customer tuples and simplifies, among other things, join processing.

In contrast, for *vertical fragmentation* a set of columns is assigned to a partition. This can be specified by a projection operation, e.g. customer information needed for order processing are stored in one partition and other marketing-related columns are stored in another table (Fig. 3.7).

A fragmentation scheme should always be complete (all tuples or columns belong to at least one partition), reconstructable (the original relation can be built from the partitions), and disjoint in the sense that the data is stored in not more than one partition. The latter requirement does not hold for vertical fragmentation where a common key column is needed in all partitions to guarantee reconstructability.

In large-scale systems, horizontal fragmentation is the most commonly used strategy. If the partitions are placed on multiple isolated instances of a database system (which could even be distributed worldwide) this strategy is sometimes called *sharding*.

Various criteria are possible for defining partitions in horizontal fragmentation. One of the main goals is to exploit the processing power of multiple nodes by decomposing operations into parallel processable sub-operations. This requires that all partitions are equally sized and support the processing of the operations. Classic criteria known from parallel and distributed databases are:

- **Round robin fragmentation:** With round robin fragmentation, tuples are assigned in a round-robin manner to the different partitions. The round robin fragmentation scheme is usually well suited to achieve good load-balancing behavior when accessing the partitions in parallel.
- **Range fragmentation:** When using range fragmentation, partitions are defined based on ranges of data values, e.g. orders with an order date between 2009 and 2011 are assigned to a partition, order entries for 2012 and younger are

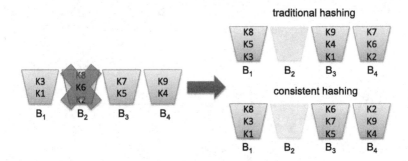

Fig. 3.8 Traditional versus consistent hashing

assigned to another partition. Range fragmentation schemes are usually applied to time values to implement some sort of data aging. For example older database entries are stored in partitions residing on slower disks or having a lower degree of redundancy and availability. More recent entries are stored in faster storage subsystems and potentially with a higher degree of redundancy.

- **Hash fragmentation:** The hash fragmentation schemes applies a hash function to data values (e.g. to the key value or a subset of a composite key) in order to determine the partition to which the tuple belongs to. Hash fragmentation is usually deployed if the system tries to evenly distribute the data without considering any application-specific semantics.

Out of these fragmentation criteria, hash fragmentation is particularly well suited to large-scale systems. Round robin simplifies a uniform distribution of records but does not facilitate the restriction of operations to single partitions. While range fragmentation does supports this, it requires knowledge about the data distribution in order to properly adjust the ranges.

3.3.3   Consistent Hashing

Hash fragmentation based on traditional hash functions has a major drawback in distributed systems. When some of the nodes go offline, i.e., the number of hash buckets changes, a reshuffling of all tuples becomes necessary, which is often not acceptable in large systems. This problem is illustrated in Fig. 3.8: four buckets are used for managing the data based in the (traditional) simple hash function $h(x) = x \mod 4$, and – each bucket is stored on a different node. When the node of bucket B_2 goes offline, all of the tuples – not only the tuples in bucket B_2 – must be transferred to other nodes using the new hash function $h(x) = x \mod 3$.

In order to tackle this problem, we can use *consistent hashing*. This technique aims at minimizing the degree of reshuffling in the case of node addition or removal. For K keys/tuples and n buckets/nodes, consistent hashing typically requires that, on

Fig. 3.9 Consistent hashing

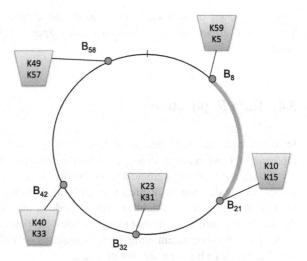

average, only $\frac{K}{n}$ keys must remapped. This is shown in Fig. 3.8: using this hashing scheme, only the tuples of the bucket at node B are reshuffled.

Another property of consistent hashing is a roughly even distribution of the tuples over the set of nodes. Furthermore, the load of the nodes – the number of tuples stored at each node – and the spread of tuples – the number of nodes responsible for a certain tuple – are only increasing logarithmically with the number of views. In this context, view means the number of nodes a given user is aware of. In a large-scale system this number may vary from user to user because the information about a newly added node cannot be propagated synchronously to all users or nodes.

Consistent hashing can be implemented using a rather simple scheme. Nodes (buckets) are mapped to points on a keyring using a standard hash function. Then, each key k on the keyring is assigned to the bucket whose point is the first clockwise successor of k on the keyring. Ideally, this mapping should distribute tuples to nodes randomly. The idea is illustrated in Fig. 3.9. Each bucket B_i (where i denotes the bucket's point on the keyring) is stored on its own node. If B_i's clockwise predecessor bucket on the keyring is B_j, then b_i is responsible for the range $(j,i]$ of the keyring, so a key k is stored in bucket B_i for $j < k \leq i$. For instance, the node of B_{21} is responsible for the range marked with the thick line segment and key 15 is assigned to B_{21}.

Let us assume the node responsible for bucket B_{32} is leaving the network. In this situation, only the keys stored in this bucket need to be transferred to bucket B_{42}. Adding a new node works in a very similar way: the node chooses a random point x on the keyring for its bucket B_x. When inserting this bucket, all keys k with $k \leq y - j$ from the successor bucket B_y on the keyring are moved to the new bucket – all other keys are untouched.

In summary, selecting a data fragmentation scheme has a significant impact on processing costs and load balancing, but also on scalability. Apart from classic schemes known from parallel and distributed databases, consistent hash-based horizontal fragmentation is a very promising approach for large-scale distributed systems.

3.4   Data Replication

In distributed data management systems with fragmented databases data is often replicated for two reasons. First, performance is improved by having local copies of data instead of requiring remote access. Furthermore, multiple copies of data allow a better load balancing in the presence of multiple requests. The second reason is an increasing availability and fault tolerance: node failures can be compensated when the data of the node is replicated to other nodes. However, the benefits of replication do not come for free: maintaining replicas requires not only additional storage space but also implies a higher effort for updates.

The main task in data replication is replica control to keep the existing replicas consistent. This involves several subtasks:

- **Update propagation:** The task of update propagation is responsible for disseminating updates to all replicas.
- **Concurrency control:** Concurrency control ensures global serializability even if different replicas are updated by concurrently running transactions.
- **Failure detection and recovery:** The task of failure detection and recovery deals particularly with updates in case of network partitioning.
- **Handling of read transactions:** Picking the "optimal" replica or set of replicas to satisfy a read request is the main requirement for the tasks of handing reading transactions. Typically, this involves a tradeoff between fast and cheap local access and freshness of data.

In the following sections we discuss several replication strategies addressing these issues. Based on a classification of possible strategies and a brief overview on classic database replication protocols, we particularly discuss techniques for large-scale systems.

3.4.1   Classification of Replication Strategies

Though, replica control can be performed in different ways, the basic idea is always the same: translating an operation on a logical object (e.g. read or update) to physical operations on the replicas. An obvious, but rather naïve approach is the *Read One Write All (ROWA)* strategy which translates a logical read into a read operation on any replica and a logical write into a write operation on all replicas. This simple strategy has a major problem: if any of the replicas is not available, then the update transaction cannot be finished successfully. To overcome this problem several strategies have been developed in the past. The strategies can

WHERE?

	primary copy	update anywhere

eager	☑ strong consistency
	  simple concurrency control
	
	☒ inflexible
		☑ strong consistency
		  flexible
		
		☒ complex concurrency control

lazy	☑ fast
	  simple concurrency control
	
	☒ inflexible
		☑ fast
		  flexible
		
		☒ conflict resolution
		  inconsistency

(left side label: **WHEN?**)

Fig. 3.10 Classification of replication strategies (After [23])

be classified according to Gray et al. [18] by only two basic parameters: when and where (Fig. 3.10).

The "when" parameter describes the propagation strategy, i.e. when are updates propagated to replicas to achieve consistency. Two possible strategies are available:

- **Eager replication:** With eager replication the updates are propagated to all replicas synchronously as part of the originating transaction.
- **Eager replication:** In contrast, with lazy replication the update of the originating transaction is performed on only one replica, but then propagated asynchronously to the other replicas, typically as part of a separate transaction.

The "where" parameter determines the way how updates are controlled and therefore implicitly the transaction location. Again, two different approaches are possible:

- **Primary copy:** The first solution is based on defining a dedicated master node for each object which maintains the primary copy. Updates are performed only on this primary copy and the master node is responsible for propagating the update to the other replicas.
- **Update anywhere:** The alternative solution is called update anywhere and allows to perform the update on any of the replicas.

Based on these two dimensions, different replication protocols can be designed which inherit the following advantages and disadvantages of the basic models. The big advantage of a primary copy approach is that concurrency control is basically the same as in non-replicated systems. However, because all nodes have to know that all updates have to be performed on the primary copy and which node is responsible for this copy. This limits the transparency and flexibility of the overall approach. In contrast, update anywhere provides this flexibility but this advantage is gained by a higher complexity of concurrency control which includes – for instance – distributed deadlock detection.

Furthermore, no inconsistencies or anomalies in serialization can occur with eager strategies. Therefore, there is no need for reconciliation. However, the probability of deadlocks increases with the number of nodes which limits the scalability. Lazy strategies – particularly in combination with update anywhere – allow any node to update its local data and also two nodes to update the same object. However, such conflicts have to be detected and reconciled to make sure that no updates will get lost.

3.4.2   Classic Replication Protocols

We start the discussion on replication protocols by first looking at some well-known classic strategies. The straightforward ROWA approach as briefly described above has a major drawback: it limits the availability of the overall system because an update transaction fails already when one of the replicas is not available. A simple way to address this issue is the ROWAA strategy (*Read One Write All Available*) where the physical write operations are executed on *all available* replicas. This requires that replicas which are not available at the time of the update have to recover their state when they are back. According to the classification in Fig. 3.10, both ROWA and ROWAA are eager update anywhere strategies.

For primary copy protocols one of the replicas has to be selected as primary copy or primary master N_P which is responsible for updates, all other replicas are called secondary. Furthermore, a client connects always to one of the replicas N_R and submits all operations of a given transaction to this replica. Read and write operations are handled differently:

- Reads are processed locally by N_R but require the acquisition of a shared lock on the data object.
- Writes are always submitted to the primary copy N_P. This node acquires an exclusive lock and performs the update. It then propagates the update in FIFO order to all secondaries. On receiving the update propagation, a secondary also acquires an exclusive lock on the data object.

In order to check whether all replicas have successfully executed the transaction and to guarantee that all agree on to the same result, a two-phase commit protocol (2PC) has to be executed for the commit of an update transaction (Sect. 3.5). Obviously, this variant of a primary copy protocol represents an eager strategy.

This protocol can be easily modified to implement a lazy strategy. As in the eager primary copy approach, read-only transactions are processed locally at any of the replicas. To implement the lazy strategy, update transactions are executed always on the primary node, i.e. all operations of a transaction are executed at one replica. Only *after* the commit the updates are propagated as soon as possible to the other replicas in FIFO order. When the secondaries receive the update propagation, they acquire the necessary exclusive locks to guarantee that the updates are serialized on the same order as the primary copy. This variant of a replication protocol was originally proposed by Alsberg and Day [3] as well as Stonebraker for Distributed Ingres [33]. Though, the lazy primary copy strategy allows an efficient processing of updates and provides better availability compared to ROWA, the delayed propagation of updates may lead to read inconsistencies: clients reading from the secondary nodes could see outdated data. Different alternatives have been proposed to address this problem: The primary could already propagate the exclusive locks to the secondaries to implement a distributed locking approach for the price of a higher communication overhead or reads could require shared locks on the primary copy, too. However, with the latter strategy the secondary copies are not really employed resulting in a rather centralized solution. Finally, failures of the primary copy require a special handling (e.g. electing a new primary copy) which becomes difficult in case of network partition events.

An implementation of an eager update anywhere strategy typically requires that each read or write operation acquires a quorum of copies to be successful. This means that before a read or write is executed, an appropriate lock has to be acquired on the majority of copies. This ensures that an data object is not modified concurrently at different nodes and – in combination with timestamps or reference counters – that replicas used for reading or writing are up-to-date. This strategy does therefore not require a dedicated replica node and allows to process updates even when some nodes fail or the network is partitioned – as long as a majority of nodes is still available. A concrete example is the *majority consensus* approach [35]. It is based on a timestamp strategy and assumes a fully replicated database. The nodes are organized in a logical ring along which requests and votes are forwarded. An update is issued on any of the nodes which sends a request to all other nodes together with the read sets RS and write sets WS with $WS \subseteq RS$ and their timestamps ts_R for voting. Requests are assigned priorities which are used for determining the votes. A simple approach is to interpret the timestamps of the requests as priority value. Each receiving node compares these timestamps with the local timestamps ts_L and votes according the following rules:

- If any of the local data objects o corresponding to an object $o' \in RS$ has been modified since the request was issued, i.e. $ts_R(o') < ts_L(o)$, vote REJECT.
- If all $o' \in RS$ are current, i.e. $ts_R(o') = ts_L(o)$ for all objects and the request does not conflict with a pending request, vote OK and mark the request as pending. Vote PASS, if the request conflicts with a pending request of higher priority. "Pending" is the state of a request between a vote and the final resolution, i.e., the commit or abort.
- Otherwise – that means in case of a conflict with a pending request of lower priority or if $ts_R(o') > ts_L(o)$ for any $o' \in RS$ – defer voting. The latter can happen when an update of o was already executed but not yet received by this node (the commit request is still on the way).

Two requests are in conflict if the intersection of the write set of one request and the read set of the other request is not empty.

If the majority of the nodes have voted OK the request is accepted and the transaction is terminated successfully. If there is a majority for REJECT the transaction has to be aborted. In both cases all nodes are notified about the result. Special handling is required for PASS and deferred voting. If the vote was PASS but a majority consensus is not possible anymore, the result is REJECT. For deferred voting, a request with the accumulated votes is sent to the nodes which have not voted yet.

The main problem of this strategy is the communication overhead: each update operation requires to obtain a majority of the votes. One possible solution is *weighted voting* [16] where each replica is assigned some number of votes. Each transaction has to collect a read quorum V_R to read an object and a write quorum V_W to perform a write. A quorum is the minimum number of votes that must be collected. Given the total number of available votes V_T the quorums have to be chosen according the following rules:

- $V_w > \frac{V_T}{2}$: Only one transaction is allowed to update a data object and in the presence of a partitioning event an object can be modified in only one partition.
- $V_r + V_w = V$: A given data object cannot be read and written at the same time.

To collect the necessary quorum a node sends requests to other nodes together with timestamps or version numbers, e.g. by first contacting the fastest nodes or the nodes with the highest number of votes.

Several variations of voting have been proposed, for instance approaches which define majority dynamically, hierarchical approaches as well as multidimensional voting strategies. An detailed evaluation of quorum-based approaches and a comparison to ROWAA strategy can be found in [22].

In [18] Gray et al. argue that eager replication does not scale. The reason is that the probability of deadlocks increases quickly with the number of nodes as well as with the transaction size. An analysis discussed in [18] shows that a 10-fold increase in the number of nodes results in a 1,000-fold increase in aborted transactions due to deadlocks.

3.4.3 Optimistic Replication

Optimistic replication strategies – also known as lazy replication – are based on the assumptions that problems caused by updating to the different replicas occur rather rarely and could be fixed when they happen. Thus, in contrast to pessimistic approaches which coordinate the replicas for synchronizing the data accesses, they allow access to the replicas without an a priori synchronization. By this, optimistic strategies promise two main advantages: first, a better availability because updates can be performed even when some nodes maintaining the replicas or some links between them fail. Second, due to the low synchronization overhead they provide better scalability in terms of the number of nodes.

Though, there is a wide variety of optimistic replication strategies, some basic steps can be identified. For the following discussion we assume a set of interconnected nodes maintaining replicas of a data object and operations (updates) which can be submitted at these nodes independently. Basically, optimistic replication works as follows [31]:

1. **Local execution of updates:** Update operations are submitted at some of nodes maintaining replicas and are applied locally.
2. **Update propagation:** All these operations are logged locally and propagated to the other nodes asynchronously. This could be done either by sending a description of the update operation (operation transfer) or by propagating the whole updated object (state transfer).
3. **Scheduling:** At each node, the ordering of the performed operations has to be reconstructed because it may happen that propagated operations are not received in the same order at all nodes. Therefore, the goal is to determine an ordering which produces an equivalent result across all affected nodes.
4. **Conflict detection and resolution:** When the same object is updated independently at different nodes at the same time and without any synchronization between the nodes, conflicts may occur, i.e., the same object is updated in different ways or updates get lost. In order to avoid such problems, these conflicts have to be detected, e.g. by checking some preconditions such as timestamps, and resolved by applying appropriate strategies.
5. **Commitment:** Finally, the state of all replicas has to be converged. This requires that all nodes agree on the set of operations, their ordering, and the conflict resolution.

In the following sections we will discuss selected representative techniques addressing the main steps.

3.4.4 Conflict Detection and Repair

To avoid problems such as lost updates due to conflicting operations at different sites, it is necessary to detect and repair these conflicts. The space of possible solutions ranges from simply prohibiting conflicts (by allowing updates only at a single master site), ignoring conflicts (Thomas write rule) over reducing the probability of conflicts (e.g. by splitting objects into smaller parts which can be updated independently) to real detection and repair techniques [31]. For the latter we can distinguish between syntactic and semantic policies. Syntactic policies use the timing of the operation submission, whereas semantic policies exploit application-specific knowledge to detect conflicting operations. An example of such a strategy is an order-processing application: as long as there enough items for shipping available a product can be ordered concurrently by multiple customers. Even if one of the updates results in a backorder, the order could be processed by triggering a reorder.

In the following we will focus on *vector clocks* [25] as a syntactic policy which can be used without a priori knowledge about the application. Vector clocks are a

Send a message *msg* at process *p*	Receive a message at process *p*

self.clock[p] := self.clock[p] + 1;
send(msg, self.clock);
	(msg, clock) := **receive**();
	self.clock[p] := self.clock[p] + 1;
	foreach i in $p_1 \ldots p_n$ **do**
	  self.clock[i] := max(self.clock[i], clock[i]);
	done

Fig. 3.11 Vector clocks

technique for determining a partial ordering of events in distributed systems. For a system of n processes a vector/array of n logical clocks is maintained – one clock for each process. A clock is typically just a counter. Each process keeps a local copy of this clock array and updates its entry in case of internal events (updates), send or receive operations.

Assuming a process p with a clock self.clock[1 ...n] for n processes and all clocks initially set to 0. The procedures for updating the clocks while sending and receiving messages are shown in Fig. 3.11. Each time a process p wants to send a message it increments its clock and sends the vector together with the message. On receiving a message, the receiver increments its clock entry and updates each element in vector by taking the maximum of its own clock value and the corresponding value of the received clock.

To order two events e_1 and e_2, we have to check if e_1 happened before e_2, i.e. $e_1 \rightarrow e_2$, e_2 before e_1 or of both events are in conflict. The happened-before relation is defined as: if $e_1 \rightarrow e_2$ then e_1.clock $< e_2$.clock. For the clocks it holds:

$$e_1.\text{clock} < e_2.\text{clock} \Longleftrightarrow$$

$$\forall p : e_1.\text{clock}[p] \leq e_2.\text{clock}[p] \wedge \exists q : e_1.\text{clock}[q] < e_2.\text{clock}[q]$$

Vector clocks are used for example in Amazon Dynamo [12] and Basho's Riak[1] for capturing causalities between different versions of the same object caused by updates at different sites.

Figure 3.12 shows an example of using vector clocks for this purpose. We assume a distributed system of the nodes A, B, C, D, E which process order transactions on a product database which is replicated over all nodes. First, node A processes an order which changes the stock of a certain product. After this update u_1, A sends a message to B with the clock $[A : 1]$. Next, node B processes another order on the same product and updates the clock with u_2 to $[A : 1, B : 1]$. Because, any non-existing entry in the clock is set to 0, node B can derive $u_1 \rightarrow u_2$. After u_2 the two nodes C and D process each another order on the product. Node C updates in u_3 the clock to $[A : 1, B : 1 :, C : 1]$, node D with u_4 to $[A : 1, B : 1, D : 1]$. Finally, another order is to

---

[1] http://wiki.basho.com/Riak.html.

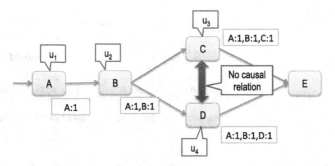

Fig. 3.12 Conflict detection with vector clock

be processed at node E. By comparing the two clocks $[A:1,B:1:,C:1,D:0]$ and $[A:1,B:1:,C:0,D:1]$, node E can detect a conflict between u_3 and u_4 because there is no causal relation between them.

3.4.5   Epidemic Propagation

In pessimistic replication, typically a predefined communication structure is used for update propagation. In the primary-copy strategy the master propagates updates to all replicas, majority consensus approaches send the updates along a logical ring. However, this results in limited scalability and reliability in cases of a huge number of sites or unreliable links and sites.

An alternative idea is to follow an epidemic dissemination strategy which is inspired by the spreading of infectious diseases. Such a strategy, which is also known as gossiping, is based on the following principles:

- Sites communicate pairwise: a site contacts other sites which are randomly chosen and sends its information, e.g. about a update.
- All sites process incoming messages in the same way: the message is processed and forwarded to other randomly chosen sites.

The randomized selection of receiving sites results in a proactive behavior: if one site is not reachable, the message will be forwarded to other sites. In this way, no failure recovery is necessary.

In the context of database replication, an update is first performed locally and then propagated to other sites – either as state transfer (database content) or operation transfer (update operation). This pairwise interaction involves an exchange and comparison of the content, because a site may have received the update over another link. There are several possible strategies, among them are anti-entropy and rumor mongering:

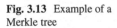

Fig. 3.13 Example of a
Merkle tree

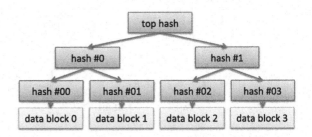

- **Anti-entropy:** Following the anti-entropy strategy, each site chooses another site randomly at regular intervals. In a second step, the two sites exchange their database contents (or a compact representation of them) and try to resolve any differences.
- **Rumor mongering:** In rumor mongering, a site that receives an update becomes a "hot rumor". In this state, it periodically chooses another site randomly and propagates the update. When too many of the contacted sites have already seen this update, the site stops propagating – the rumor is not "hot" anymore.

Anti-entropy is a reliable strategy but exchanging and comparing the database contents can become expensive. In contrast, rumor mongering requires less effort at each site, but it may happen that an updates will not reach all sites [13].

Merkle Trees

The actual comparison can be performed using different techniques. The main goal is to reduce the amount of data to be exchanged and the effort for comparison. Beside vector clocks as described in the previous section or event logs, so-called Merkle trees [29] are an appropriate technique which are used for example in Amazon Dynamo, Cassandra and Riak. Merkle trees are in fact hash trees where leaves are hashes of keys and non-leaves are hashes of their child nodes. Usually, Merkle trees are implemented using binary trees but are not restricted to them. Figure 3.13 shows an example of a Merkle tree. The inner nodes contain hash values for the data blocks or their children respectively. To compute the hash values cryptographic hash functions such as SHA-1 or Tiger functions are used.

For replica synchronization each of the site provides a Merkle tree representing its content, for instance, the keys the data objects. Using these two trees the hash nodes can be compared hierarchical: if two nodes are equal, there is no need to check the children. Otherwise, by going down in the tree, smaller and smaller hashes can be compared to identify the content which is out-of-sync.

3.5 Consensus Protocols

In distributed systems it is often necessary that several independent processes achieve a mutual agreement – even in cases where any process fails. This problem is known as *consensus problem* and allows a system to act as a single entity which is essential for the transparency we expect from a distributed system. Furthermore, it is a fundamental concept for fault tolerance in such systems. There are many examples of consensus problems: Among a set of processes one process has to be selected as leader for coordinating some activities, synchronizing local clocks of multiple nodes, deciding whether a transaction spawing multiple nodes can commit, and managing consistency of replicas.

In the absence of failures reaching a consensus is rather easy. As an example, let us assume n processes $p_1, \ldots, p_n$ which have to agree on a certain value (e.g., a vote, global time etc.). Each process sends its vote to all other processes. After receiving all votes, each process can determine locally the majority of the votes (or the average of time respectively). Furthermore, all processes will come to the same decision.

However, in the presence of failures, the situation is much more difficult [14]: Messages could be lost or a process reports a certain local value to one process and a different value to another process. Therefore, a consensus protocol or algorithm should satisfy the following properties:

- **Agreements:** All processes decide on the same (valid) result.
- **Termination:** All processes eventually decide.
- **Validity:** The value that is decided upon was proposed by some process.

In data management, distributed commit protocols are one of the main applications of consensus protocols. They are used to ensure atomicity and durability for transactions which span multiple nodes. Such transactions have to be decomposed into multiple sub-transactions which can be processed locally. However, guaranteeing atomicity also for the global transaction requires that all participating nodes come to the same final decision (commit or abort), commit is achieved only if all participating nodes vote for it, and all processes terminate.

Obviously, this is not achievable if sub-transactions are processed at the local nodes independently: if a process p_i decides to commit its sub-transaction and later, another process p_j at a different node aborts its sub-transaction, then the global transaction has to be aborted, too. However, because p_i has already committed the abort is not possible anymore.

In order to avoid this problem, an additional voting phase can be introduced leading to the *Two-Phase Commit (2PC)* protocol. In this protocol, processes can take one of two roles: one process acts as coordinator – usually the process at whose node the transaction was initiated – and the other nodes form the cohorts or workers. Furthermore, the protocol requires a write-ahead log at each node.

Figure 3.14 shows the basic steps of the 2PC. At the end of a transaction, the coordinator writes the state to the log and sends a prepare message to all

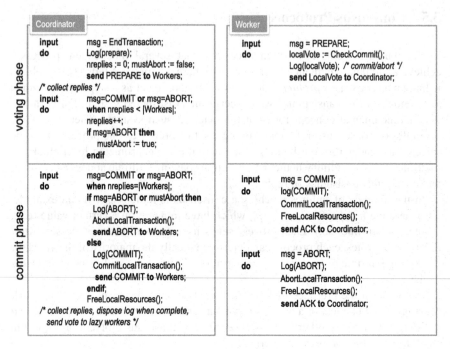

voting phase

Coordinator

input	msg = EndTransaction;
do	Log(prepare);
	nreplies := 0; mustAbort := false;
	send PREPARE **to** Workers;
/* collect replies */	
input	msg=COMMIT **or** msg=ABORT;
do	**when** nreplies < |Workers|;
	nreplies++;
	if msg=ABORT **then**
	mustAbort := true;
	endif

Worker

input	msg = PREPARE;
do	localVote := CheckCommit();
	Log(localVote); /* commit/abort */
	send LocalVote **to** Coordinator;

commit phase

Coordinator

input	msg=COMMIT **or** msg=ABORT;
do	**when** nreplies=|Workers|;
	if msg=ABORT **or** mustAbort **then**
	Log(ABORT);
	AbortLocalTransaction();
	send ABORT **to** Workers;
	else
	Log(COMMIT);
	CommitLocalTransaction();
	send COMMIT **to** Workers;
	endif;
	FreeLocalResources();
/* collect replies, dispose log when complete,	
send vote to lazy workers */	

Worker

input	msg = COMMIT;
do	log(COMMIT);
	CommitLocalTransaction();
	FreeLocalResources();
	send ACK **to** Coordinator;
input	msg = ABORT;
do	Log(ABORT);
	AbortLocalTransaction();
	FreeLocalResources();
	send ACK **to** Coordinator;

Fig. 3.14 2PC protocol

workers participating on this transaction. Each worker checks locally whether its sub-transaction can be finished successfully, writes its vote on commit or abort to its log and sends it back to the coordinator. After the coordinator has received the votes from all workers, it decides: if any worker has voted for abort, the transaction must be globally aborted, only if all votes are commit, the coordinator decides to global commit. This decision is written to the log at the coordinator's site and sent to all workers. The workers perform the commit or abort according to the global decision and send a completion notification back to the coordinator.

The 2PC protocol is widely used in distributed data management solutions, but unfortunately not resilient to all possible failures. Figure 3.15 illustrates two critical cases:

Case #1: Assuming the workers have sent their votes, but the coordinator is permanently down due to a failure. The only way to address this and to proceed is to abort the transaction at all workers, e.g. after timeout. However, this requires to know that the coordinator has not already decided and could result in undoing a decision made before.

Case #2: After sending the global commit to the first worker, the coordinator and this worker fail. Now, none of the remaining workers knows the global decision and can simply abort.

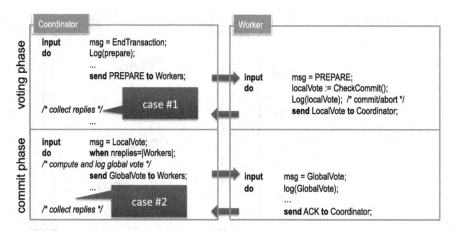

Fig. 3.15 Critical cases in the 2PC protocol

In summary, 2PC achieves consensus for commits, but it is a blocking protocol: after the workers have sent their vote and the coordinator is permanently down (fail-stop failure), the workers will block indefinitely. In contrast, fail-stop-return failures, i.e. a node is able to recover, can be handled. In this case, the coordinator can read its decision from the log and resend the messages.

The discussed protocol is the classic centralized variant of the 2PC family. In the literature several variations and extensions have been proposed, for instance, protocols for distributed communication structures as well as so-called presumed variants which try to reduce the number of messages to be transmitted.

The problem of 2PC can be avoided by switching to a nonblocking protocol. With such a protocol the participating processes can still decide if the transaction is committed or not even if one process fails without recovering. A possible solution are the so-called Three-Phase Commit (3PC) protocols. These protocols are typically based on the idea of choosing another coordinator if the first one failed. However, they are not widely used in practical implementations.

A consensus protocol that is able to handle all important cases of failures safely is Paxos. Paxos is in fact a family of protocols. It was first presented in 1989 by Leslie Lamport and published in [26]. The name Paxos comes from a fictional parliament at the Aegean island Paxos where each legislator maintained his own ledger for recording the decrees that were passed. The goals are to keep these ledgers consistent and to guarantee that enough legislators stayed for a long enough time in the chamber.

Paxos assumes processes (called acceptors or replicas) which operate at arbitrary speed, can send messages to any other process asynchronously, and may experience failures. Each process has access to a persistent storage used for crash recovery. Acceptors submit values for consensus via messages, but the network may drop messages between processes.

Fig. 3.16 Paxos consensus
protocol

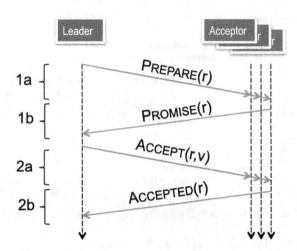

The protocol (Fig. 3.16) runs in a sequence of several rounds numbered by nonnegative integers. Each round i has a single coordinator or leader which is elected among the processes and which tries to get a majority for a single value v_i. If round i achieves a majority for v_i, i.e. acceptors have sent acknowledges to the coordinator, then v_i is the result. In case of failures, another round is started which could include electing a new leader if the previous leader failed.

The challenging situation is when multiple processes think they are the leader. Here, Paxos ensures consistency by not allowing to choose different values. A leader is elected by one of the standard algorithms, e.g. as discussed in [1]. Then, any process that thinks to be the new leader initiates a new round and performs the following protocol which is structured in two phases. Note that several phases can run concurrently since there could be multiple leaders. Furthermore, there is phase 1 needed in the first round.

- **Phase 1a:** The leader chooses a number r for the round for which it believes that it is larger than any other round already completed in phase 1. Then r is sent to all (or a majority of) acceptors as part of a prepare message.
- **Phase 1b:** When an acceptor receives a prepare message with round number r, it checks if it has already performed any action for r or greater. If this is the case, the message is ignored, otherwise it responds with a promise message saying that it promises not to accept other proposals for rounds with numbers less than r. For this purpose, the promise message contains the current state consisting of the highest round number (if any) it has already accepted and the largest r received in a prepare message so far.
- **Phase 2a:** If the leader has received responses to its prepare message for r from a majority of acceptors, then it knows one of two possible things. Some acceptors of the majority have sent an accept message of phase 2b, then the leader takes the value v of the highest-numbered reported round and all messages from this round have the same value. Then, it tries to get v chosen by sending an accept request

with r to all acceptors. Otherwise, if none of the majority of acceptors has sent an accept message, no value has been chosen yet. In this case, the leader can try to get accepted any value, e.g. one value proposed by the client.

- **Phase 2b:** When the acceptor receives an accept message for a value v and the round number r, it accepts that message unless it has already responded to a prepare message for a higher-numbered round. In the latter case, it just ignores the message.

Paxos guarantees progress as long as a new leader is selected and a majority of nodes is running for a long enough time. It also guarantees that at most one value v is chosen if processes execute the algorithm correctly. Basically, Paxos can tolerate F faults if there are $2F + 1$ acceptors. Detailed statements and proofs are given for instance in [11].

The algorithm presented here is only the basic protocol. Several optimizations and variations have been proposed in the literature. Other works like [9] discuss the practical deployment, in this case in the context of Google's distributed locking mechanism Chubby.

Paxos can be also used to implement a transaction commit protocol [19]. Here, multiple coordinators are used and the protocol makes progress as long as a majority of coordinators is working. In the Paxos commit protocol, each worker runs one instance of the consensus protocol to choose a value Prepared or Aborted. A transaction commit is initiated by sending a BeginCommit message to the leader which then sends a Prepare message to all workers. A worker that receives this message decides whether it is able to prepare and in this case sends in its instance of Paxos an accept request containing the value Prepared and the round number $r = 0$. Otherwise, it sends a request with the value Aborted and $r = 0$. For each instance of the consensus protocol, an acceptor sends its accept message to the leader. As soon as the leader has received $F + 1$ accept messages for round $r = 0$, the outcome of its instance is available.

If a decision cannot be reached in round $r = 0$ in one or more Paxos instances, the leader assumes that the workers in these instances have failed and start a new round with a higher number by sending a prepare message.

However, the transaction is committed only if every workers instance of Paxos chooses the value Prepared, otherwise it has to be aborted. The Paxos transaction commit protocol has the same properties like the 2PC but in contrast to this, it is a *nonblocking* protocol. This follows from the Paxos progress property: each instance of the protocol eventually chooses one of the values Prepared or Aborted if a majority of workers is non faulty. A detailed discussion of the properties can be found in [19].

The properties of Paxos make the protocol very useful to implement fault-tolerant distributed systems in large networks of unreliable computers. In Cloud databases where partitioning and replication are essential techniques to achieve scalability and high availability, Paxos is used for instance to implement replication and commit protocols. Known uses of the protocol are Google's lock service Chubby [8] as well as MegaStore [4], Amazon Dynamo [12], and cluster management for Microsoft Bing [21].

3.6 Summary

Transactions are a fundamental concept of database and distributed systems to build reliable and concurrent system. Applications performing data entry, update, and retrieval tasks typically require that integrity and consistency of data are guaranteed and data are stored persistently. Classic database systems provide techniques to ensure these properties since decades and support even small-scale distributed scenarios. In this chapter we have given an overview on fundamental techniques from the database domain for these purposes.

However, for managing big data or serving many customers, large-scale distributed settings with hundreds or even thousands of servers are needed. Scalability can be achieved only by partitioning the data and replication is needed for guaranteeing high availability in clusters of a large number of servers. But, in these settings consistency between replicas, availability and tolerance in case of partitioning events cannot be longer guaranteed at the same time. We have discussed the CAP theorem that explains the reasons for this. As a consequence of this theorem, the requirements of scalable cloud data management have lead to system designs which no longer favor strict consistency for availability and partition tolerance by using, among others, optimistic replication techniques. Thus, highly-scalable cloud databases provide mostly only weaker forms of consistency as well as limited support for transactions, such atomicity only for single items or last-writer-wins strategy instead of full transaction isolation. This may be sufficient for many Web applications, but if more advanced transaction support is needed, e.g. atomic operations on multiple items, this functionality has to be implemented on top of the storage service [6], either in the application or a in middleware like dedicated transaction services. The need for higher level of atomic operations may result not only from application transactions but also from scenarios where data are stored at different sites (e.g. user data and indexes). In any case, increasing levels of consistency and isolation also increases operation cost. Ideally, such transaction services would allow customers to choose the specific level matching the requirements of their applications at a finer granularity (e.g. data level) and to pay only for what is needed. An example of such a strategy to dynamically adapt consistency levels (called consistency rationing) is described in [24].

Another direction of research addresses the challenges resulting from a separation of the transaction service (or coordinator) and the data storage layer [28], such as that both components may fail independently and that concurrency control is more difficult. Some possible solutions are discussed in [27]. Finally, there are several active research projects aiming at scalable transactional support. Examples are, among others, Sinfonia [2], G-Store [10], and Scalaris [32].

References

1. Aguilera, M.K., Delporte-Gallet, C., Fauconnier, H., Toueg, S.: Stable leader election. In: DISC, pp. 108–122 (2001)
2. Aguilera, M.K., Merchant, A., Shah, M.A., Veitch, A.C., Karamanolis, C.T.: Sinfonia: A new paradigm for building scalable distributed systems. ACM Trans. Comput. Syst. **27**(3) (2009)
3. Alsberg, P.A., Day, J.D.: A principle for resilient sharing of distributed resources. In: Proceedings of the 2nd international conference on Software engineering (ICSE '76), pp. 562–570 (1976)
4. Baker, J., Bond, C., Corbett, J., Furman, J.J., Khorlin, A., Larson, J., Leon, J.M., Li, Y., Lloyd, A., Yushprakh, V.: Megastore: Providing scalable, highly available storage for interactive services. In: CIDR, pp. 223–234 (2011)
5. Bernstein, P.A., Hadzilacos, V., Goodman, N.: Concurrency Control and Recovery in Database Systems. Addison-Wesley (1987)
6. Brantner, M., Florescu, D., Graf, D.A., Kossmann, D., Kraska, T.: Building a database on s3. In: SIGMOD Conference, pp. 251–264 (2008)
7. Brewer, E.: Towards Robust Distributed Systems. In: PODC, p. 7 (2000)
8. Burrows, M.: The chubby lock service for loosely-coupled distributed systems. In: OSDI, pp. 335–350 (2006)
9. Chandra, T.D., Griesemer, R., Redstone, J.: Paxos made live: an engineering perspective. In: PODC, pp. 398–407 (2007)
10. Das, S., Agrawal, D., El Abbadi, A.: G-store: a scalable data store for transactional multi key access in the cloud. In: SoCC, pp. 163–174 (2010)
11. De Prisco, R., Lampson, B., Lynch, N.: Revisiting the paxos algorithm. Theor. Computer Science **243**(1–2), 35–91 (2000)
12. DeCandia, G., Hastorun, D., Jampani, M., Kakulapati, G., Lakshman, A., Pilchin, A., Sivasubramanian, S., Vosshall, P., Vogels, W.: Dynamo: amazon's highly available key-value store. In: SOSP, pp. 205–220 (2007)
13. Demers, A., Greene, D., Hauser, C., Irish, W., Larson, J., Shenker, S., Sturgis, H., Swinehart, D., Terry, D.: Epidemic algorithms for replicated database maintenance. In: Proceedings of the sixth annual ACM Symposium on Principles of distributed computing, PODC '87, pp. 1–12 (1987)
14. Fischer, M., Lynch, N., Paterson, M.: Impossibility of Distributed Conensus with One Faulty Process. Journal of the ACM **32**(2), 374–383 (1985)
15. Fox, A., Gribble, S.D., Chawathe, Y., Brewer, E.A., Gauthier, P.: Cluster-based Scalable Network Services. SIGOPS **31**, 78–91 (1997)
16. Gifford, D.: Weighted Voting for Replicated Data. In: SOSP, pp. 150–162 (1979)
17. Gilbert, S., Lynch, N.: Brewer's Conjecture and the Feasibility of Consistent, Available, Partition-Tolerant Web Services. SIGACT News (2002)
18. Gray, J., Helland, P., O'Neil, P., Shasha, D.: The Dangers of Replication and a Solution. In: SIGMOD, pp. 173–182 (1996)
19. Gray, J., Lamport, L.: Consensus on Transaction Commit. ACM Transactions on Database Systems **31**(1), 133–60 (2006)
20. Härder, T., Reuter, A.: Principles of Transaction-Oriented Database Recovery. ACM Computing Surveys **15**(4), 287–317 (1983)
21. Isard, M.: Autopilot: automatic data center management. SIGOPS Oper. Syst. Rev. **41**(2), 60–67 (2007)
22. Jimenez-Peris, R., Patino-Martinez, M., Alonso, G., Kemme, B.: Are Quorums an Alternative for Data Replication? ACM Transactions on Database Systems **28**(3), 257–294 (2003)
23. Kemme, B., Jiménez-Peris, R., Patiño-Martínez, M., Alonso, G.: Database replication: A tutorial. In: B. Charron-Bost, F. Pedone, A. Schiper (eds.) Replication, *Lecture Notes in Computer Science*, vol. 5959, pp. 219–252. Springer (2010)

24. Kraska, T., Hentschel, M., Alonso, G., Kossmann, D.: Consistency rationing in the cloud: Pay only when it matters. PVLDB 2(1), 253–264 (2009)
25. Lamport, L.: Time, clocks, and the ordering of events in a distributed system. Commun. ACM 21(7), 558–565 (1978)
26. Lamport, L.: The Part-Time Parliament. ACM Transactions on Computer Systems 16(2), 133–160 (1998)
27. Levandoski, J.J., Lomet, D.B., Mokbel, M.F., Zhao, K.: Deuteronomy: Transaction support for cloud data. In: CIDR, pp. 123–133 (2011)
28. Lomet, D.B., Fekete, A., Weikum, G., Zwilling, M.J.: Unbundling transaction services in the cloud. In: CIDR (2009)
29. Merkle, R.C.: Method of providing digital signatures. US Patent 4309569 (1982). http://www.google.com/patents/US4309569
30. Pritchett, D.: BASE: An ACID Alternative. ACM Queue 6, 48–55 (2008)
31. Saito, Y., Shapiro, M.: Optimistic Replication. ACM Computing Surveys 37(3), 42–81 (2005)
32. Schütt, T., Schintke, F., Reinefeld, A.: Scalaris: reliable transactional p2p key/value store. In: Erlang Workshop, pp. 41–48 (2008)
33. Stonebraker, M.: Concurrency Control and Consistency of Multiple Copies of Data in Distributed INGRES. IEEE Transactions on Software Engineering SE-5(3), 188–194 (1979)
34. Terry, D., Demers, A., Petersen, K., Spreitzer, M., Theimer, M.: Session Guarantees for Weakly Consistent Replicated Data. In: PDIS, pp. 140–149 (1994)
35. Thomas, R.: A Majority Consensus Approach to Concurrency Control for Multiple Copy Databases. ACM Transactions on Database Systems 4(2), 180–209 (1979)
36. Vogels, W.: Eventually Consistent. ACM Queue 6, 14–19 (2008)
37. Weikum, G., Vossen, G.: Transactional Information Systems. Morgan Kaufmann Publishers (2002)

Chapter 4
Web-Scale Analytics for BIG Data

The term *web-scale analytics* denotes the analysis of huge data sets in the range of hundreds of Terabytes or even Petabytes that occur for example in social networks, Internet click streams, sensor data, or complex simulations. The goal of web-scale analytics is to filter, transform, integrate, and aggregate these data sets, and to correlate them with other data. Parallel processing across many machines and computing cores is the key enabler for queries and other complex data processing operations against large data sets.

Challenges in the field of web-scale analytics are (1) the definition of complex queries in a format that leads itself to parallelization and (2) the massively parallel execution of those analytical queries. To address the first issue, a simple functional programming paradigm based on the higher-order functions *map* and *reduce*, with a simple data model based on keys and values has been popularized by the industry and open-source community. *MapReduce* programs on the one hand can express the relational operations used in SQL. On the other hand, one can specify more complex data analysis tasks, such as statistical analysis or data mining in MapReduce. The MapReduce programming model allows for a rather simple execution model which features straightforward concepts for fault-tolerance, load balancing, and resource sharing – crucial aspects in any massively parallel environment. In this section, we will discuss foundations of query processing, fault-tolerance, and programming paradigms, before describing the MapReduce programming model and its functional programming background in detail. We will highlight applications, strengths, and weaknesses of the MapReduce model. We will also discuss query languages for web-scale analytics that have been built on top of MapReduce, such as Facebook's Hive, IBM's JAQL, and Yahoo's Pig.

4.1 Foundations

Web-scale analytics aims at pushing the known concepts from parallel data processing further to orders of magnitude larger systems. At the same time, it extends the

W. Lehner and K.-U. Sattler, *Web-Scale Data Management for the Cloud*,
DOI 10.1007/978-1-4614-6856-1_4, © Springer Science+Business Media New York 2013

application domain from the classical relational data analysis to deep analysis of semistructured and unstructured data. In order to achieve that, novel approaches and paradigms have been developed. In this section, we discuss the foundations of data analysis, briefly recapitulating the basics of query processing in relational databases which are needed to understand the advanced techniques, before jumping into the specifics of parallel data processing. Section 4.2 discusses the novel approaches for massively parallel scale-out at the example of the MapReduce paradigm.

4.1.1   Query Processing

Query processing describes the process of analyzing data, typically integrating it with data from other sources and applying operations such as filters, transformations, and aggregations. One distinguishes two query types:

- **Imperative Queries:** Imperative queries describe exactly *how* the analysis is performed by giving the express control flow. The query is typically specified in a low level imperative language. A common example is the analysis of log files with Python or traditional shell scripts.
- **Declarative Queries:** Declarative queries describe *what* the analysis should accomplish rather than how to do it. They make use of an algebra or calculus and typically describe which operators or functions need to be applied in order to compute the result. One of the best known representatives is the *relational algebra*, which forms the basis for the declarative query language SQL.

The relational algebra [6] is particularly simple and clear, yet powerful. Many other query algebras have related concepts at their core. The relational algebra is based on the relational model where data are represented as unordered sets of tuples, called relations. All tuples of the same relation share the same structure, i.e. the same set of attributes. Relations can hence be viewed as tables, the attributes of the tuples as the table columns. At its core, the relational algebra consists of five operations: The *selection* (σ_c), which filters out tuples from the relation based on a predicate c; the *projection* ($\pi_{c1,c2,c3}$), which discards all columns from the tuples except $c1, c2, c3$; the *set union* ($\cup$) and *set difference* ($-$) of two relations, and the *Cartesian product* ($\times$) of two relations. Extended versions [25] add operators, like set intersection ($R \cap S = R - (R - S)$), joins ($R \bowtie_c S = \sigma c(R \times S)$), and grouping with aggregations (γ). The join is of special importance: It essentially concatenates tuples that have equal attribute values in a subset of their attributes. The join is used heavily to re-create tuples that were split and stored in different tables in the process of *normalization* [12] to avoid redundancies.

Many operators have properties such as commutativity ($R \times S = S \times R$), associativity ($(R \times S) \times T = R \times (S \times T)$), or distributivity ($\sigma_{R.a='A' \wedge S.b='B'}(R \bowtie S) = \sigma_{R.a='A'}(R) \bowtie \sigma_{S.b='B'}(S)$). Therefore, multiple semantically equivalent representations of the same expression exist.

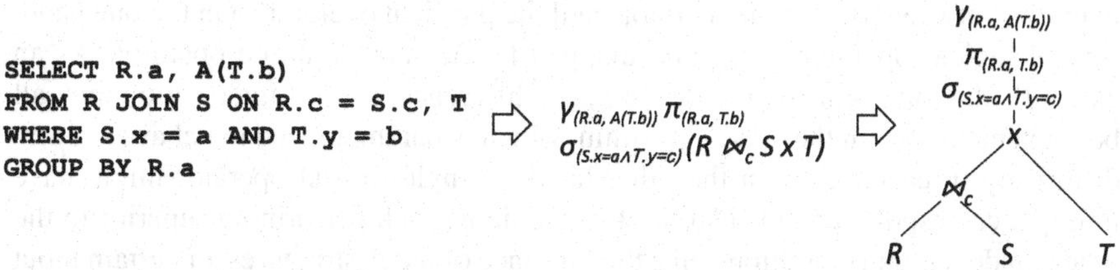

```
SELECT R.a, A(T.b)
FROM R JOIN S ON R.c = S.c, T
WHERE S.x = a AND T.y = b
GROUP BY R.a
```

$\Rightarrow \quad \gamma_{(R.a, A(T.b))} \, \pi_{(R.a, T.b)} \\ \sigma_{(S.x=a \land T.y=c)} (R \bowtie_c S \times T) \quad \Rightarrow$

$$\gamma_{(R.a, A(T.b))}$$
$$|$$
$$\pi_{(R.a, T.b)}$$
$$\sigma_{(S.x=a \land T.y=c)}$$
$$|$$
$$\times$$

$\bowtie_c$

$R \qquad S \qquad T$

Fig. 4.1 Relational algebra expression

When processed by a database (or a similar analytical tool), a relational algebra expression is often represented as a tree, as shown in Fig. 4.1. The tree defines an explicit order in which the operators are evaluated, by requiring that an operator's children must be evaluated before the operator is. The relational algebra tree can also be viewed as a dataflow: The base relations (here R, S, and T) are the data sources. The data flows upwards into the next operator, which consumes it and produces a new data stream for its parent operator. For the topics discussed in this book, the given basics about the relational algebra are sufficient. For a details, we refer the reader to the literature on database systems [12].

Query Execution

A declarative query, represented by means of algebraic operators, is executed by a runtime system that provides algorithmic implementations for the processing steps described by the logical operators. In most cases, the runtime has a collection of *runtime operators* that encapsulate an isolated operation, such as for example a sorting operation that orders the data set, or a filter that applies a selection. The encapsulation of small units of functionality in operators is flexible and allows the engine to use the same operation for different purposes. A sort can for example be used to sort the final result, but also to eliminate duplicates or to order the data as a preprocessing for an efficient join. A common terminology names the query algebra the *logical algebra* with *logical operators*, whereas the operators available to the runtime system are called *physical operators*, sometimes defining a *physical algebra* [18]. The physical operators are composed to trees that resemble dataflows, much as the query can be represented as a tree of logical operators. The data sources of the flow are operators accessing the base data. The root operator of the tree returns the result. The tree of physical operators is also called *execution plan* or *query plan*, as it describes exactly how the query is evaluated by means of physical data structures and algorithms.

A runtime system might have a single physical operator implementation for each algebraic operator. In that case, the logical and physical algebra would be equivalent and the query operator tree would be an explicit description of the query execution by the runtime system, modulo certain parameters, like the maximum allowed memory consumption for each operator. In practice, however, there is no one-to-one mapping between the logical operators and the physical operators. On the one hand, several logical operators might be mapped to the same runtime operator. As an example, the join, semi-join, outer-join, set difference, and set intersection may all be implemented with the same algorithm, which is parameterized to behave slightly differently in each case. On the other hand, a single logical operator might have multiple corresponding physical implementations, each performing superior to the others under certain conditions, like the presence of index structures, or certain input set sizes. A common example is the join, which has implementations that make use of sorting, hashing, or index structures. The mapping of the logical operators to the most efficiently evaluated combination of physical operators is the task of the query compiler.

For a detailed description of the algorithms typically used by the physical operators, we would like to refer the reader to a database systems textbook [12]. In the following, we sketch the three main classes of algorithms implemented by physical operators in data processing systems:

- **Sort-based Operators:** Sort-based operators work on ordered streams of tuples, where the order is defined with respect to a subset of attributes. The order is established by either reading the data from an ordered data structure, or by a preceding sort. In an ordered stream, all tuples that have the same value in the ordered fields are adjacent. Duplicate elimination and aggregation operators are easily implemented on top of ordered streams, as well as joins, which work by merging the sorted streams of the two input relations.

- **Hash-based Operators:** Hash-based operators create a hash table, using a subset of the attributes as the hash key. Tuples with equal attribute values hash into the same hash table slots, making hash tables a good data structure for grouping tuples (aggregation) or associating them (join). A detailed description of a hash based operator for joining and grouping is given by Graefe et al. [17].

- **Index-based operators:** Index-based operators use an index structure (such as a B-Tree) to efficiently retrieve tuples by their attribute values. Therefore, they are particularly suitable for evaluating predicates, such as in selections or joins. Their main advantage is that they retrieve only the relevant tuples, rather than retrieving all of them and filtering out irrelevant ones. Graefe gives a good overview of indexes and index-based query processing [16].

A dataflow of physical operators has two possible ways of execution: In the first variant, each operator fully creates its result before its parent operator starts processing the result. The advantage is that each operator knows its input sizes (and possibly other characteristics, like data distributions) before it starts processing. On the downside, the materialization of the intermediate results may consume enormous amounts of memory and even spill to disk, if memory is insufficient. Many data processing systems therefore choose to *pipeline* the data between operators, meaning that an operator consumes records as they are produced by its child. The operator itself produces records as it consumes them, forwarding the records to its own parent. The speed at which a parent operator consumes the records regulates the speed at which the records are produced by its child. Pipelining may happen at

Fig. 4.2 Processing
of a declarative query

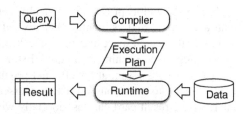

the granularity of a single record or a batch (vector) of records. Certain operations however require the materialization of intermediate results. An example is the sort, where the last input record must be consumed before the first output record is produced. The hash tables, created for example for hash-based join processing, are another example. We refer the reader to the literature [12] for details.

Query Compilation

An essential advantage of declarative query languages, like the relational algebra, is that they can be transformed automatically into semantically equivalent queries, using rules and properties of the underlying algebra. Most database systems make use of that fact and employ an optimizer to transform the relational algebra expression from the SQL statement into an equivalent physical algebra expression that is efficient to evaluate. Aside from relieving the application programmer from hand-tuning a query, the optimizer separates the actual persistent data representation from the application's view – a property referred to as *data independence*. The separation allows the hardware and physical design to change, while the application can still issue the same queries. Figure 4.2 sketches the compilation process.

The component named "compiler" in Fig. 4.2 consists typically of several sub-components called *parser*, *semantical analyzer*, *optimizer*, and *plan generator*. The parser has the simple task of parsing the query syntactically and produces a syntax tree as a result. The semantical analyser checks all semantical conditions, such as the existence of referenced relations or attributes and the compatibility of data types and functions. It typically simplifies the query's predicate expressions.

The by far most complicated sub-component is the optimizer. Its task is to find the most efficient execution plan for the given logical query. The optimizer can choose from a variety of plans for each logical query, spanning an often large search space. The size of the search space is mainly due to algebraic degrees of freedom: To join n relations, there exist $C_{n-1} * n!$ (C_n being the n-th Catalan number) possible join orders [12], due to the associativity and commutativity of joins and cross products. But also the choice of the according physical operator for a logical operator increases the number of possible execution plans. The difference in execution time between plans with different join orders and join algorithms can easily be several orders of magnitude [26].

The optimization process is typically centered around enumerating different plan alternatives and estimating their execution cost, discarding expensive plans. To reduce the search space and minimize the number of plans to consider, optimizers employ aggressive pruning techniques. Estimating the costs of an execution plan (or sub-parts of it) is essential for efficient pruning. Since the costs of each operation relate directly to the amount of data processed, a central aspect is the estimation of intermediate result cardinalities, normally with the help of catalogued statistics or data samples. For a more detailed overview of query optimization techniques, please refer to the surveys on query optimization [5, 27].

The plan generator, as the final component of the query compiler, translates the optimizer's plan into an efficiently executable form that the runtime can interpret with minimal overhead [28].

4.1.2   Parallel Data Processing

Parallelizing query processing permits to handle larger data sets in reasonable time or to speed up complex operations and, therefore, represents the key to tackle the big data problem. Parallelization implies that the processing work is split and distributed across a number of *processors*, or processing *nodes*. "*Scale-out*" refers to scenarios where the amount of data per node is kept constant, and nodes are added to handle large data volumes while keeping the processing time constant. Similarly, "*speed-out*" means that the data volume is kept constant and nodes are added to speed up the processing time. The ideal scale-out behavior of a query has a linear relationship between the number of nodes and the amount of data that can processed in a certain time. The theoretical linear scale-out is hardly achieved, because a certain fraction of the query processing is normally not parallelizable, such as the coordinated startup of the processing or exclusive access to shared data structures. The serial part of the computation limits its parallel scalability – this relationship has been formulated as *Amdahl's Law*: Let f be the portion of the program that is parallelizable, and p be the number of processors (or nodes). The maximal speedup S_{max} is then given by:

$$S_{max} = \frac{1}{(1-f) * \frac{f}{p}}$$

Figure 4.3 shows the scaling limits of programs, depending on the fraction of the code that is parallelizable. It is obvious that for a totally parallelizable program ($f = 1$), the speedup is p. However, since in practise, $f < 1$, the speedup is sub-linear and is in fact bounded by a constant, which it asymptotically approaches with an increasing number of processors (Fig. 4.3, bottom). A very high percentage of parallelizable code is imperative for a program to be scalable. Even programs that have 99% parallelizable code are only sped up by factor of 50, when running on 100 nodes!

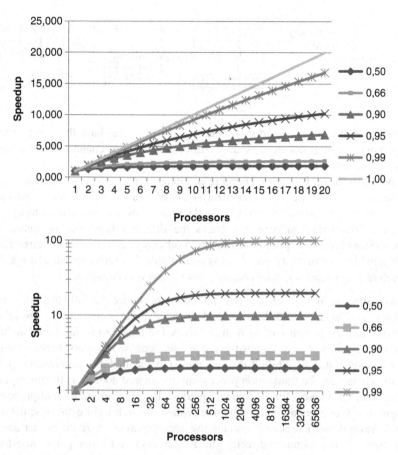

Fig. 4.3 Scalability according to Amdahl's Law. Comparison of scalabilty (*top*) and bounded speedup (*bottom*). The *lines* represent different parallelizable fractions

Parallel Architectures

Parallel architectures are classified by what shared resources each processor can directly access. One typically distinguishes *shared memory*, *shared disk*, and *shared nothing* architectures, as depicted in Fig. 4.4:

- **Shared memory:** In a *shared memory* system, all processors have direct access to all memory via a shared bus. A typical example are the common symmetric multi-processor systems, where each processor core can access the complete memory via the shared memory bus. To preserve the abstraction, processor caches, buffering a subset of the data closer to the processor for fast access, have to be kept consistent with specialized protocols. Because disks are typically accessed via the memory, all processes also have access to all disks.

Fig. 4.4 Parallel
architectures: shared memory
(*left*), shared disk (*middle*),
shared nothing (*right*)

- **Shared disk:** In a *shared disk* architecture, all processes have their own private memory, but all disks are shared. A cluster of computers connected to a SAN is a representative for this architecture.

- **Shared nothing:** In a *shared nothing* architecture, each processor has its private memory and private disk. The data is distributed across all disks and each processor is responsible only for the data on its own connected memory and disks. To operate on data that spans the different memories or disks, the processors have to explicitly send data to other processors. If a processor fails, data held by its memory and disks is unavailable. Therefore the shared nothing architecture requires special considerations to prevent data-loss.

When scaling out the system, the two main bottlenecks are typically the bandwidth of the shared medium and the overhead of maintaining a consistent view of the shared data in the presence of cache hierarchies. For that reason, the shared nothing architecture is considered the most scalable one, because it has no shared medium and no shared data [9]. While it is often argued that shared disk architectures have certain advantages for transaction processing, the shared nothing is the undisputed architecture of choice for analytical queries. Even in modern multiprocessor designs, one sees a deviation from the shared-memory architecture due to scalability issues. Several multiprocessor systems use architectures, where cores can access only parts of the memory directly (local memory) and other parts (non-local memory) only indirectly, for example though a message interface [20]. The result is a Non Uniform Memory Access (NUMA) architecture.

Classifying Parallelization

Parallelization can happen between queries, with multiple queries running concurrently on different processors, and within a query, with multiple processors cooperating on the evaluation of a query. While the former variant is particularly relevant for frequent and simple transactional queries, the later variant is necessary for the complex analytical queries which are the scope of this chapter.

When multiple processors cooperate on a single query, they can do so in different ways. When each processor executes a different set of operators, one speaks of *inter-operator* parallelism, or *pipeline parallelism*. Figure 4.5, left, illustrates that using the example of an execution plan consisting of three operators and two input data sets. Each operator is processed by a different node. This parallelization strategy requires a pipelined mode of execution (cf. Sect. 4.1.1) in order to gain

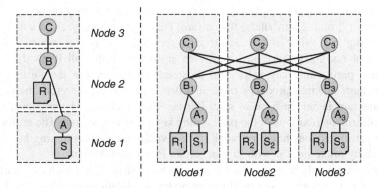

Fig. 4.5 Inter-operator parallelism (*left*) vs. data parallelism (*right*)

speedup though the parallelization. The speedup is naturally limited by the number of operators in the query.

When multiple nodes cooperate on the evaluation of an operator, one speaks of *intra-operator* parallelism. As special case, called *data parallelism*, all nodes cooperate on an operator by executing the full operator on a different subset of the input data. When all nodes execute an instance of the same execution plan (or a sub-part of it), but on different partitions of the input data, one speaks of *data-parallel pipelines*. This processing flavor is the natural match for shared-nothing systems. It is depicted in Fig. 4.5, right hand side. In the course of a data parallel pipeline, there may be the requirement to re-distribute the intermediate result among the participating nodes (here between operators *B* and *C*) in order to co-locate items that need to be handled by the same operator instance.

Data Placement

As mentioned before, shared nothing systems require to distribute the data among the nodes. *Horizontal partitioning* or horizontal *fragmentation* (see Sect. 3.3) splits the data into disjoint subsets, stored on the individual nodes. The partitioning scheme can be purely random, in which case any data item may end up at any node – an example is the *round-robin partitioning*, where the k-th data item is stored on k mod n-th of the n nodes. This partitioning scheme assigns each node an equal amount of data.

A scheme called *range partitioning* assigns data items to nodes based on which range a certain attribute falls into. Consider for example sales data, which include an attribute for the date of the sale. The data is partitioned in such a way that node 1 stores the sales data from year x, node 2 stores the sales data from year $x + 1$ and so on. Each node stores the data for a certain range of dates (here a year). The date attribute is referred to as the *partitioning key*. All items that share the same partitioning key value will be stored on the same node. Care must be taken when defining the ranges such that each node stores a similar amount of data.

The *hash partitioning* scheme assigns data to partitions by evaluating a hash function $h(x)$ on the attribute(s) that is (are) the partitioning key. A data item with partitioning key value of k is assigned to partition $h(k) \bmod n$, where n is the number of nodes. Because hash functions are deterministic, all items that share the same partitioning key value will be stored on the same node. Furthermore, a good hash function produces rather uniform hash values; therefore the created partitions are rather uniform in size. For carefully picked hash functions, many non-uniform distributions of the partitioning key are smoothed out. The uniformity of the partitions does however break, if few values of the partitioning key occur particularly often, such as with Zipf or certain Pareto distributions.

Data can not only be partitioned, it can also be *replicated*, in which case multiple copies of the item are stored on different nodes. Replication (see also Sect. 3.4) is essential for availability in shared nothing systems, but it may also aid in query processing, as we discuss later. If a copy of the data item is stored on every node, the item is said to be *fully replicated*.

Essential Parallelization Strategies

We will briefly discuss the basic approaches to parallelize some essential data analysis operations. For a more detailed overview of parallel query execution algorithms, please refer to reference [15]. In the following, we assume a shared nothing system with data-parallel pipelines.

A fundamental paradigm in parallel dataflow systems is that each instance of an operator must work completely independent from the other instances. To achieve that, the instances are provided with data subsets that permit independent processing. For example, a duplicate elimination operator can work in independent parallel instances, if we ensure beforehand that duplicates are always within the same node only. If the data is not distributed accordingly, it must be re-distributed in a pre-processing step of the operator. There, the nodes send each record to its designated processing node(s), typically via the network. Redistribution requires node-to-node communication channels, as the dataflow in Fig. 4.5 (right) shows between operators B and C.

Re-distribution steps typically establish a partitioning or replication scheme on the intermediate result. In the above example of duplicate elimination, a suitable re-distribution step is to create a hash-partitioning on the operator's input. The attributes relevant to duplicate elimination act as the partitioning key k. That way, all duplicates produce the same hash value and are sent to the same node. In order to *hash partition* the input of the duplicate elimination operator O with its n instances, O's predecessor sends each data item to the i-th instance of O, where i is $h(k) \bmod n$. In a similar way, data could also be *range partitioned*. Since range partitioning requires a table defining the range boundaries and hash partitioning works without extra metadata, hash partitioning is typically preferred. In the following, we refer to the re-distribution steps as *data shipping* and to the succeeding independent execution of the operator instances as *local processing*.

All **tuple-at-a-time** operations can be parallelized trivially. Parallel instances of those operations are executed on different subsets of the input without special consideration. Representatives for such operations are filters, projections (without duplicate elimination), or any kind of computation of a derived field within a tuple.

In a parallel **aggregation**, all instances of the grouping/aggregation operator process disjoint groups. Each operator instance has all records belonging to its groups and may use a standard local grouping and aggregation algorithm. Hash-partitioning the input data, using the grouping attributes as the partitioning key, ensures that. If an aggregation functions can be broken down into a pre-aggregation and final aggregation, parallel aggregation is often broken down into three phases: (1) A local aggregation without prior partitioning. The same group may occur on multiple nodes, so the aggregated result is not final, but in most cases much smaller than the aggregation's input. (2) A hash-partitioning step, and (3) the final aggregation which aggregates the pre-aggregated results from step (1). This is possible with all additive, semi-additive and algebraic aggregation functions, like COUNT, SUM, MIN, MAX, AVG, STDEV. For example, a sum can be computed by first computing partial sums and finally adding those up.

Equi-joins can be parallelized by co-locating all joining items (i.e. items that share the same join key) on the same node. Hash-partitioning both join inputs with the same hash function, using the join keys as partition keys, accomplishes that. After the partitioning is established, any local join algorithm is suitable for the local processing. This join strategy is referred to as a *partitioned join*. Based on the existence of partitions, the partitioned joins are often called differently. The *re-partition join* re-partitions both inputs. In *co-located* joins, both inputs are already partitioned the same way and no re-partitioning is required – all processing is local. If one of the inputs is partitioned on the join key (or both are partitioned, but differently), only one of the input must be re-partitioned, using the same partitioning scheme as the other input. This is also known as *directed join*.

An alternative strategy is to fully replicate one input to all nodes and leave the partitioning of the other input as it is. Naturally, each item from the non-replicated input can find all its join partners in the full replica. This join flavor is called *broadcast join* or *asymmetric-fragment-and-replicate join*. The choice between the partitioned joins and broadcast join is made on the base of the input sizes. Consider a join with two inputs R and S, executed in parallel on n nodes. Let $B(R)$ and $B(S)$ be the sizes of R and S respectively. A partitioned join costs $\frac{n-1}{n} * (B(R) + B(S))$ in communication, if both inputs need repartitioning. The communication costs of the broadcast join are $(n - 1) * B(R)$ when replicating R and $(n - 1) * B(S)$ when replicating S. Here, the costs obviously depend only on the size of the replicated relation. In general, the broadcast join is beneficial if one relation is much smaller than the other.

A parallel **sort** can be realized by a range partitioning, followed by a local sort. The range partitioning ensures that contiguous intervals are sorted, and the sorted result is simply the concatenation of the results from the individual operator instances.

4.1.3   Fault Tolerance

While in general, fault tolerance applies also to non-distributed systems, fault tolerance is an especially crucial feature for massively parallel shared nothing systems. Fault tolerance refers to the ability of a system to continue operation in the presence of failures. Failure types include hardware failures that render a processing node unusable until fixed, software failures that require a restart and causing a temporary outage, as well as operator failures (especially when interpreting user defined functions with errors) that leave the processing node intact.

Let us illustrate that with a little example: Assume a single computer has an availability of 99.9%, i.e. the chance that it fails within a certain day is 0.1%. This corresponds to an up-time of more than 364.5 days a year, a good value for commodity hardware. In a cluster of 100 machines, the probability that all machines are available within a certain day is $0.999^{100} = 0.9$, meaning that a failure of a one of the machines is not unlikely. In a cluster of 1,000 machines, the probability that all machines are available is only 37%, meaning you see a failure more likely than none. The computation is highly simplified and assumes independence of failure reasons, which is not always the case when count in reasons as network hardware failures or overheating. One can see immediately, that large analytical clusters require fault tolerance to provide acceptable availability.

Fault tolerant systems that tolerate the failure of up to k nodes are called *k-safe*. To achieve k-safety in a shared nothing system, $k+1$ copies of each data item need to be maintained. The different copies need not necessarily be in the same format, and the different formats can be used for efficient query processing [33].

In the context of fault tolerant query processing, one distinguishes between systems that restart the complete query upon a failure and systems that need only restart a subset of the operators. If one of the n processing nodes fails during query execution, the former approach simply restarts the query on $n-1$ nodes. The data processing originally performed by the failed node is spread among one or more of the remaining nodes. In the case where the various copies of the data were each in a different format, the execution plan naturally needs to be adapted.

The second approach persists intermediate results so that the data stream at a certain point can be replayed, similarly to forward recovery with redo-logs (cf. Sect. 3.1). Figure 4.6 illustrates both cases. Consider the previous example of a parallel grouping/aggregation, where the data is hash-partitioned by the grouping attributes. Each processor runs a parallel instance of the operator (C_1 to C_3) and processes a partition of groups. The parallel instance of the operator is dependent on data from all parallel instances of its predecessor operator. In the presence of a node failure (node 3 in this example), the input of the affected operators (A_3, B_3, C_3) has to be recreated. On the left-hand side of the figure (no persisting of intermediate results), all operators that are predecessors of the failed operators ($A_1, B_1, A_2, B_2, A_3, B_3$) have to be restarted in order to re-produce C_3's data. On the right hand side, only the failed operators (A_3, B_3) have to be restarted and the input to C_3 from B_1 and B_2 is provided by means of the persisted intermediate result.

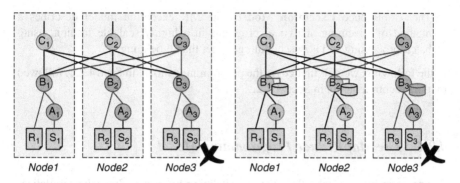

Fig. 4.6 Query recovery in a data-parallel system

One can create materialization points for intermediate results either artificially, or by piggy-baging on an operator that fully materializes the intermediate results anyways, such as hash tables or sorts. The materialized result might be kept in memory, or persisted to disk, based on memory availability. If persisting to disk is required, the costs may be significant.

4.2 The MapReduce Paradigm

As mentioned before, parallel processing of analytical queries has been researched in the field of database systems since the 1980s, leading to systems like Gamma [8] or Grace [11]. Since then, several concepts have been suggested and introduced, regarding the parallelizability of user defined code, or the runtime system's resilience to failures. The MapReduce[1] paradigm [7], however, marks one of the biggest breakthroughs in the field of parallel query processing. Created out of the need to parallelize computation over thousands of computers (an order of magnitude more than the database systems supported), MapReduce suggested simple but feasible solutions for both the question how to specify a query in a parallelizable way and how to execute it in a scalable way.

While its efficiency is highly controversial [34], MapReduce has evolved to widespread model for scalable parallel execution, and is therefore explained in detail here. When talking about MapReduce, one typically distinguishes two aspects:

1. The MapReduce **Programming Model**: The MR programming model refers to the MapReduce style of writing analytical queries in a parallelizable fashion. The programming model uses concepts inspired by functional programming.

---

[1] Different styles of spelling the term "MapReduce" exist, like "map/reduce" or "map-reduce". We stick to the spelling used by the authors of the original paper [7].

2. The MapReduce **Execution Model**: The MR execution model describes a method of executing analytical programs in a highly scalable fashion, using batch-processing and lazy scheduling, rather than pipelining.

In the following, we will first cover the programming model in Sect. 4.2.1, followed by the execution model in Sect. 4.2.2.

4.2.1   The MapReduce Programming Model

The programming model is the key to parallelizing a program. Since the parallelization of arbitrary code is hard to impossible, the programming model must provide mechanisms or primitives that describe how to parallelize the code. MapReduce's programming model is inspired by functional programming. We will cover the theoretical basics first and then look at the MapReduce specifics.

Functional Programming Background

Functional programming languages do not have any side effects that persist after a function terminates. One particular aspect of functional programming are higher-order functions, which take functions as input arguments in addition to values, lists, or complex data structures. Because of the lack of side effects and the potential of independently processing functions that are called by a higher order function, functional programs can be parallelized much more effectively than imperative programs that are written in languages like C++ or Java.

In the following, we will discuss three higher order functions that are of particular interest for data analysis: *map*, *reduce*, and *filter*. All of these functions take as input a first-order function and a data structure, for our consideration a list that consists of a head member that is concatenated to a remaining tail list. The style of stating the examples follows the syntax of the Haskell Language.

The *map* function applies a first-order function f to all members of the input list. For example, map sqrt 9 25 169 will apply the square root function to each list element and yield the list 3 5 13.

Below a recursive definition of *map* in Haskell Syntax is given. The first line defines the *map* of a function f for the empty list as the empty list. Then the map of a list consisting of a *head* member and a remaining *tail* list is defined recursively, by concatenating the result of the function application of f on the *head* element to the *map* of the remaining *tail* list with the function f.

```
map f [] = []
map f (head:tail) = f head : map f tail
```

One can parallelize the higher-order function *map* very easily. We can compute the function f independently for each list member. Partitioning the list into sublists and assigning them to different processors yields a degree of parallelism that is proportional to the number of available processors. The parallelization of *map* therefore is often called *embarrassingly simple parallelization.*

The *reduce* function (in functional programming also known as *fold, accumulate, aggregate, compress* or *inject*) computes a single value from a list by applying a first order binary function to combine all list members into a single result. For example, reduce + 1 2 3 4 5 combines the set of integer numbers from 1 to 5 with the operation + and thus yields 1+2+3+4+5=15.

For non-associative functions, the result of a reduce depends on the order, in which the first-order function was applied. Functional programming languages usually distinguish left-recursive and right-recursive definitions of reduce. A right-recursive reduce recursively combines the head member of the list with the results of the combination of the list tail.
For example, right-reduce - 1 2 3 4 5 yields 1-(2-(3-(4-5)))=3. A left-recursive reduce combines all but the rightmost member with the rightmost one, e.g. left-reduce - 1 2 3 4 5 yields (((1-2)-3)-4)-5=-13.

The definition of right-reduce and left-reduce in Haskell syntax is shown below. In addition to a binary function *f* and a list consisting of a *head* member and a remaining *tail* list, the definitions also use an additional parameter, *neutral*, which can be thought of as the neutral element of the binary function (e.g., 0 for +, or 1 for ∗).

```
right-reduce f neutral []    = neutral
right-reduce f neutral (head:tail)
    = f head (right-reduce neutral default tail)

left-reduce f neutral []     = neutral
left-reduce f neutral (head:tail)
    = left-reduce f (f neutral head) tail
```

The *filter* function takes as input a predicate (i.e., a function with a boolean result) *p* and a list and returns as result all members of the input list that satisfied *p*. For example, filter odd 1 2 3 4 5 yields 1 3 5.

Below find the definition of filter in Haskel syntax. In the first line, the filter of the empty list is defined as the empty list. The second and third line defines the filter of a list consisting of a *head* member and a remaining *tail* list as the *head* member concatenated with the filter of the remaining *tail* list, if the *head* member satisfies the predicate *p*. The third line defines the result as the filter of the remaining *tail*, if *p* is not satisfied by the head member.

```
filter p []                  = []
filter p (head:tail)
    | p head         = head : filter p tail
    | otherwise      = filter p tail
```

Map, filter, and reduce are three basic operations that allow processing (ordered) lists (or unordered sets) of data. They bear strong resemblance to the extended projection, selection, and aggregation operations of relational database systems and allow for filtering, transforming, and aggregating data sets. Map and filter can be easily parallelized, as each of their inputs can be processed independently. The parallelization of generic reduce is not straightforward. However, in the case of associative first-order functions the usual divide-and-conquer parallelization strategies can be also applied for reduce.

4.2.1.1 Basic MapReduce Programming

The MapReduce programming model has been proposed by [7] for processing large data sets, with special consideration for distributed computation. It distinguishes itself from the classic map/filter/reduce concepts of functional programming in the following ways:

- **Generalized Map:** The signature of the map operator is relaxed in that map may compute none, one, or multiple results for each input. In contrast to that, map in functional programming produces exactly one result for each input.
- **Generalized Reduce:** The reduce operator includes a partitioning step (also called grouping step) before the combination step that defines reduce in functional programming. The Reduce operator computes an output of none, one, or multiple results for each input group, by calling the first order function for each group.
- **No Filter:** There is no explicit filter operator. The filter function can be expressed by the generalized map operator, returning either one result (if the boolean function argument to map returns *true*), or none (if the boolean function returns *false*).
- **Key Value Data Model:** The input and output of the map and reduce operators are pairs that consist of a key and a value. The input pairs form a set; their order is irrelevant. The key has special meaning for the reduce operation: values with identical key form a group and will be combined during one invocation of the first-order function. The keys and values are arbitrary data structures that are only interpreted by the first-order function. The only requirement for the data types that act as keys are that they are comparable, in order to establish the grouping.
- **Fix MapReduce Pipeline:** A MapReduce program consists always of a map followed by a reduce. The input of the map is created by a reader, which produces a set of key/value pairs. In most cases, the reader obtains the data from a distributed file system, but it may also connect to a database or a web service. The result of the reduce function is collected by a writer, which typically persists it in a (distributed) file system. If a program cannot be represented by a single MapReduce program, it must be broken into a sequence of MapReduce sub-programs that are executed in sequence.

Figure 4.7 shows the logical dataflow of a MapReduce program. The notations use the following formal definition: with the set of keys K, the set of values V, the

Fig. 4.7 Basic dataflow of a MapReduce program

Kleene star (*) and the Kleene plus (+),[2] as well as two first-order functions on key/value sets, m: $K \times V \to (\overline{K} \times \overline{V})^*$ and r: $\overline{K} \times \overline{V}^* \to (K' \times V')^*$, the signatures of map and reduce are:

- map m : $(K \times V)^+ \to (\overline{K} \times \overline{V})^*$
- reduce r : $(\overline{K} \times \overline{V}^*)^+ \to (K' \times V')^*$

We use different symbols for the input and output keys and values, because the first order functions are allowed to change the types of the keys and values. The key is actually only used to define the groups for the reduce function, it has no special meaning for the input of the map function. The programming model could be changed in such a way that the map function's input is a set of values rather than key/value pairs. Likewise, the reduce function's output could be values rather than key/value pairs as well.

The following example in Java notation illustrates how to count the number of times each word occurs in a set of text files. In order to achieve that, we define the first order function $m()$ that is called for each line of a text file, with the key *filename* and the value *text*. The function $m()$ parses the text and emits each word as a key with the associated count value 1. We also define the first-order function $r()$ that takes as input a word and all associated count values for that word. The function r sums up all counts associated with that word and emits the word as the key, and the sum of all counts as the new value.

```
1  m(Key filename, Value text) {
2         foreach (word : text)
3             emit(word, 1);
4  }
5
6  r(Key word, Value[] numbers) {
7         int sum = 0;
8         foreach (val : numbers) {
9            sum += val;
10        }
11        emit(word, sum);
12 }
```

---

[2]The Kleene star is a unary operation over an alphabet (set) and denotes all strings that can be built over that alphabet, including the empty string. In our notation, it denotes zero, one or more occurrences of the elements of the base set. The Kleene plus denotes all strings but the empty set. In our notation, the Kleene plus denotes one or more occurrences of the elements of the base set. The Kleene star and plus operations are commonly used in regular expressions.

Fig. 4.8 Word-count example as a MapReduce dataflow

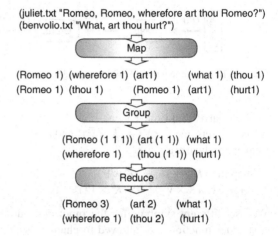

(juliet.txt "Romeo, Romeo, wherefore art thou Romeo?")
(benvolio.txt "What, art thou hurt?")

Using the two textfiles juliet.txt ("Romeo, Romeo, wherefore art thou Romeo?") and benvolio.txt ("What, art thou hurt?") as input arguments, the MapReduce program with the above defined functions yields the following list of key value pairs: (Romeo 3), (art 2), (thou 2), (art 2), (hurt 1), (wherefore 1), (what 1).

The internal processing of this program is graphically illustrated in Fig. 4.8. The map function $m()$, applied to the input key/value pairs, produces a list of key value pairs, where each word occurs together with a 1. The intermediate grouping step groups together all values that have the same key, resulting in key/value pairs where the value is actually a list of all the values for that specific key. Finally, the reduce function $r()$ is evaluated for each key with the corresponding list of values as argument, yielding the final result.

The MapReduce programming model can be viewed as simple sequence of a "value-at-a-time" operation (map), followed by a "group-at-a-time" operation (reduce). Since the *reduce* function does not necessarily fold the data, as in the functional programming definition, this view is often useful. While seemingly very simple, many algorithms can be mapped to those operations, making them very powerful generic building blocks. Most importantly, they allow for a highly efficient distributed implementation, which we discuss in the next section.

4.2.2   The MapReduce Execution Model

The MapReduce execution model has been first described in Dean et al. in [7]. The targeted execution environment is a massively parallel setup of up to thousands of commodity computers, so the main design objective was high scalability. The following points are the cornerstones of its design:

- A shared nothing architecture, where the MapReduce program runs in a data-parallel fashion.
- Decomposition of the work into smaller *tasks*, which can run independently from each other. A task is for example the application of the map function to a subset of the data.
- Simple recoverability of a task in case it fails or its output is lost, because failures for various reasons are considered common (see Sect. 4.1.3).
- Co-locating functions with the input data where possible, to reduce data transfer over the network.
- Lazy assignment of tasks to workers. Tasks are not assigned when the program is started. Instead, a worker, upon reporting availability of resources, is assigned a task.

In the following, we describe the MapReduce processing pipeline with the above mentioned points in more detail. Most of the architecture is described in the original paper [7]. For further details, we would like to refer the reader to the description of the open source MapReduce implementation *Hadoop*,[3] which follows that architecture and is extensively described in [39]. One major distinction is that the MapReduce framework described in [7] is implemented in C++, while Hadoop is implemented in Java. Other than that, the differences relevant in this scope concern only the naming of components and the way a program is deployed for parallel execution.

The Distributed File System

Shared nothing systems require that the data is distributed across the processing nodes. As the most generic mechanism of distributing the data, MapReduce makes use of a *distributed file system* (DFS), which spans the nodes.[4] Data is stored as files – the most generic storage format. [14] describes the architecture of the file system in detail. Files are broken down into blocks, typically 64–256 MB in size. For each block, a number of copies (typically 3) is distributed across the nodes, to prevent data loss upon node failure (Fig. 4.9).

The file system consists of a master and a number of storage nodes. Following the Hadoop project's terminology, the master is called *name node* and the storage nodes are called *data node*. The storage nodes simply store the blocks. The master manages the metadata, i.e., which blocks a file consists of, where the blocks are stored, and how many replicas for each block exist. In addition, the master tracks the available storage nodes by receiving periodic heartbeat messages from them. If a storage node fails, the master ensures that additional copies of the lost node's blocks are created.

---

[3]http://hadoop.apache.org.

[4]In principle, MapReduce can obtain its input from other sources as well. The distributed file system is however the most common case.

Fig. 4.9 The distributed file
system architecture

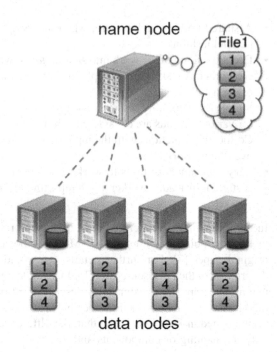

Communication is not transparently handled by the master to eliminate it as a transfer bottleneck. Instead, clients retrieve only the meta data from the master and connect to the storage nodes directly to read the file blocks. A file can be read in parallel by creating multiple connections to different storage nodes and simultaneously reading multiple blocks. If a file stores a relation as a sequence of tuples, the blocks can be considered partitions of that relations, which can be read in parallel.

The MapReduce Engine

The MapReduce framework follows a master-worker architecture as well. The master receives the MapReduce program (in Hadoop terms also called *jobs*), assigns work to the workers and monitors the progress. The worker processes are normally started on the same nodes as the DFS storage nodes, such that they have local access to a part of the data (e.g., in the form of files in the DFS). Figure 4.10 illustrates the execution model, which we sketch in the following: the master splits a MapReduce program into a number of map and reduce *tasks*. A map task is the application of the map function to a partition of the input file (often referred to as the mapper's *input split*), a reduce task is the application of the reduce function to a subset of the keys; tasks are therefore parallel instances of a data-parallel operator. The number of map tasks corresponds to the number of blocks that the input file has in the DFS, such that each block has its own map task. The number of reduce tasks is often

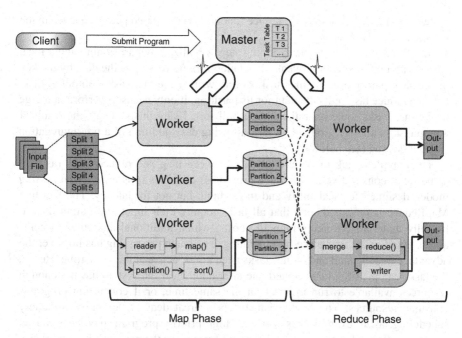

Fig. 4.10 Conceptual execution of a MapReduce program. The *solid lines* indicate local read/write operations, while the *dashed lines* represent remote reads

chosen close the number of computing cores in the cluster, or a multiple thereof. It is fundamentally limited by the number of distinct keys produced by the mappers.

Each map task is assigned to a worker, preferably to one that has a copy of the input split that was assigned to the mapper. Map tasks that cannot find their input locally can nevertheless read it through the DFS, albeit with the overhead of network traffic. By scheduling map tasks to their input splits, the majority of the initial reading happens from a local disk, rather than across the network, effectively moving the computation to the data. Inside the map task, the reader is invoked to de-serialize the input split and produce a stream of key/value pairs from it. The map function is invoked for each key/value pair. Its produced key/value pairs are partitioned into as many partitions as there are reduce tasks, by default using a hash-partitioning scheme. The data inside each partition is written to the worker's local disk. The intermediate result created by each map task is hence partitioned for the reduce tasks.

Each reduce task corresponds to one partition of the keys. It connects to all workers and copies from the intermediate results its designated partition, using a mechanism like Remote Procedure Calls or a file server run by the worker. After all partitions are read, it groups the keys by sorting the key/value pairs. The task invokes the reduce function for each consecutive set of key/value pairs with the same key. The result of the reduce function is written back to the distributed file system – hence, the result of the reduce function is considered persistent even in the presence of node failures.

MapReduce's intermediate grouping step is realized by partitioning and a local sort. As an implementation tweak, the Hadoop framework sorts the data by the key inside each partition in the map task, before writing the map task's output to disk. When a reduce task pulls the data for its partition, it only needs to perform a merge of the map tasks' outputs, rather than a full sort. Using this strategy, the result of a map task is already grouped by key, allowing easy addition of a pre-aggregation steps, if desired (see below).

The complete lack of pipelining data between map and reduce tasks (as well as between consecutive MapReduce programs) classifies it as a *batch-processing* model, designed for scalability and throughput, but not for latency. The fact that MapReduce is designed such that all tasks require their input and output data to be fully materialized incurs high I/O costs, which traditional analytical systems aim to avoid in the first place by pipelining. The batch processing has however the advantage that the map and reduce tasks need not be active at the same time. Hence, the tasks can possibly be executed one after another, if the system has not enough resources available to run them all at the same time, or if concurrent programs consume resources. The mechanism offers a great deal of flexibility for query scheduling: as an example, tasks from a high-priority program may be preferred over those from other programs, when the master picks the next task for a worker.

A key aspect of the MapReduce framework is elasticity, meaning that worker nodes can drop in and out of a running MapReduce cluster easily. While not many details are published about Google's MapReduce implementation, the open source variant Hadoop realizes the elasticity conceptually by making the workers loose participants of a cluster. A worker sends a periodic heartbeat message to its master. The heartbeat signals the worker's availability, reports the available resources to execute mappers or reducers, and reports on the progress of currently running mappers and reducers. The master maintains a table of available workers and their current work, updating it with received heartbeats. When not receiving a heartbeat in a certain time, it labels a worker unavailable and its tasks failed. The master may send a response to the heartbeat, assigning new tasks to the worker.

Using periodic heartbeats for the communication increases the latency of MapReduce jobs, because it takes a heartbeat plus response in time until a worker is notified of pending work. It does however keep the master thin and, most importantly, keeps the logic of entering and leaving the cluster simple and robust.

Fault Tolerance

Fault tolerance in the MapReduce execution model is surprisingly simple. MapReduce does not differentiate between different failure reasons. If a task is not reported to be alive for a certain amount of time, it is considered failed. In that case, a new attempt is started at another worker node. The restarted task behaves exactly like the initial task attempt. The number of attempts for each task is tracked and a MapReduce program is considered failed, if a task does not complete within a certain number of attempts.

A restarted map task will be able to obtain another copy of its input split from a another copy of the file in the distributed file system. A restarted reduce task connects to the workers and pulls the data for its partition, exactly like the original reduce task. When a worker node fails, one may loose the results from completed map tasks. If there remain reduce tasks that have not yet pulled those map tasks' data, the map tasks have to be restarted as well. The MapReduce fault tolerance model bears high similarity with the one discussed in Sect. 4.1.3.

MapReduce programs fail mostly due to erroneous user code, or faulty data. The possibility of an unrecoverable failures due to system outages exists in MapReduce as well, but it requires enough simultaneous occurring node outages that parts of the original input data are lost. The DFS, however, detects outages of storage nodes as well and triggers the creation of additional copies for file segments that are affected by the outages. Hence, data loss does occur only if sufficient ($k + 1$ for a k-safe DFS) outages occur within a short window of time.

Extension to the Core Model

Both MapReduce systems [7] and [39] introduce an additional function, called *combine*. This function is merely an optimization for efficiently implementing reduce operations in a distributed setting. Combine performs a local reduce before data is transmitted over the network for a final reduction phase. For many reduce functions, such pre-reductions are possible and may help to significantly reduce the amount of data to be transferred. In the word-count example from Sect. 4.2.1.1, the combine function may sum up the 1s, computing a partial sum. Instead of transferring all ones, only the partial sum is transferred per key and map task. When the number of distinct keys is significantly lower than the number of key/value pairs (hence resulting in a high number of duplicate keys), the combine function can make a big runtime difference. Relating to the parallelization strategies in Sect. 4.1.2, the combine function resembles the pre-aggregation, while the reduce function resembles the final aggregation.

While the core MapReduce model describes only two user functions (*map* and *reduce*) plus the *reader* and *writer*, the Hadoop implementation allows the programmer to specify several more functions of the processing pipeline. In addition to the above discussed *combine* function, those include:

- The partitioner for the original input, creating the above mentioned *input splits*.
- The partitioner for the reducer partitions, computing which partition a key is assigned to.

- The comparator that established the order between keys during the sort.
- The grouper, which determines when a new key starts in the sequence of sorted keys.

Making the pipeline parameterizable widens the applicability of Hadoop to algorithmic problems. We will see in an example in Sect. 4.2.4 how that helps to express programs that do not fit the original MapReduce model. More details on how to specify those functions can be found in the Hadoop Definitive Guide [39]. A good discussion about Hadoop's processing pipeline, its customizability, and how it can be viewed as a generic distributed database runtime is given by [10].

4.2.3   Expressing Relational Operators in MapReduce

Having discussed the programming abstraction and execution of MapReduce, we will now take a look at how to represent the essential physical relational operators through MapReduce. Please refer to Sect. 4.1.1 to see how physical relational operators relate to the logical operators of the relational algebra. We assume in this section, that the relational data is represented the following way: Each key/value pair represents one tuple, where the value holds the tuple's fields. For some operations, a subset of the fields is extracted from the value and used as the key (cf. join keys):

- **Filter:** A filter is represented as a *map* function, because each tuple can be filtered independently. The function reads the relevant fields from the value and evaluates the predicate function on them. As discussed in Sect. 4.2.1.1, the map function returns the exact same key/value pair as it was invoked with, if the predicate function evaluated to *true*, otherwise it ignores the tuple. The key is irrelevant for this operation.
- **Projections:** In the specific setup, projections that do not eliminate duplicates and solely remove fields are in many cases combined with other functions, by crafting the key/value pair to be returned to hold only the projected fields. As a stand-alone operation, the projection is the natural equivalent to a map function. The first-order function takes the tuple (value) it is invoked with, extracts the relevant fields and puts them into a new tuple, which is returned from the function. Any other form of transformation, such as deriving new fields by the application of a mathematical formula to a set of fields in the tuple, is represented the same way. The key is irrelevant for this operation. A projection with duplicate elimination works similar to a grouping and aggregation step – instead of aggregating the tuples of a group, the first-order function merely selects an arbitrary tuple to return.
- **Grouping and Aggregation:** The combination of grouping and aggregation maps naturally to a reduce operation, because it operates on the set of tuples, which agree on the values of their grouping columns. As a MapReduce program, the map function sets the key to the column(s) that is (are) grouped. The intermediate grouping step of the MapReduce pipeline ensures that the reduce function

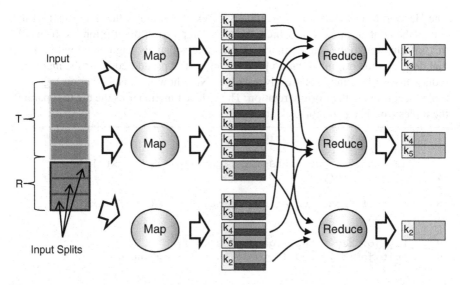

Fig. 4.11 A reduce-side join in MapReduce

is invoked exactly with the tuples of a group, which must be aggregated to a single result tuple. The first-order reduce function implements the aggregation function by, for example, counting or summing up the values. Multiple different aggregations can be performed in the same first-order function. The function invocation returns a single result tuple, containing the aggregated values.

- **Joins:** Joins are a little more tricky to express in MapReduce. There is an obvious mismatch between the fact that the map and reduce function have only a single input data set and the requirement of a join operator to process two data sets. To overcome that problem, one uses a trick that is very common in MapReduce programs: recall from Sect. 4.2.2 how the input to the individual map tasks is represented by a collection of so called *input splits*, which represent the partitions of the input to the map functions. It is straightforward to create those splits for both relations to be joined and use the union of the splits as the input to the mapper. That way, both input relations are fed into the same MapReduce program. The map function sets the key of its result to the join-key, so that all tuples from both relations are grouped together by their join key. All tuples that need to joined are given to the same reduce function, which in turn separates them based on the relation they stem from. Finally, the reduce function needs to build the cross product of all tuples with the same join key.

Figure 4.11 shows the dataflow of the join. The intermediate results created by the map functions contain values from both relations grouped by key. The join must naturally treat tuples from the different relations differently (for example the fields that make up the join key may be at different positions), so it needs a means to determine which relation the current tuple it processes originated from.

The Hadoop MapReduce implementation for example allows the map function to access the context of its task, which reveals the input split description. To forward that information to the reduce function, the tuple is usually augmented with a tag, that describes the original relation for each tuple. The pseudo-code for the map and reduce first-order functions are given below. Note how the map function tags the tuples according to their origin relation. The reduce function uses the tag to separate the tuples from the two input relations:

```
 1  map (Key key, Value tuple) {
 2      char tag;
 3      if (context.getInputSplit().getFile() = 'R.txt') {
 4          tag = 'R';
 5      }
 6      else if (context.getInputSplit.getFile() = 'S.txt') {
 7          tag = 'S';
 8      }
 9      Key joinkey = tuple.getFields(...);
10      emit(joinkey, tag ++ tuple);      // tag tuple
11  }
12
13  reduce (Key joinkey, Value[] tuplesWithTag) {
14      Tuple[] rTuples = new Tuple[];
15      Tuple[] sTuples = new Tuple[];
16
17      for (t : tuplesWithTag) {
18          if (t.tag == 'R') {      // distinguish based on origin
19              rTuples.add(t.tuple);
20              for (s : sTuples) {
21                  emit(joinkey, t.tuple ++ s) // concat t and s
22              }
23          } else {
24              sTuples.add(t.tuple);
25              for (r : rTuples) {
26                  emit(joinkey, s ++ t.tuple) // concat s and t
27              }
28          }
29      }
30  }
```

The above mentioned variant is typically called a *reduce-side* join in the MapReduce community. In terms of parallel database operations (Sect. 4.1.2), this variant would be a *repartition sort-merge join* – it partitions the data by the join key to create suitable partitions and uses a sort-merge strategy for local processing. Because the sorting is hardwired in the MapReduce execution model, sorting cannot be circumvented, rendering other local join strategies impracticable.

A second variant of MapReduce joins implements the join in the map function and typically referred to as a *map-side join*. It makes use of the fact that the first-order map function may contain arbitrary code and in fact create side-effects. To realise a map-side join, one of the inputs (normally the smaller one) is read into an in memory data structure when the map task is initialized, i.e. prior to the first invocation of the map function.[5] That data structure is typically a hash table, indexed by the join key(s). At each invocation, the first-order map function extracts the join key from its tuple and probes the hash table. For each tuple with matching join keys, the function creates a result tuple by concatenating the tuples' fields and returns it. In the terms of parallel database operations, this variant would be called a *broadcast hash join*, because one input is replicated to all parallel instances. The local processing could of course be done with a different strategy than an in-memory hash join. Partitioned hash-joins or sort-merge strategies are possible options. However, since the broadcasting of one input in a massively parallel setup is only efficient if that input is very small, the in-memory hash join is the most common method (see [30, 35]). We see that for both variants of the join, the MapReduce abstraction is actually not the perfect fit, since the functional abstraction has to be relaxed to realize the join.

The **Union** without duplicate elimination is not realized via a map or reduce function. Instead, it is expressed by taking all inputs to be united and making them together the input to the MapReduce program for the operation succeeding the union. The mechanism is the same as the trick used in the repartition-join (reduce-side-join).

Subqueries occur in two major forms: correlated and uncorrelated [22]. Uncorrelated subqueries can be executed like an independent query and their result is typically input to a join or a predicate. Correlated subqueries, being part of a predicate, pose a challenge, because their semantics requires to evaluate them for each tuple that the predicate is applied on. Their parallelization is not always possible in an efficient manner. Triggering a separate MapReduce program for each tuple that the subquery needs to be evaluated for is impossible due to the overhead of a MapReduce program. A good start is to decompose the subquery into a correlated and an uncorrelated part [32], and evaluate the uncorrelated part once in parallel. Its result is then read by all parallel instances of map function and cached, similar as in the map-side join. The map function finally evaluates the correlated part for each tuple it is invoked with. If the result of the uncorrelated part is very large (in the worst case, there is no uncorrelated part and the result corresponds to the entire involved relations), this strategy might be inapplicable. In that case, the query might not be suited for parallelization with MapReduce, and would need to be restated. This is however not a specific problem of MapReduce – database systems face the same challenges regarding the general efficient evaluation of correlated subqueries.

Each MapReduce job has a certain overhead cost, which is incurred in addition to the cost of the first-order functions that are evaluated. The overhead cost results from the communication between master and workers, the costs for setting up the tasks and their requires data structures, shuffling the data across the nodes for the grouping, sorting the data by the keys, and from reading and writing both the original input, the final output, as well as the intermediate results between the map

---

[5]Implementations like Hadoop offer special *setup* and *cleanup* functions that allow to create and tear down such data structures.

and reduce phase. For that reason, one typically aims at reducing the number of MapReduce sub-programs that are required to represent a program. Easy approaches to do that are for example to combine successive map functions into a single map function. Likewise, successive reduce functions that use the same subset of fields from the tuple as the key can typically combined. A good overview of those rules and further optimization heuristics are given in [29].

4.2.4 Expressing Complex Operators in MapReduce

The map and reduce functions are typically implemented in imperative programming languages like C++ and Java. In principle, arbitrary programs can be written using MapReduce as long as the task can be formulated as data-parallel problem. Apart from document processing as one of the first MapReduce applications in Google and classic relational query operators as described in Sect. 4.2.3 also complex operators can be implemented. In the following, we give some examples of such operators and describe how sorted neighborhood blocking, clustering, and set-similarity joins can be expressed in MapReduce.

Sorted neighborhood blocking. Blocking is a technique frequently used for entity resolution, also known as duplicate detection or deduplication. The goal of entity resolution is to identify pairs of records representing the same real-world object (e.g. persons, products) but differ in some attributes. A naïve strategy to perform this matching is to compare each record to all others by performing a pairwise similarity comparison of the attributes. To reduce the high effort of comparison a blocking technique is used: records with the same values regarding a given key (one or more attributes or a key constructed from some attributes), e.g. the same city, year of birth, product category etc. are assigned to the same block. Then, the matching is computed only for pairs of records within the same block. This can be easily mapped to MapReduce by implementing the blocking in a map function and the matching step in a reducer. However, this strategy is not optimal for MapReduce for several reasons [23]. Blocking produces a disjoint partitioning, i.e. records from different blocks are not compared which may miss some pairs representing the same object. Furthermore, load balancing is difficult to achieve because blocks can have very different sizes.

A better approach is sorted neighborhood blocking [19] where for each record a key is constructed, e.g. the concatenation of last name and zip code of the address of a person. The records are sorted on this key. Then, while scanning the records a window of fixed size is moved over the records and only records within this window are compared. An implementation of this sorted neighborhood technique for MapReduce was proposed by Kolb et al. in [23]. The approach extends the idea for implementing the basic blocking technique described above to preserve the order during repartitioning (i.e. all records sent to reducer R_i have a smaller blocking key than records sent to R_{i+1}) and to allow to compare also records across different reducer partitions which is needed to implement the sliding window. This is achieved by constructing composite keys, extending the reduce function, and replicating records across multiple reducers.

Composite keys are constructed from the blocking key k by adding a prefix $p(k)$ where $p : k \to i$ is a function with $1 \leq i \leq r$ with r is the number of reducers. Then, the key $p(k).k$ is used to route the record to the appropriate reducer, i.e. all keys of records at reducer i have the same prefix i and the records are sorted on the actual blocking key k. Based on this, the reducer can process the sliding window and construct pairs of matching records.

A sliding window does not produce a disjoint partition, therefore, some records have to be shared by two reducers. If it is guaranteed that the window size w is always smaller than the size of a block processed by a reducer then this can be achieved by making the last $w - 1$ records of reducer i also available to reducer $i + 1$. For this purpose, [23] introduces an additional boundary key as prefix to the composite key which is constructed by the map process. The resulting key is equal to $p(k).p(k).k$ for the original records with key k sent to reducer i and $p(k) + 1.p(k).k$ for the replicated records sent to reducer $i + 1$. In order to avoid duplicate pairs of matching records, each reducer produces only matches containing at least one record of its actual (non-replicated) partition. In [23] some problems with load imbalance for skewed data are discussed which are addressed e.g. in [24].

Clustering. Clustering is a data mining task to group objects in a way that within a group all objects are similar (or close) to one another and different from objects in other groups. A simple but popular technique is K-Means which is based on partitioning of data objects. The algorithm is iterative and works as follows:

1. Initially, K data objects (points) are chosen as initial centroids (cluster center points). This can be done randomly or by some other strategies.
2. Assign each data object to its closest centroid based on a given distance function such as euclidian distance.
3. Update the centroids by recomputing the mean coordinates of all members of its group.
4. Repeat step 2–3 until centroids do not change anymore.

K-Means clustering is well-suited for parallelization and a parallel implementations for different platforms have been proposed in the literature. The main idea of a parallel approach for MapReduce[6] is to partition the data, calculate the centers for each partition, and finally calculate the actual centers (i.e., for the whole dataset across all partitions) from the average of the centers from each partition. Fig. 4.12 illustrates this approach. All worker share a global file containing the centroid information $c_1, \ldots, c_k$ with $c_j = (x_j, y_j, z_j)$ for each iteration. Then, the map function uses this information while reading the data objects $o_i = (x_i, y_i, z_i)$ to calculate the distance of each data object to each centroid. Based on these distance values

---

[6]http://blog.data-miners.com/2008/02/mapreduce-and-k-means-clustering.html.

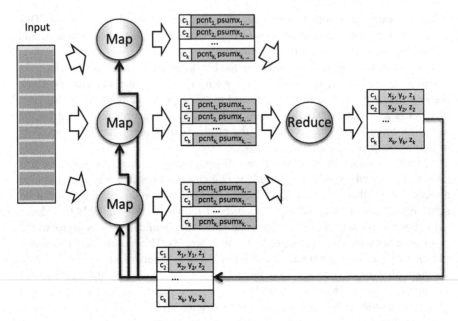

Fig. 4.12 K-Means clustering with MapReduce

the object is assigned to the closest centroid. For each centroid c_j the number of assigned objects $pcnt_j$ as well as the partial sum $psumx_j, psumy_j, psumz_j$ of each coordinate are maintained. Thus, the result of the map step is a record for each cluster containing the cluster id, the number of data objects assigned to it, and the sum of each coordinate. Finally, in the reduce function the cluster information of all partitions are simply aggregated to calculate the actual cluster centers which are then written back to the global file. These two steps are combined in a MapReduce job and are iteratively executed until the centroids do not change.

Set-similarity join. The idea of the set-similarity join is to detect similar pairs of records containing string or set-based data. This is a problem which occurs in many applications, e.g. master data management, CRM, and document clustering. In [36] the authors study how to implement this efficiently using MapReduce. The proposed approach works in three stages:

Stage 1: For all records a signature from the join value is constructed. The signature is defined in a way that similar values have at least one signature in common. In order to reduce the number of candidate keys prefix filtering is applied: string values are splitted into tokens which are ordered based on a given global ordering (e.g. frequency of tokens). The prefix of a string of length n is the first n tokens of the ordered set. This idea implements the pigeonhole principle: if n items are put into $m < n$ pigeonholes then at least one pigeonhole must contain more than one item. Assuming a string containing the tokens [aa, bb, cc, dd] where the ordering of tokens is bb, dd, aa, cc the prefix with length 2 would be [bb, dd]. For the set-similarity problem that means that similar strings need to share at least common tokens in their prefixes. Both the steps of compute frequencies of tokens and sorting them by frequency can be easily implemented in MapReduce very similar like in the word count example.

Stage 2: Using the token ordering obtained in stage 1, the input relation is scanned and the prefix of each record is constructed. This prefix together with the record identifier (RID) and the join attribute values are distributed in a map step to the reducers. The routing is achieved either for each of the prefix tokens (which leads basically to a replication of the records) or for groups of tokens. The reducers perform a nested loop operation on all pairs of incoming records to compute the similarity of join attributes. As output, pairs of RIDs and the similarity value are produced (filtered by a threshold).

Stage 3: Finally, the RID pairs generated in stage 2 are used to join their records.

In the paper [36] several alternative strategies for the individual stages are discussed and also two different cases of the self join and joining two different relations of records are discussed.

4.2.5   MapReduce Shortcomings and Enhancements

MapReduce has earned frequent criticism stating that MapReduce programs resemble a low level imperative form of specifying the query. It looses the advantages gained through higher-level declarative query languages, such as independence from the actual storage model and operator implementations with the potential to optimize the queries. The MapReduce programmer must for example decide manually how to realize a join and implement and parameterize many parts by himself. Implementing the operations efficiently and robust is difficult and hardly achieved by most programmers. In large parts, this problem is alleviated by the fact that many analytical programs are stated in higher level languages (Sect. 4.3), which generate MapReduce programs. Here, MapReduce becomes merely the runtime used by a query language with a compiler and optimizer.

Map-Reduce-Merge

The inherent problem of handling operations on two input has first been addressed by an extension called *MapReduceMerge* [40]. It builds upon the MapReduce model, but adds an additional *merge* phase. The merge phase is the designated point for two-input operations, like for example joins or set intersections. If used, it gets its input from two different MapReduce programs and makes use of the fact that the data in the reduce phase is partitioned and sorted. Each parallel instance of the merge function may select an arbitrary subset from both its inputs partitions, therefore being able to combine the data flexibly. With proper selections of the partitions and

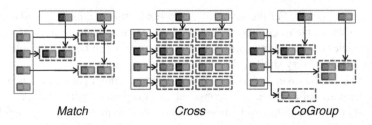

Match   *Cross*   *CoGroup*

Fig. 4.13 Three example PACTs for functions taking two input data sets

suitable merge code, many relational operations are expressible, such as joins (hash and sort-based), semijoins, set intersections, and set differences.

All of the above mentioned operations can be realized in pure MapReduce as well, typically using the tagged reducer, as described for joins in Sect. 4.2.3. While MapReduceMerge simplifies that, the programmer must still manually specify how exactly the operation is performed and implement the local processing logic himself. As a runtime for higher-level languages that generate MapReduce programs, MapReduceMerge has a limited additional benefit.

PACTs

A generalization of MapReduce are the Parallelization Contracts (PACTs) of the Stratosphere system [1]. Like map and reduce, PACTs are second-order functions that apply the first-order user function to the input data set. The core idea behind PACTs is that they do not specify a fix processing pipeline like MapReduce. Instead, they define how the input data is divided into the subsets that are processed by the first-order function invocations. The system compiles programs composed of PACTs to DAG dataflows (Sect. 4.2.6) to execute them in parallel. The compilation process picks the best suited execution strategies for each PACT. Hence a Reduce-PACT does not necessarily come with a partitioning step and a sort, but it may reuse prior partitioning schemes and use hash-based grouping, if the compiler deems that the best strategy. The PACT programming model hence exhibits a declarative property.

The Stratosphere system offers additional second-order functions to map and reduce, as shown in Fig. 4.13. The little boxes represent key/value pairs, where the color indicates the key. The grey dotted rectangles correspond to the subsets that the PACTs invoke their first-order function with. These functions ease the implementation of operations like for example joins or certain subqueries. The Match-PACT is easily used to implement an inner join and the compiler frees to programmer from the burden to choose between the variants of broadcasting or hash-partitioning (cf. map-side vs. reduce-side) and sort-merging vs. hashing. Using a lightweight mechanism called *OutputContracts*, certain properties of the user code are made explicit and can be exploited by the compiler to perform optimizations across multiple PACTs. PACTs hence have adopted some of the

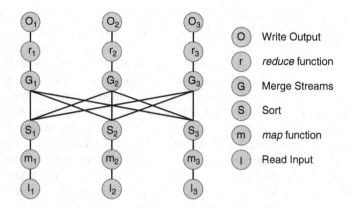

Fig. 4.14 The MapReduce execution pipeline as a DAG dataflow

optimization techniques from relational databases and applied them to the data-centric programming paradigm. The exact parallel execution and the mechanism of exchanging data between nodes depends on the runtime system executing the program.

4.2.6 Alternative Model: DAG Dataflows

A powerful alternative to the MapReduce execution model are *Directed Acyclic Dataflow Graphs*, often called *DAG Dataflows*. As the name suggests, programs are represented as directed acyclic graphs. The vertices execute sequential user code, while the edges describe communication channels. The user code in a vertex consumes the records from its inward pointing edges and selects for each produced record one or more outward pointing edges. The program is hence composed of sequential building blocks that communicate through channels. DAG dataflows directly represent the data-parallel pipelines illustrated in Fig. 4.5. The communication channels (edges) can typically be of different types (in-memory FIFO pipes, network channels, files), depending on the co-location and co-execution of the vertices they connect. It is possible to represent the MapReduce execution pipeline though a DAG dataflow, as described in Fig. 4.14.[7]

Representatives for DAG Dataflow Engines are *Dryad* [21], *Nephele* [37] (which executes the compiled PACT programs), and *Hyracks* [3]. A big advantage of the DAG abstraction is that more complex programs can be represented as a single dataflow, rather than multiple MapReduce jobs – hence intermediate result

---

[7]A common heuristic in DAG dataflows is to reduce the number of vertices and edges. For that reason, the code of the vertices I, m, and S might be combined to one vertex. Likewise could the code from G, r, and O be combined.

materialization can be avoided. While the abstraction is far more generic than the MapReduce execution pipeline, it has to handle all problems in a more generic way as well. The MapReduce fault-tolerance model (simply execute a task again) and load balancing mechanism (lazy task assignment) are not directly applicable to DAG dataflows and have to generalized to more generic mechanisms, as described in Sect. 4.1.3 for the example of fault tolerance. The implementation of the channels is up to the system. They can be implemented in the form of pipelines, such that no larger portions of the data are materialized, and the speed of the receiver naturally limits the speed at which the sender can produce the data. Another way to implement them is by writing the channel data to files and pulling the files to the receiver, which is very similar to the MapReduce execution model. The Dryad system implements its network channels that way to decouple the processing on the sender from the receiver. For more details on the specifics of DAG engines, we would like to refer the reader to [3, 21, 37].

4.3   Declarative Query Languages

An important observation from the previous sections is that while many data processing operators can be implemented using the standard MapReduce extension points, expressing them in terms of the new parallel programming model might be a challenging task. Moreover, the choice of a bad parallelization strategy or the use of unsuited data structures can cause a significant performance penalty. To ease the burden on inexperienced programmers and shorten development cycles for new jobs, a number of projects provide a higher-level language or application programming interface and compile higher-level job specifications into a sequence of MapReduce jobs. The translation based approach facilitates the use of optimization techniques and ensures a base level of quality for the generated physical plans. This section reviews the specifics of the most popular higher-level languages to this date.

4.3.1   Pig

Apache Pig[8] was the first system to provide a higher-level language on top of Hadoop. Pig started as an internal research project at Yahoo (one of the early adopters of Hadoop) but due to its popularity subsequently was promoted to a production level system and adopted as an open-source project by the Apache Software Foundation. Pig is widely used both inside and outside Yahoo for a wide range of tasks including ad-hoc data analytics, ETL tasks, log processing, and training collaborative filtering models for recommendation systems.

---

[8]http://wiki.apache.org/pig/FrontPage.

Pig queries are expressed in a declarative scripting language called Pig Latin [13], which provides SQL-like functionality tailored towards BIG Data specific needs. Most notably from the syntax point of view, Pig Latin enforces implicit specification of the dataflow as a sequence of expressions chained together through the use of variables. This style of programming is different from SQL, where the order of computation is not reflected at the language level, and is better suited to the ad-hoc nature of Pig as it makes query development and maintenance easier due to the increased readability of the code. A Pig workflow starts with `load` expressions for each input source, defines a chain of computations using a set of data manipulation expressions (e.g. `foreach`, `filter`, `group`, `join`) and ends with one or more `store` statements for the workflow sinks. The word-count example from Sect. 4.2.1.1 can be specified in Pig Latin as follows:

```
1  TEXTFILES   = load  '/path/to/textfiles-collection';
2  TOKENS      = foreach TEXTFILES generate
3                    flatten(tokenize((chararray)$0)) as word;
4  WORDS       = filter TOKENS by word matches '\\w+';
5  WORDGROUPS  = group WORDS by word;
6  WORDCOUNTS  = foreach WORDGROUPS generate
7                    count(WORDS) as count,
8                    group as word;
9  store WORDCOUNTS into '/path/to/word-count-results';
```

Unlike traditional SQL systems, the data does not have to be stored in a system specific format before it can be used by a query. Instead, the input and output formats are specified through storage functions inside the `load` and `store` expressions. In addition to ASCII and binary storage, users can implement their own storage functions to add support for other custom formats.

Pig uses a dynamic type system to provide native support for non-normalized data models. In addition to the simple data types used by relational databases, Pig defines three complex types – `tuple`, `bag` and `map` – which can be nested arbitrary to reflect the semi-structured nature of the processed data. For better support of ad-hoc queries, Pig does not maintain a catalog with schema information about the source data. Instead, input schema is defined at the query level either explicitly by the user or implicitly through type inference. At the top level, all input sources are treated as bags of tuples. The tuple schema can be optionally supplied as part of the `load` expression, e.g.

```
1  A  = load '/path/to/logfiles' USING PigStorage()
2         AS (date: int, ip: int, msg: chararray);
```

If the `AS` clause is not provided, the query compiler will try to infer the tuple schema from the types of the subsequent transformation expressions.

A common design goal for all discussed higher-level languages is the ability to incorporate custom user code in the data processing pipeline. Pig provides two standard ways to achieve that: user-defined functions (UDFs) and Pig Streaming. UDFs are realized as Java classes implementing Pig's UDF interface and have synchronous behavior – when a UDF is invoked with a single input data item, it produces a single output item and returns control to the caller. In contrast, the Streaming API can be used to asynchronously redirect the data processing pipeline through an external executable implemented in an arbitrary language.

The lifecycle of a Pig query consists of several phases. Submitted queries are first parsed and subjected to syntax and type checks and a schema inference process to produce a canonical representation of the input program. During the logical optimization phase a number of algebraic rewrites (e.g. filter pushdown) are applied to the logical plan. The optimized logical plan is then translated into a physical plan and each of the physical operators is mapped to the map or reduce function of a single MapReduce job. To minimize the number of executed jobs, structurally similar operations (e.g. aggregations that require grouping on different keys) may be embedded into a single job using the special pair of physical operators SPLIT (on the map side) and MULTIPLEX (on the reduce side). Once the MapReduce DAG has been created, final optimizations are performed at the job level. For instance, in this step algebraic aggregation functions are aggressively decomposed into a combine and reduce phase in order to minimize the number of shuffled records and reduce the skew of the number of elements associated with each group. Finally, the actual MapReduce jobs are created by specifying a subplan for each map and reduce stage in the Hadoop job configuration. The subplans are used by the jobs to configure the execution logic of the different mappers and reducers at runtime. The generated MapReduce jobs are executed in a topological order to produce the final result.

4.3.2 JAQL

Jaql,[9] a declarative query language for analyzing large semistructured data sets, is developed by IBM and bundled into its InfoSphere BigInsights[10] solution (a Hadoop based data analytics stack). Jaql's design is influenced by high-level languages like Pig and Hive as well as by declarative query languages for semistructured data like XQuery. Jaql aims to provide a unique combination of features, including a flexible data model, reusable and modular scripting language, the ability to pin down physical aspects of the specified queries, referred to as *physical transparency* and scalability [2]. Jaql is a viable substitute for Pig for most of the use cases described above, but due to its features is particularly well suited towards scenarios with partially known or evolving input schema. In addition, because of its tight integration with System T,[11] Jaql can also facilitate information extraction and semantic annotation processes on large data sets such as crawled web or intranet data.

---

[9]http://www.jaql.org/.

[10]http://www-01.ibm.com/software/data/infosphere/biginsights/.

[11]http://www.almaden.ibm.com/cs/projects/systemt/.

Jaql's data model is an extension of JSON – a simple and lightweight format for semistructured data. Similar to Pig, the data model supports arbitrary nesting of complex data types such as records and lists. A key difference between Jaql and Pig with that respect is that Jaql uses the same type for records and maps. This means that the canonical representation of a Jaql record must explicitly encode all field names, e.g. a movie record might be encoded like this:

```
1  {
2    title: "The skin I live in",
3    director: "Pedro Almodovar",
4    genres: [ drama ],
5    year: 2011
6  }
```

While this notation is more readable than the standard tab separated format used by most other languages, it could be too verbose for large datasets. Fortunately, in such cases Jaql can utilize schema information for more compact data representation in its pipelines. As in Pig, schema definition can be provided by the user at the query level as an optional parameter of the I/O functions. However, Jaql's schema language is more flexible as it provides means to specify incomplete types and optional fields. For example, the following schema describes a list of movies as the one presented above, but allows the definition of arbitrary fields at the record level:

```
1  [
2    {
3      title: string,
4      director: string,
5      genres: [ string ... ],
6      year?: integer,          // optional field
7      *: any                   // open type
8    }
9    ...
10 ]
```

This is very practical for exploration of datasets with unknown structure because the user can incrementally refine the schema without the need to change the associated query logic.

Jaql scripts consist of a sequence of statements, where each statement is either an import, an assignment or an expression. The following Jaql script implements the word-count example presented above:

```
1  // register the string function
2  split = javaudf("com.acme.jaql.ext.SplitFunction");
3
4  // word count expression
5  read(hdfs("/path/to/textfiles-collection"))
6    -> expand split($, " ")
7    -> group by w = $ into { word: w, count: count($) }
8    -> write(hdfs("/path/to/word-count-results"));
```

As in Pig, the dataflow is encoded in the query – in Jaql this is done explicitly at the syntax level through the use of the pipes (denoted by the "->" symbol). The core expressions for manipulating data collections provided by Jaql roughly correspond to the ones available in Pig (e.g. transform, filter, group by, join), but unlike Pig here they are not restricted to the top level and can be applied in a nested manner. This means that certain operations like nested grouping are easier to express in Jaql.

A key aspect of Jaql with respect to usability is the rich support for function extensions. User-defined functions (UDFs) and user-defined aggregates (UDAs) come in two flavors: external Java implementations registered with the javaudf function and in-script function definitions:

```
1  // variant 1: external UDF
2  sum1 = javaudf("com.acme.jaql.ext.SumFunction");
3  // variant 2: in-script function definition
4  sum2 = fn(a, b) ( a + b );
```

Jaql also supports specific syntax for the definition of algebraic aggregation functions that facilitates the use of combiner in the compiled MapReduce jobs. In addition, for improved reusability common Jaql statements (e.g. groups of function definitions) can be packaged in modules and imported by other Jaql scripts.

The query lifecycle in Jaql is similar to Pig. An abstract syntax tree (AST) is constructed from the input query and rewritten using greedy application of algebraic rewrite rules. In addition to heuristic rules as filter and projection push-down, the rewrite engine also performs variable and function inlining (e.g. substitution of variables with their values and functions with their definitions). After simplifying the script, Jaql identifies sequences of expressions that can be evaluated in parallel and rewrites them as one of the two higher-order functions mrAggregate() or mapReduceFn(). During the rewrite, the original expressions are packed inside lambda functions and passed as map or reduce parameters to the newly created MapReduce expression. The compiled AST of the query is either decompiled to Jaql and presented back to the user or translated into a DAG of sequential and parallel (MapReduce) steps and passed to the Jaql interpreter. The interpreter evaluates all sequential expressions locally and spawns parallel interpreters using the MapReduce framework for each mrAggregate or mapReduceFn statement.

A key property of the source-to-source translation scheme described above is that all physical operators (e.g. the mrAggregate and the mapReduceFn functions) are also valid Jaql language expressions. This means that the advanced user can pin down the evaluation semantics of a query either through the direct use of physical operators in the input or by tweaking the Jaql code representing the compiled physical plan (available through the "explain" expression). The ability to mix logical and physical operators in the query language in Jaql, referred to as *physical transparency*, provides the means for sophisticated custom optimization of runtime critical queries at the language level.

4.3.3 Hive

Apache Hive[12] is a data warehouse infrastructure built on top of Hadoop provided by Facebook. Similar to Pig, Hive was initially designed as an in-house solution for large-scale data analysis. As the company expanded, the parallel RDBMS infrastructure originally deployed at Facebook began to choke at the amount of data that had to be processed on a daily basis. Following the decision to switch to Hadoop to overcome these scalability problems in 2008, the Hive project was developed internally to provide the high-level interface required for a quick adoption of the new warehouse infrastructure inside the company. Since 2009 Hive is also available for the general public as an open-source project under the Apache umbrella.

Inside Facebook Hive runs thousands of jobs per day on different Hadoop clusters ranging from 300 nodes to 1200 nodes to perform a wide range of tasks including periodical reporting of click counts, ad-hoc analysis and training machine learning models for ad optimization.[13] Other companies working with data in the Petabyte magnitude like Netflix are reportedly using Hive for the analysis of website streaming logs and catalog metadata information.[14]

The main difference between Hive and the other languages discussed above comes from the fact that Hive's design is more influenced by classic relational warehousing systems, which is evident both at the data model and at the query language level. Hive thinks of its data in relational terms – data sources are stored in tables, consisting of a fixed number of rows with predefined data types. Similar to Pig and Jaql, Hive's data model provides support for semistructured and nested data in the form of complex data types like associative arrays (maps), lists and structs which facilitates the use of denormalized inputs. On the other hand, Hive differs from the other higher-level languages for Hadoop in the fact that it uses a catalog to hold metadata about its input sources. This means that the table schema must be declared and the data loaded before any queries involving the table are submitted to the system (which mirrors the standard RDBMS process). The schema definition language extends the classic DDL CREATE TABLE syntax. The following example defines the schema of a Hive table used to store movie catalog titles:

```
1  CREATE EXTERNAL TABLE movie_catalog (
2    title                    STRING,
3    director                 STRING,
4    genres                   list<STRING>,
5    year                     INT)
6  PARTITIONED BY (region INT)
7  CLUSTERED BY (director) SORTED BY (title) INTO 32 BUCKETS
8  ROW FORMAT DELIMITED
```

[12]http://wiki.apache.org/hadoop/Hive.

[13]http://www.slideshare.net/ragho/hive-icde-2010.

[14]http://www.slideshare.net/evamtse/hive-user-group-presentation-from-netflix-3182010-3483386, http://www.youtube.com/watch?v=Idu9OKnAOis.

```
9          FIELDS TERMINATED BY '|'
10    STORED AS TEXTFILE
11    LOCATION '/path/to/movie/catalog';
```

The record schema is similar to the one presented in the discussion of Jaql. In contrast to the Jaql schema, Hive does not provide support for open types and optional fields, so each record must conform to the predefined field structure. However, the DDL syntax supports the specification of additional metadata options like HDFS location path (for externally located tables), table storage format and additional partitioning parameters. In the example above we have indicated that the movie catalog is stored as a delimited plain text files outside the default Hive warehouse path using the STORED AS and LOCATION clauses. Hive provides several bundled storage formats and the ability to register custom serialization/de-serialization logic per table through the ROW FORMAT SERDE <format> WITH SERDEOPTIONS <options> clause. In addition, table records will be partitioned on market region code, each partition will be clustered into 32 buckets based on the director value and the movie titles in each bucket will be sorted incrementally by title. Table partitioning and clustering layout will reflect in the following HDFS directory structure:

```
1   # partition 1
2   /path/to/movie/catalog/region=1/bucket-01
3   ...
4   /path/to/movie/catalog/region=1/bucket-32
5
6   # partition 2
7   /path/to/movie/catalog/region=2/bucket-01
8   ...
9   /path/to/movie/catalog/region=2/bucket-32
10
11  ...
```

The available metadata will be used at compile time for efficient join or grouping strategy selection and for aggressive predicate-based filtering of input partitions and buckets. Upon definition, table data can be loaded using the SQL-like LOAD DATA or INSERT SELECT syntax. Currently, Hive does not provide support for updates, which means that any data load statement will enforce the removal of any old data in the specified target table or partition. The standard way to append data to an existing table in Hive is to create a new partition for each append set. Since appends in an OLAP environment are typically performed periodically in a batch manner, this strategy is a good fit for most real-world scenarios.

The Hive Query Language (HiveQL) is a SQL dialect with various syntax extensions. HiveQL supports many traditional SQL features like from clause subqueries, various join types, group bys and aggregations as well as many useful built-in data processing functions which provide an intuitive syntax for writing Hive queries to all users familiar with the SQL basics. In addition, HiveQL provides native support for inline MapReduce job specification. The following statement

defines the word-count example as a HiveQL MapReduce expression over a docs
schema which stores document contents in a STRING doctext field:

```
1  FROM (
2    MAP doctext USING 'python wc_mapper.py' AS (word, count)
3    FROM docs
4    CLUSTER BY word
5  ) a
6  REDUCE word, count USING 'python wc_reduce.py';
```

The semantics of the mapper and the reducer are specified in external scripts
which communicate with the parent Hadoop task through the standard input and
output streams (similar to the Streaming API for UDFs in Pig).

The Hive query compiler component works in a very similar manner to Jaql
and Pig. An AST for the input query is produced by the parser and augmented with
missing information in a subsequent type checking and semantic analysis phase. The
actual optimization phase is performed out by a set of loosely coupled components
which cooperate in a rule application process. A *Dispatcher* component employs a
GraphWalker to traverse the operator DAG, identifies matching rules at each node
and notifies the corresponding *Processor* component responsible for the application
of each matched *Rule*. The set of commonly applied rules include column pruning,
predicate push-down, partition pruning (for partitioned tables as discussed above)
and join reordering. The user can influence which rules are applied and enforce
the use of certain physical operators like map-side join, two phase aggregation for
skewed group keys or hash based partial map aggregators by providing compiler
hints inside the HiveQL code. The compiled physical plan is packed into a DAG
of MapReduce tasks which similar to the other languages use custom mapper and
reducer implementations to interpret the physical subplans in a distributed manner.

Hive also provides means for custom user extensions. User-defined functions
(UDFs) are be implemented by subclassing a base UDF class and registered as valid
HiveQL syntax extensions using the CREATE TEMPORARY FUNCTION...
statement. In addition, advanced users can also extend the optimizer logic by
supplying custom *Rule* and *Processor* instances.

4.4 Summary

Cloud infrastructures are an ideal environment for analytical applications dealing
with big data in the range of Terabytes and Petabytes. However, writing parallelizing
the analytical tasks as well as providing a reliable parallel execution environment
are big challenges. In this chapter, we have introduced the MapReduce paradigm as
programming model originally developed by Google which gained a lot of attraction
in the last few years and has already established as a de-facto standard for web-scale
analytics.

Based on an introduction on foundations of parallel query processing we have
discussed both the programming model and the execution model of MapReduce.

Furthermore, we have shown how to implement standard database query operators but also more complex analytics operators in MapReduce. Additional details on how to use the MapReduce model for programming specific tasks and how to operate the system can be found for example in [39].

However, MapReduce is mainly a programming model and therefore provides only a low-level form for specifying tasks and queries. These shortcomings have triggered the development of alternative approaches such as DAG models and engines which we have also discussed. Finally, several languages have been developed allowing a higher-level specification of jobs which are then translated into MapReduce jobs. We have presented the most popular among these languages Pig, Jaql, and Hive.

Another declarative programming language for parallel analysis of large sets of records is *Sawzall* developed by Google [31]. Sawzall programs define a set of *table aggregators* and side effect free semantics that associate record values with the different aggregators on a per-record basis. The Sawzall runtime utilizes Google's MapReduce engine to processes large amount of records[15] in a parallel manner. To do so, the Sawzall engine initializes a distributed runtime in the map phase of a MapReduce job. A program interpreter runs in each mapper to emit aggregation values for all records. The Sawzall runtime gathers the interpreter results and, if possible, performs partial aggregation before emitting them to a set of complementary components called *aggregators*, which run on the reduce side and implement various types aggregation logic (e.g. sum, avg, percentile). Sawzall precedes the higher-level languages described above and provides a limited subset of their functionality targeted towards a particular subclass of domain-specific problems relevant for Google. Since 2010, the compiler and runtime components for the Sawzall language are also available as an open-source project.[16]

The *Cascading* project [38] provides a query API, a query planner and a scheduler for defining, sharing, and executing complex data processing workflows in a scale-free and fault-tolerant manner. The query API is based on a "pipes and filters" metaphor and provides means to create complex data processing pipelines (*pipe assemblies*) by wiring together a set of pipes. The API defines five basic *pipe* types specifying different dataflow semantics – Pipe, Each, GroupBy, CoGroup, Every, and SubAssembly. The processing logic of the concrete pipe instances is provided at construction time by different *function* or *filter* objects. The constructed pipe assemblies are decoupled from their data inputs and outputs per se and therefore represent an abstract dataflow specification rather than an actual physical dataflow. Concrete dataflows are created by a *flow connector* from a plan assembly and a set of data sinks and sources (*taps*). When a new flow is constructed, the flow connector employs a planner to convert the pipe assembly to a graph of dependent MapReduce jobs that can be executed on a Hadoop cluster. In addition, a set of flows that induce an implicit consumer/producer dependency relation

---

[15]typically specified and encoded using Google's *protocol buffers*.

[16]http://code.google.com/p/szl/.

through their common taps can be treated as a logical entity called *cascade* and executed as a whole using a topological scheduler. The Cascading project provides a programming metaphor very similar to the PACT programming model described above on top of Hadoop – the parallelization contract concept corresponds to the concept of pipes and PACT DAGs correspond to a pipe assemblies or workflows.[17]

Tenzing is a query engine developed by Google and supporting SQL on top of MapReduce [4]. It allows querying data in row stores, column stores, Bigtable, GFS and others. In addition to standard relational query operators Tenzing provides different join strategies, analytical functions (`over` clauses for aggregation function) as well as the `rollup` and `cube` operators all implemented in map and reduce functions. The query engine is tightly integrated with Google's internal MapReduce implementation but has added several extensions to reduce latency and increase throughput. These include streaming and in-memory chaining of data instead of serializing all intermediate results to disk as well as keeping a constantly running worker pool of a few thousand processes.

References

1. Battré, D., Ewen, S., Hueske, F., Kao, O., Markl, V., Warneke, D.: Nephele/pacts: a programming model and execution framework for web-scale analytical processing. In: Proceedings of the ACM symposium on Cloud computing, pp. 119–130 (2010)
2. Beyer, K., Ercegovac, V., Gemulla, R., Balmin, A., Kanne, M.E.C.C., Ozcan, F., Shekita, E.J.: Jaql: A scripting language for large scale semistructured data analysis. PVLDB (2011)
3. Borkar, V.R., Carey, M.J., Grover, R., Onose, N., Vernica, R.: Hyracks: A flexible and extensible foundation for data-intensive computing. In: ICDE, pp. 1151–1162 (2011)
4. Chattopadhyay, B., Lin, L., Liu, W., Mittal, S., Aragonda, P., Lychagina, V., Kwon, Y., Wong, M.: Tenzing a sql implementation on the mapreduce framework. PVLDB **4**(12), 1318–1327 (2011)
5. Chaudhuri, S.: An overview of query optimization in relational systems. In: PODS, pp. 34–43 (1998)
6. Codd, E.F.: A relational model of data for large shared data banks. Commun. ACM **13**(6), 377–387 (1970)
7. Dean, J., Ghemawat, S.: Mapreduce: simplified data processing on large clusters. In: Proceedings of the conference on Symposium on Opearting Systems Design & Implementation, pp. 10–10 (2004)
8. DeWitt, D.J., Gerber, R.H., Graefe, G., Heytens, M.L., Kumar, K.B., Muralikrishna, M.: Gamma – a high performance dataflow database machine. In: Proceedings of the International Conference on Very Large Databases (VLDB), pp. 228–237 (1986)
9. DeWitt, D.J., Gray, J.: Parallel database systems: The future of high performance database systems. Communications of the ACM **35**(6), 85–98 (1992)
10. Dittrich, J., Quiané-Ruiz, J.A., Jindal, A., Kargin, Y., Setty, V., Schad, J.: Hadoop++: Making a yellow elephant run like a cheetah (without it even noticing). PVLDB **3**(1), 518–529 (2010)

---

[17]depending on whether you include the `DataSource` and `DataSink` contracts as part of the PACT graphs or not

11. Fushimi, S., Kitsuregawa, M., Tanaka, H.: An overview of the system software of a parallel relational database machine grace. In: Proceedings of the International Conference on Very Large Databases (VLDB), pp. 209–219 (1986)
12. Garcia-Molina, H., Ullman, J.D., Widom, J.: Database systems – the complete book (2. ed.). Pearson Education (2009)
13. Gates, A., Natkovich, O., Chopra, S., Kamath, P., Narayanam, S., Olston, C., Reed, B., Srinivasan, S., Srivastava, U.: Building a highlevel dataflow system on top of mapreduce: The pig experience. PVLDB 2(2), 1414–1425 (2009)
14. Ghemawat, S., Gobioff, H., Leung, S.T.: The google file system. SIGOPS 37(5), 29–43 (2003)
15. Graefe, G.: Parallel query execution algorithms. In: Encyclopedia of Database Systems, pp. 2030–2035. Springer US (2009)
16. Graefe, G.: Modern b-tree techniques. Foundations and Trends in Databases 3(4), 203–402 (2011)
17. Graefe, G., Bunker, R., Cooper, S.: Hash joins and hash teams in microsoft sql server. In: VLDB, pp. 86–97 (1998)
18. Graefe, G., McKenna, W.J.: The volcano optimizer generator: Extensibility and efficient search. In: ICDE, pp. 209–218 (1993)
19. Hernández, M.A., Stolfo, S.J.: The merge/purge problem for large databases. In: SIGMOD Conference, pp. 127–138 (1995)
20. Howard, J., Dighe, S., Hoskote, Y., Vangal, S., Finan, D., Ruhl, G., Jenkins, D., Wilson, H., Borkar, N., Schrom, G.: Dvfs in 45nm cmos. IEEE Technology 9(2), 922–933 (2010)
21. Isard, M., Budiu, M., Yu, Y., Birrell, A., Fetterly, D.: Dryad: distributed data-parallel programs from sequential building blocks. In: Proceedings of the ACM SIGOPS/EuroSys European Conference on Computer Systems, pp. 59–72 (2007)
22. Kemper, A., Eickler, A.: Datenbanksysteme: Eine Einf?hrung. Oldenbourg Wissenschaftsverlag (2006)
23. Kolb, L., Thor, A., Rahm, E.: Parallel sorted neighborhood blocking with mapreduce. In: BTW, pp. 45–64 (2011)
24. Kolb, L., Thor, A., Rahm, E.: Load balancing for mapreduce-based entity resolution. In: ICDE, pp. 618–629 (2012)
25. Maier, D.: The Theory of Relational Databases. Computer Science Press (1983)
26. Markl, V., Lohman, G.M., Raman, V.: Leo: An autonomic query optimizer for db2. IBM Systems Journal 42(1), 98–106 (2003)
27. Neumann, T.: Query optimization (in relational databases). In: Encyclopedia of Database Systems, pp. 2273–2278. Springer US (2009)
28. Neumann, T.: Efficiently compiling efficient query plans for modern hardware. PVLDB 4(9), 539–550 (2011)
29. Olston, C., Reed, B., Silberstein, A., Srivastava, U.: Automatic optimization of parallel dataflow programs. In: USENIX Annual Technical Conference, pp. 267–273 (2008)
30. Olston, C., Reed, B., Srivastava, U., Kumar, R., Tomkins, A.: Pig latin: a not-so-foreign language for data processing. In: Proceedings of the ACM International Conference on Management of Data (SIGMOD), pp. 1099–1110 (2008)
31. Pike, R., Dorward, S., Griesemer, R., Quinlan, S.: Interpreting the data: Parallel analysis with sawzall. Scientific Programming 13(4), 277–298 (2005)
32. Rao, J., Ross, K.A.: Reusing invariants: A new strategy for correlated queries. In: SIGMOD, pp. 37–48 (1998)
33. Stonebraker, M., Abadi, D.J., Batkin, A., Chen, X., Cherniack, M., Ferreira, M., Lau, E., Lin, A., Madden, S., O'Neil, E.J., O'Neil, P.E., Rasin, A., Tran, N., Zdonik, S.B.: C-store: A column-oriented dbms. In: VLDB, pp. 553–564 (2005)
34. Stonebraker, M., Abadi, D.J., DeWitt, D.J., Madden, S., Paulson, E., Pavlo, A., Rasin, A.: Mapreduce and parallel dbmss: friends or foes? Communications of the ACM 53(1), 64–71 (2010)
35. Thusoo, A., Sarma, J.S., Jain, N., Shao, Z., Chakka, P., 0002, N.Z., Anthony, S., Liu, H., Murthy, R.: Hive – a petabyte scale data warehouse using hadoop. In: ICDE, pp. 996–1005 (2010)

36. Vernica, R., Carey, M.J., Li, C.: Efficient parallel set-similarity joins using mapreduce. In: SIGMOD, pp. 495–506 (2010)
37. Warneke, D., Kao, O.: Nephele: efficient parallel data processing in the cloud. In: Proceedings of the Workshop on Many-Task Computing on Grids and Supercomputers, pp. 1–10 (2009)
38. Wensel, C.K.: Cascading: Defining and executing complex and fault tolerant data processing workflows on a hadoop cluster (2008). http://www.cascading.org
39. White, T.: Hadoop: The Definitive Guide. O'Reilly Media (2009)
40. Yang, H.c., Dasdan, A., Hsiao, R.L., Parker, D.S.: Map-reduce-merge: simplified relational data processing on large clusters. In: Proceedings of the ACM International Conference on Management of Data (SIGMOD), pp. 1029–1040 (2007)

Chapter 5
Cloud-Specific Services for Data Management

Cloud-based data management poses several challenges which go beyond traditional database technologies. Outsourcing the operation of database applications to a provider who, on the one hand, takes responsibility not only for providing the infrastructure but also for maintaining the system and, on the other hand, can pool resources and operate them in a cost-efficient and dynamic way promise cost savings and elasticity in usage. However, most customers are willing to move their on-premise setup to a hosted environment only if their data are kept securely and privately as well as non-functional properties such as availability or performance are guaranteed.

In this chapter, we present techniques to address these challenges of cloud-based data management. Based on an introduction of the basic notions of quality of service and service level agreements we present techniques to provide database-oriented service guarantees. Particularly, we present concepts of database workflow management as well as resource provisioning for cloud environments. One of the key distinguishing features of cloud computing in contrast to traditional application hosting is the pay-per-use or utility-based pricing model where customers pay only as much for the cloud resources as they use. We give an overview on the cost and subscription types underlying typical pricing models in cloud computing. Finally, we present also approaches for secure data management in outsourced environments. Beside appropriate encryption schemes we describe the implementation of basic database operations like joins, aggregation and range queries on encrypted databases.

5.1 Service Level Agreements

Providing cloud services to customers requires not only to manage the resources in an cost-efficient way but also to run these services in certain quality satisfying the needs of the customers. The quality of delivered services is usually formally defined in an agreement between the provider and the customer which is called

W. Lehner and K.-U. Sattler, *Web-Scale Data Management for the Cloud*, DOI 10.1007/978-1-4614-6856-1_5, © Springer Science+Business Media New York 2013

service level agreement. In the following sections we introduce the basic ideas of such agreements from the technical perspective of cloud computing and give an overview on techniques to achieve the technical goals of service quality.

5.1.1   The Notion of QoS and SLA

Quality of service (QoS) is a well-known concept in other areas. For example, in networking QoS is defined in terms of error rate, latency, or bandwidth and implemented using flow control, resource reservation or priorization. Other examples of QoS are jitter or subjective measures like experienced quality in multimedia which can be implemented using appropriate coding/encoding schemes or scheduling of disk requests.

For IT service providers, QoS is typically used in the context of service level agreements (SLA). Service level agreements define the common understanding about services, guarantees, and responsibilities. They consist of two parts:

- **Technical part:** The technical part of an SLA (so-called service level objectives) specifies measurable characteristics such as performance goals like response time, latency or availability and the importance of the service.
- **Legal part:** The *legal part* defines the legal responsibilities as well as fee/revenue for using the service (if the performance goals are met) and penalties (otherwise).

Supporting SLAs requires both the monitoring of resources and service providing as well as resource management in order to minimize the penalty cost while avoiding overprovisioning of resources.

5.1.2   QoS in Data Management

In classic database system operation, QoS and SLAs are mostly limited to provide reliable and available data management. Query processing typically aims at executing each query as fast as possible, but not to guarantee given response times. However, for database services hosted on a cloud infrastructure and provided as multi-tenant service, more advanced QoS concepts are required. Important measures are the following:

- **Availability:** The availability measure describes the ratio of the total time the service and the data are accessible during a given time interval and the length of this interval. For example, Amazon EC2 guarantees an availability of 99.95% for the service year per region, which means downtimes in a single region up to 4.5 h per year are acceptable.
- **Consistency:** Consistency as service guarantee depends on the kind of service provision. In case of a hosted database like Amazon RDS or Microsoft Azure

SQL, full ACID guarantees are given, whereas scalable distributed data stores such as Amazon SimpleDB guarantee only levels of eventual consistency (Sect. 3.2).

- **(Query) response time:** The response time of a query can either be defined in the form of *deadline constraints*, e.g. response time of a given query is $\leq 10\,\text{s}$, or not per query but as *percentile constraints*. The latter means for example, that 90% of all requests to be processed within $10\,\text{s}$, otherwise the provider will pay a penalty charge.

In order to provide guarantees regarding these measures, different techniques are required. Availability can be achieved by introducing redundancies: data is stored at multiple nodes and replication techniques (Sect. 3.4) are used to keep multiple instances consistent. Then, only the number of replicas and their placement affect the degree of availability. For instance, Amazon recommends to deploy to EC2 instances in different availability zones to increase availability by having geographically distributed replicas, which is done for data in SimpleDB automatically.

Techniques for ensuring different levels of consistency are described in Chap. 3 or are standard database techniques which can be found in textbooks and are not covered here in more detail.

Though response time guarantees are not the domain of standard SQL database systems, there exist some techniques in realtime databases [21]. The goal of these systems is to complete database operations within given time constraints. For this purpose, time semantics are associated with data, i.e. data is valid for specific time intervals. Furthermore, transactions (database operations) are specified with timing constraints, e.g. a completion deadline, a start time or periodic invocation. Finally, the correctness criteria require that a transaction T is meeting its timing constraints: either as absolute time consistency where all data items used by T are temporally valid, or as relative time consistency where all items used by T are updated within specific interval of each other.

In addition to timing constraints, transactions are specified with further characteristics such as arrival pattern (periodic, sporadic), the data access (random or predefined, read or write) and – one of the most important – the implication of missing the deadline. This is usually modeled using a transaction value depending on the time. Figure 5.1 illustrates this with an example. Transaction T_1 has always the same value (or revenue) independent of the time of finishing. In contrast, the value of executing transaction T_2 decreases after some time to zero and for T_3 the value becomes even negative after the deadline, i.e. penalty costs have to be paid.

In realtime DBMS these characteristics are used in time-cognizant protocols to schedule the execution order of transactions. However, this works only in case of lock conflicts and is therefore not directly applicable to guarantee response times of queries. For this problem, several approaches can be used:

- **Provide sufficient resources:** Adding more resources is a straightforward solution but requires accurate capacity planning to avoid over- or under-provisioning.

Fig. 5.1 Value of transactions with respect to deadlines

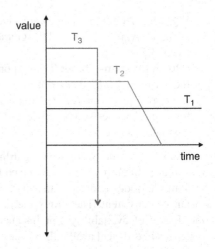

- **Shielding:** The technique of shielding means to provide dedicated (but possibly virtualized) systems to customers. QoS guarantees are given on a system level as long as the system can handle the workload.
- **Scheduling:** Scheduling aims at the ordering of requests and allocating resources on priority. It allows a fine-grained control on QoS provisioning.

In the following, we briefly discuss workload management as the most cost-efficient but also challenging approach.

5.1.3 Workload Management

The goal of workload management in database systems is to achieve given performance goals for classes of requests such as queries or transactions. This technique is particularly used in the mainframe world. For example, IBM's mainframe platform z/OS provides a sophisticated workload manager component. Similar solutions are available for other commercial DBMS such as Oracle, Sybase or EMC Greenplum. Workload management concerns several important aspects:

- The specification of service-level objectives for the workload consisting of several requests (queries, updates) and services classes,
- Workload classification to classify the requests into distinct service classes for which performance goals are defined,
- Admission control and scheduling, i.e. limiting the number of simultaneously executing requests and ordering the requests by priority.

Figure 5.2 illustrates the basic principle of workload management. Incoming transactions are classified into service classes. The admission control and scheduling component selects requests from these classes for executing. Depending on the

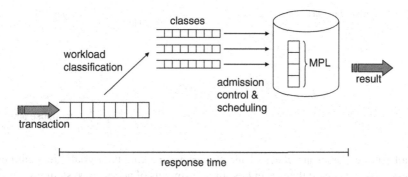

Fig. 5.2 Principle of workload management

service class, some requests are prioritized. Furthermore, the number of simultaneously running requests can be limited to avoid performance degradation of all
currently processed requests. This is typically achieved by the multiprogramming
level (MPL) – the maximum number of tasks which can be active at a time. The
whole time from arriving at the system until producing the result represents the
response time.

For admission control and scheduling several techniques such as static priorization and goal-oriented approaches are available.

Static priorization approaches which are used by some commercial DBMS, e.g.
IBM DB2 with the Query Patroller or Oracle's Resource Manager. This component
intercepts incoming queries and determines if they should be blocked, queued or run
immediately. This is decided based on user-given thresholds such as the number of
simultaneously running queries (i.e. the multiprogramming level) or the maximum
cost of a single query or concurrently running queries obtained from the query
optimizer. The thresholds can be also determined by the system, for example using
historical analysis.

An example of a goal-oriented approach is IBM's Workload Manager (WLM) [8]
for the mainframe platform z/OS. It allows to dynamically allocate and redistribute
server resources (CPU, I/O, memory) across a set of concurrent workloads based
on user-defined goals. Furthermore, it does not only manage database processes but
also units of work spanning multiple address spaces (e.g. middleware components).

WLM uses services classes specified by the system administrator. For each
service class an importance level and performance goals are defined. Goals are
expressed for instance in terms of response time or a relative speed (called velocity).
The WLM measures the system continuously to determine a performance index PI
for each service class. In case of a response time goal, PI is calculated by

$$PI = \frac{\text{achieved response time}}{\text{response time goal}}$$

A PI value ≈ 1 means that the goal is met, $PI < 1$ indicates that the goal is
overachieved and $PI > 1$ that the goal is missed. In this way, the goal achievements

Fig. 5.3 Utility function

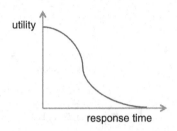

of all service classes are checked and classes not meeting their goals are identified. These classes become then receivers for adjustments of access to system resources. The measured system data are used to forecast the improvement for receivers and degradation for donors. If such a change is found beneficially then the calculated adjustments are performed.

Another way of specifying performance goals or preferences are utility functions [16]. They allow to map possible system states such as resource provisioning to jobs or requests to a real scalar value and can represent performance features like response time, throughput etc. but also the economic value. Figure 5.3 shows an example of a utility function for response time. Given a set of utility functions for different clients or resource consumers the goal of scheduling is now to determine the most valuable feasible state, i.e. to maximize utility. This can be seen as a search problem where the space of alternative mappings is explored.

5.1.4 Resource Provisioning

Traditional database workload management as described in Sect. 5.1.3 aims at scheduling requests for a fixed amount of resources. In contrast, the elasticity of cloud infrastructures allows to size the resources to meet the given SLAs. This opens opportunities

* For clients to rent sufficient machines/resources to handle the application load,
* For providers to allocate limited resources to achieve the performance goals of their customers but also to consolidate resources in order to maximize profit.

However, for both sides the risk of underprovisioning and overprovisioning exist [3]. Overprovisioning (Fig. 5.4) typically occurs if resources are allocated for a peak load and results in a waste of resources and money. Underprovisioning means that not enough resources are provided to satisfy the performance requirements of the customers, e.g. because the resource demands have been underestimated. Thus, SLAs of (at least some) customers will be violated and usually penalty fees have to be paid. In the worst case, it could also mean that customers whose requests have not been satisfied will never come back.

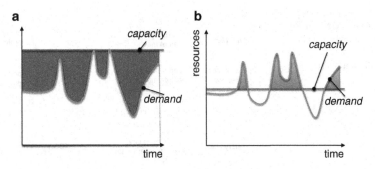

Fig. 5.4 (a) Overprovisioning vs. (b) Underprovisioning

In order to address these issues two tasks have to be solved:

- **System model:** A model is needed for estimating achievable performance for a given set of resources (CPU cycles, number of cores, memory, IO and network bandwidth, . . .), i.e. a function has to be determined

$$f(CPU, memory, IO, network) = performance$$

- **Resource allocation:** Resources have to be allocated or provided to process requests of the customers. This can be done statically, e.g. renting three machines for 1 h, or dynamically, e.g. allocate an additional machine to handle a current peak load. The latter can be done intensionally (*dynamic scaling*) by the client or fully automatically by the infrastructure (*auto scaling*).

Defining the system model is in fact the old problem of capacity planning. However, in the context of cloud computing it comprises two levels [24]: a local analysis to identify a configuration to meet the SLAs of a single client while maximizing the revenue and the global analysis to find a policy for scheduling and allocating resources among all clients, ideally by considering the current system load.

Defining a system model to predict performance of database operations is a very challenging task. Reasons are among others that database systems can process many different queries which all have different resource demands and performance characteristics. Furthermore, performance depends on the available resources (e.g. memory, IO bandwidth), data volume and even data distribution. Recent efforts try to address this challenge by leveraging statistical analysis and machine learning techniques. For example, in the work described in [24] regression analysis is used. Based on measurements of database system performance for TPC-W benchmark, a regression model is learned to predict performance for the parameters CPU, memory, number of replicas, and query rate. The performance is expressed in average SLA penalty costs for a simple step function, i.e., if the response time for a query is not met the provider pays penalty. The results reported in this paper show that regression tree analysis together with a boosting techniques achieves relative error rates of less than 30%.

Fig. 5.5 Performance
prediction of queries using
correlation analysis [11].
(**a**) Training phase.
(**b**) Prediction phase

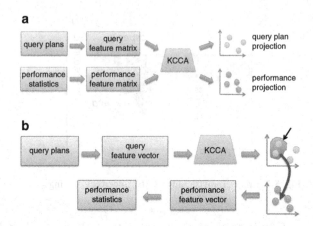

A second approach based on correlation analysis was proposed by Ganapathi
et al. in [11] and works as follows: in a training phase, a matrix of vectors of query
plan features (number of operator instances, cardinalities for each operator, etc.) and
a matrix of vectors of performance features (elapsed time, I/Os, records accessed
etc.) are used with Kernel Canonical Correlation Analysis (KCA) – a generalization
to canonical correlation analysis – to project the vectors onto dimensions of maximal
correlation across the datasets. In the predication phase for a new query, its query
feature vector is derived and mapped using KCCA to find its coordinates on
the query projection. Then, the coordinations on the performance projections are
inferred using nearest neighbor search, and finally reverse mapped from the feature
space to the prediction metrics. Experimental evaluations have shown that elapsed
times of individual queries are predicted within 20% of their time (for 85% of all
test queries including short and long-running queries) but require careful parameter
tuning (Fig. 5.5). Finally, the work of Soror et al. [23] already mentioned in Sect. 2.5
also aims to define a system model.

As mentioned above, the task of resource allocation can be done either statically
or dynamically. The static approach is typically implemented by so-called design
advisors (see Sect. 2.5). Dynamic approaches for shared-nothing databases are more
challenging because the necessary migration or replication of data causes some
additional overhead which has to be considered for the decision.

Possible approaches range from rather simple rule-based strategies to complex
decision models trying to minimize the costs and penalties. Examples of a rule-
based solutions are commercial products such as Xeround[1] or Scalebase.[2] Xeround
offers a MySQL-like database service on several cloud platforms (Amazon EC2,
Rackspace). The system consists of a two-tier architecture with access nodes for
query processing and data nodes implemented on top of a distributed hashtable.

---

[1]http://xeround.com.

[2]http://www.scalebase.com.

Data is organized in virtual partitions which are replicated to different data nodes. If predefined thresholds for data volume or throughput (requests per time) are exceeded, the system automatically scales out by allocating data nodes (data volume threshold exceeded) or processing nodes (throughput threshold exceeded). That means, Xeround combines read replicas and sharding of virtual partitions as well as multi-master replication but hides this from the application by providing a load balancer.

Scalebase offers another scaling solution for MySQL databases. A component called Data Traffic Manager serves as a middleware between the client application and the transparently sharded MySQL databases. As in Xeround, new database nodes can be added at any time and Scalebase performs the redistribution of data automatically.

Though, such basic techniques allow to allocate resources automatically, they do not support directly the provider's goal of minimizing costs while meeting SLAs. This requires to optimize the resource allocations among all clients.

In [24] the SmartSLA approach addressing this goal is presented. Based on the system performance model and the SLA penalty cost function described above and weighted with factors representing different classes of customers (gold, silver, bronze), a total SLA penalty cost function is defined as the total sum which is to be minimized. Because all possible configurations of memory, CPU, replicas etc. build a huge search space where resources represent the dimensions, a grid-based search for the optimal configuration is performed. Here, grids represent fixed amount of resources (e.g. x MB memory etc.). The dynamic resource allocation is then basically the problem of identifying the optimal search direction (which resource, increase or decrease) minimizing the total SLA penalty costs. Such a search step is performed at the end of given time intervals and processed at two levels: first, for memory and CPU shares and second for the more expensive number of replicas. For the latter, migration costs are taken into account. Experimental evaluations reported in this work show that this approach can adaptively allocate resources and reduce total costs.

5.2 Pricing Models for Cloud Systems

One of the central ideas and key success factors of the cloud computing paradigm is the pay-per-use price model. Ideally, customers would pay only for the amount of the resources the have consumed. Looking at the current market, services differ widely in their price models and range from free or advertisement-based models over time or volume-based models to subscription models. Based on a discussion of the different cost types for cloud services we present some fundamentals of pricing models in the following.

5.2.1   Cost Types

For determining a pricing model, all direct and indirect costs of a provided service have to be taken into account. The total costs typically comprise *capital expenditures (CapEx)* and *operational expenditures (OpEx)*. Capital expenditure describes all costs for acquiring assets such as server and network hardware, software licenses, but also facilities, power, and cooling infrastructure. Operational expenditure includes all costs for running the service, e.g. maintenance costs for servers, facilities, infrastructure, payroll, but also legal and insurance fees.

One of the economical promises of cloud computing is to trade CapEx for OpEx by outsourcing IT hardware and services. Furthermore, for customers there is no need for long-term commitment to resources. However this typically comes with higher OpEx. A good analogy is the rental car business: relying on rental cars instead of maintaining a company-owned fleet of cars avoids the big investment for purchasing cars (CapEx), but requires to pay the rates for each day of use (OpEx).

Cloud-based data management has some specific characteristics which have to taken into account for pricing models, because data is not a as elastic as pure computing jobs. The data sets have to be uploaded to the cloud, stored there for a longer time and usually require additional space for efficient access (indexing) and high availability (backups). Thus, the following types of operational costs are included:

- **Storage costs:** Database applications require to store data persistently on disk. In order to guarantee a reliable and high available service, backup and archiving have to be performed which need additional storage space. In addition, for efficient access, index structures are required which are also stored on disk. The disk space occupied by all these data (application data, backup, indexes) is considered part of the storage costs.
- **Data transfer costs:** This type of costs covers the (initial and regularly) transfer of application data to the service provider over the network as well as the costs for delivering requests and results between clients and the database service.
- **Computing costs:** This represents typically the main cost type for processing database services and includes processing time of running a data management system (computing time, license fee) or processing a certain number of requests (queries, transactions, read/write requests).

Further costs can be also billed for certain guarantees and service-level agreements, e.g. availability, consistency level or provided hardware (CPU type, disk type).

5.2.2   Subscription Types

Based on the individual cost types different pricing models can be built. Currently available models are often inspired by other commercial services (such as mobile

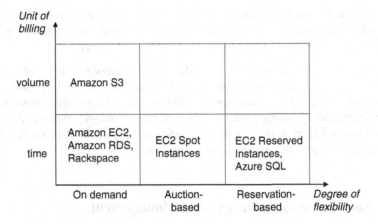

Fig. 5.6 Classification of subscription types

phone plans) and range from a pure pay-per-use approach where each type of cost is billed individually to flat-rate like subscription models for longer time periods. In principle, these models can be classified according to two dimensions: the unit for billing and the degree of flexibility (Fig. 5.6). The first dimension describes which unit is used for billing. Typical units are

- **Time of usage:** Examples are Amazon's EC2 and RDS instances or Rackspace instances which are billed in $ per hour for specific hardware configurations. Further parameters such as system load, compute cycles, bandwidth usage or number or requests are not taken into account. However, this means that it is up to the customer to choose an appropriate configuration needed to handle to load.
- **"volume-based" units:** Examples are GB per month for storage services or the number of requests per time unit. Volume-based pricing models simplify resource provisioning and SLAs for the service provider: based on the requested volume the provider can estimate the required resources (disk space, computing resources to handle the requests).

The second dimension characterizes the flexibility of service usage:

- **On-demand or pay-per-use:** This is the most flexible approach: a customer can use the service at any time as well as when he really wants to use it. Apart from the consumed units (time, volume) no additional costs are billed.
- **Auction-based:** In this model, which is, for instance, offered by Amazon with their so-called "spot instances" in EC2, customers can bid for unused capacities. The prices for such machine instances vary over time depending on supply and demand. As long as the price for these instances is below the customer's bid (e.g. a maximum price), the customer can use such instances. Of course, this makes sense only for applications which are very flexible in their usage times. Furthermore, such applications have to deal with possible interruptions which occur when prices of instances exceed the bid.

- **Reservation-based:** This means that capacity is reserved at the providers side for which the customer has to pay a one-time or regularly fee. In return, the customer receives a discount for the regular charges (time or volume).

Currently, cloud service providers use different combinations of these subscription and cost types. This allows a flexible choice for customers, but makes it sometimes difficult to select the most appropriate offer. Some providers offer basic online pricing calculators for determining the price of given configurations, e.g. Amazon[3] and Microsoft.[4] More details about prices and pricing models of currently offered cloud data management services are given in Chap. 6.

5.3   Security in Outsourced Data Management

A major obstacle to managing data in the cloud is security and privacy. There are two major aspects where cloud data management increases the risk. First, a central collection of data creates a valuable target for attacks. With the increase in benefit, attacks may become more sophisticated and better funded. Targeted attacks have proven to be very powerful.

Second, data in the cloud is entrusted to the service provider. This entails a threat to privacy from the service provider and any party granted access by that service provider, such as legal authorities. In international cloud environments this may pose a legal problem where personal data may not even be stored in the cloud due to privacy regulations.

These security and privacy threats may not be overcome as long as the service provider has access to the data. Only if the service provider is oblivious to the data stored at its site, one can reach protection against intentional or unintentional threats from the service provider's site. Encryption may protect the confidentiality of the data, but needs to be applied correctly. Disk, file or database encryption is generally not particularly useful in this context, since the key is retained at the service provider. It helps secure the data center against physical attacks, but against attacks impersonating a valid client or operating at the application layer, it is not effective.

Instead the goal is to retain the key at the client's site and only encrypt fields of the database. This approach has the advantage that a compromise of the service provider is now insufficient. An attacker has to also compromise the key at the client. It also enables a client to store person related, sensitive data in the cloud, without anyone being able to inspect it.

While this approach brings many security and privacy advantages it may also hinder data processing. In almost all data management applications the service

---

[3]http://calculator.s3.amazonaws.com/calc5.html.

[4]http://www.windowsazure.com/en-us/pricing/calculator/.

provider processes queries for the client and only returns the result. Consider the following SQL statement computing the revenue per country in stores opened since January 1st 2000

```
SELECT Country.Name, SUM(Stores.Revenue)
  FROM Country, Stores
 WHERE Country.Code = Stores.CountryCode
   AND Stores.OpenDate >= "1.1.2000" GROUP BY Country.Name
```

This query contains a join between two tables Country and Stores, an aggregation over field Revenue and a range query in the field OpenDate. Assume all data fields are encrypted. This may prevent all three database operations – join, aggregation and range query. An approach that processes the query at the client would require sending (and decrypting) all data at the client. This is – particularly for massive cloud storage – impractical. Instead we would like to enable these query operators while preserving the confidentiality properties of encryption. In the remainder of this section we will review several encryption techniques that combine these two goals.

It is not only important to consider the functionality of the data operations. The specific implementation of the operation may present different trade-offs between security and performance. We have to carefully review the security definitions and algorithms, since some implementations may not achieve the highest level of security, but provide better complexity.

5.3.1 Secure Joins

Although there are several implementations of joins in database technology, at their very core they require a comparison of values. The join operator combines two tables at rows with equal field values. This may be sped up by using index-based structures which allow a sub-linear time search in the database. Also for other operations, such as a selection (based on equality) sub-linear search is crucial for performance. Considering that databases may be several Terabytes in size, full scans can be prohibitive.

Opposed to this performance requirement there is the security and privacy requirement of the database user. As already discussed the user may not want to disclose the field content to the database, but instead encrypt it and retain the key. The database is then forced to perform the join operation on the encrypted data.

Deterministic Encryption

Unfortunately, modern definitions of privacy for encryption prevent an equality comparison on the encrypted data. Modern encryption is *randomized*.

We consider only public-key encryption schemes in this section. Public-key encryption has the advantages that sources – other than the database user – may also add data to the database, e.g. via e-mail or content distribution networks. Furthermore, any public-key encryption scheme can be reduced to a secret-key encryption scheme by simply keeping the public key secret. The reverse – reducing a secret-key encryption scheme to a public-key encryption scheme – is not possible.

A (public-key) encryption scheme consists of three algorithms:

- A *key generation* algorithm $pk, sk \leftarrow \mathcal{K}(\lambda)$ that generates a public, private key pair pk, sk given a security parameter λ,
- An *encryption* algorithm $c \leftarrow \mathcal{E}(pk, x, r)$ that computes a ciphertext c for a plaintext x given the public key pk and a random number r,
- A *decryption* algorithm $x \leftarrow \mathcal{D}(sk, c)$ that reconstructs the plaintext x from the ciphertext c given the private key sk.

The randomization parameter r is essential for achieving the desired security and privacy. The common definition for security of (public-key) encryption is indistinguishability under chosen plaintext (ciphertext) attack (IND-CPA / IND-CCA) [10, 14]. In the IND-CPA a hypothetical adversary is given the public key and the challenge to compute a single bit from the ciphertexts of two chosen plaintexts. He may not succeed with a probability non-negligibly better than guessing. Another way to put it is: Anything that can be computed from the ciphertext, must be computable without it. Note that symmetric encryption is also often randomized, depending on the cipher mode, e.g. cipher block chaining (CBC).

This security definition immediately implies the necessity of randomizing the ciphertext. Then even two ciphertexts for the same plaintext are very likely to differ. This, of course, prevents equality comparison.

Equality comparison is detrimental to the security definition. Imagine a very small plaintext space, e.g. a field with sex $\in \{$ male, female $\}$. An adversary – given the public key – could simply encrypt all field values and compare the ciphertexts. This way he could also break the challenge outlined above.

In [4] the authors try to reconcile this conflict. In order to maintain sub-linear (logarithmic) search the authors propose a *deterministic* encryption scheme and try to maintain best possible security. Any sub-linearly searchable encryption scheme needs to be deterministic. Their security definition is that anything that is computable from the ciphertext must be computable from the plaintext space. Assume there is an algorithm that chooses a plaintext and computes some auxiliary information. Then there is a second algorithm that tries to compute the same auxiliary information from a ciphertext of this plaintext and the public key. This second algorithm should not succeed with probability non-negligibly better than polynomial in the inverse of plaintext size.

The authors also propose a construction for such a scheme. Note that many common (deterministic) public-key encryption schemes, such as standard RSA, do not satisfy the security definition. The construction suggests to replace the randomization parameter r with a hash of the public key and the plaintext $r \leftarrow H(pk, x)$ in an IND-CPA (IND-CCA) secure encryption scheme. They provide proofs for this construction.

The security and privacy for the user can be further increased by a technique called *bucketization*. Bucketization has been first proposed in [15]. It maps multiple plaintext (deterministically) to the same ciphertext. The database then returns to the user more entries than actually match the query and the user filters only those that belong to the correct answer set. This can be accommodated in the above scheme by encrypting a bucket representative.

Searchable Encryption

It is possible to maintain the security properties of randomized encryption, i.e. security against chosen plaintext attacks, and nevertheless enable a secure join. This nevertheless necessitates a full scan of the database, i.e. the search operation is linear in the size of the database. The idea is to only reveal matches for a search token. The search token can only be generated by the private key holder and allows to identify ciphertexts with a matching (equal) plaintext. The database then linearly scans the encrypted table testing each ciphertext using the search token. If there is a match, then the database can include the tuple into the join, but if there is no match then the database obtains no additional information.

This security property is strictly stronger than the one of deterministic encryption. It does not reveal equality without the token, i.e. the user is in control which and how many elements he wants to reveal. The token itself does not yet reveal the plaintext, but so does not an equality match in deterministic encryption.

Searchable encryption can be based on the same techniques as identity-based encryption. Identity-based encryption is an alternative to public-key encryption where any string can be used to encrypt. This eliminates the need to distribute the public keys, since now the identity of the recipient can be used to encrypt. It is then the recipient's task to obtain the private key from a trusted third party (and prove that he is the rightful owner of that identity).

An identity-based encryption scheme consists of the following four algorithms:

- A *setup* algorithm $p, k \leftarrow \mathscr{S}_{ID}(\lambda)$ that generates public parameters p and a master key k given a security parameter λ,
- An *encrypt* algorithm $c \leftarrow \mathscr{E}_{ID}(p, id, x)$ that computes a ciphertext c for a plaintext x given the public parameters p and an identity (an arbitrary string, e.g. an e-mail address) id,[5]
- A *keygen* algorithm $k_{id} \leftarrow \mathscr{K}_{ID}(k, id)$ that retrieves the secret key k_{id} for an identity id given the master key k,
- A *decryption* algorithm $x \leftarrow \mathscr{D}_{ID}(k_{id}, c)$ that reconstructs the plaintext x from the ciphertext c given the secret key k_{id}.

---

[5]We omit the randomization parameter for clarity, but identity-based encryption is also randomized.

The first practical identity-based encryption scheme has been proposed by Boneh and Franklin and is based on bilinear maps in elliptic curves [6]. The scheme fulfills security against an IND-CPA adversary in the random oracle model.

Any anonymous identity-based encryption scheme can now be turned into a searchable encryption scheme [1]. In anonymous identity-based encryption scheme an adversary cannot infer the identity from the ciphertext. A similar indistinguishability property as for chosen plaintext attacks holds. The encryption scheme by Boneh and Franklin is anonymous.

A searchable encryption enables to match ciphertexts to the search tokens, but it is no longer necessary to provide a decryption algorithm. Instead the searchable encryption scheme can be augmented with a regular (IND-CPA secure) encryption scheme in order to enable decrypting the ciphertexts. We construct the searchable encryption scheme as follows:

- A *key generation* algorithm $pk, sk \leftarrow \mathcal{K}(\lambda) \hat{=} \mathcal{S}_{ID}(\lambda)$.
- An *encryption* algorithm $c \leftarrow \mathcal{E}(pk, w)$ for a keyword w given public key pk. It encrypts a random number r using the identity-based encryption scheme with w as identity: $c' \leftarrow \mathcal{E}_{ID}(pk, w, r)$. It then also appends r. Note that there is still a randomization parameter of the encryption not to be mixed with.
- A *trapdoor* algorithm $t \leftarrow \mathcal{G}(sk, w) \hat{=} \mathcal{K}_{ID}(sk, w)$ that generates a trapdoor t for a keyword t given the private key pk.
- A *test* algorithm $\{true, false\} \leftarrow \mathcal{T}(t, c)$ that returns whether the ciphertext c matches the search token t. It decrypts c using the identity-based encryption scheme into $r' \leftarrow \mathcal{D}_{ID}(t, c)$. Then it compares r and r' and returns true if they match.

5.3.2   Secure Aggregation and Selection

When querying data, sometimes only part of the data is interesting followed by an aggregation of several database rows. SQL offers several arithmetic functions that can be used to aggregate data at the server. Of course, using standard public-key encryption, aggregation over encrypted data is no longer possible.

Homomorphic Encryption

An alternative may provide homomorphic encryption. In homomorphic encryption a specific operation on the ciphertexts maps to another operation on the plaintexts. Let $E(x)$ denote the encryption (ciphertext) of plaintext x and $D(c)$ the decryption of the corresponding ciphertext c. Then the homomorphism can be expressed as

$$D(E(x) \odot E(y)) = x \oplus y$$

Already simple encryption schemes, such as textbook RSA (which is not secure against chosen plaintexts attacks) or El-Gamal are homomorphic. The homomorphic operation is multiplication, i.e. $\oplus \hat{=} \cdot$. The operation on the ciphertexts is also multiplication (in case of El-Gamal each element is multiplied with the element of the other operand), i.e. also $\odot \hat{=} \cdot$.

Such encryption scheme are not yet particularly useful for secure aggregation. In additively homomorphic encryption systems the homomorphic operation is addition, i.e. $\oplus \hat{=} +$. This can be used for computations such as summation (SUM ()) or counting (COUNT ()). The selected elements are simply added using the ciphertexts. The encrypted result is returned to the application. The most prominent such encryption scheme is Paillier's [20].

Paillier's encryption scheme works in an RSA modulus and is based on the security of factoring. It is secure against chosen plaintext attacks and can perform additions in the group $\mathbb{Z}_n^*$ of the RSA modulus. For details of the encryption system we refer to the reference, but many implementations are publicly available. Its performance is comparable to standard public-key cryptography. For Paillier encryption we can then write

$$D(E(x) \cdot E(y)) = x + y$$

This immediately leads to another interesting arithmetic property. If one can "add" ciphertexts, then one can also multiply with a plaintext. In the simplest case by repeated addition, but more elegant procedure of course is exponentiation. This can be written as

$$D(E(x)^y) = x \cdot y$$

These homomorphic properties are achieved by encrypting the plaintext in the exponent. This could, of course, also be done in standard encryption schemes, such as El-Gamal, but the challenge is to retrieve the plaintext efficiently. This needs to be possible without the need to solve the discrete logarithm problem. Paillier encryption achieves this by doubling the ciphertext length, i.e. the ciphertext is in group $\mathbb{Z}_{n^2}^*$.

Private Information Retrieval

Additively homomorphic encryption allows the implementation of several primitive aggregation functions, but it can also be used to solve selection in private databases. In the selection problem (called private information retrieval in the cryptographic literature) there is a querier and a database. The querier has an index i which represents the element he wants to retrieve and the database has a number of records. The protection goal in this case is that the querier does not have to reveal its query, i.e. index. In the simplest form the database may have access to the plaintext of the data.

The basic private information retrieval problem can be solved using additively homomorphic encryption [17, 19]. For example let $E(x)$ denote Paillier encryption. Then the querier encrypts either a 1 for each index he wants to retrieve – in case of aggregation this can be multiple – or a 0 otherwise. Let $E(x_j)$ denote the ciphertexts ($x_j = 1$, if $i = j$ and $x_j = 0$ otherwise). There are as many ciphertexts as entries in the database ($0 \leq j < n$).

The database then linearly scans each row. Let y_j denote the value of the j-th row. Then the database computes $c = \prod_{j=0}^{n-1} E(x_j)^{y_j}$. It is easy to see that $D(c) = y_i$.

In a rigorous definition of privacy it is unavoidable that the database performs a linear scan. Every row that is not included in the computation may not be the index queried. The database therefore would obtain partial knowledge about the index. Nevertheless the communication complexity can be reduced.

The basic construction still requires that the querier sends as many as ciphertexts as database rows. The first improvement can be achieved by arranging the data in a square. Then the querier sends an index for the row i' of the square its result resides in. The database responds with a result for each column. This reduces the communication complexity to $O(\sqrt{n})$.

One can further reduce the sending communication complexity of the server. The ciphertext for each is broken into pieces. This is necessary since the size of the ciphertexts commonly exceeds the size of the plaintexts. Alternatively one can use a different key or parameters for homomorphic encryption scheme. Particularly, Damgård and Jurik's variant of Paillier encryption [9] may provide such an alternative using a parameter of the encryption, but the same key. The pieces of the ciphertext are then also added in the same fashion as the elements of the column. The querier provides an index for the column it wants to obtain and the database homomorphically adds the ciphertext pieces. Depending on the piecing of the ciphertext the communication tradeoff may vary. Let l be the expansion of the ciphertext. Certainly $l > 1$ also due to the randomization of the ciphertext, but a factor of $l < 2$ is achievable using Damgård-Jurik encryption.

If one wants to combine encryption storage and private information retrieval, additively homomorphic encryption is no longer sufficient. In additively homomorphic encryption schemes it is not possible to multiply two ciphertexts. A solution may provide more powerful homomorphic encryption scheme. The encryption scheme by Boneh, Goh and Nissim [7] allows one homomorphic multiplication of ciphertexts of fan-in two in addition to an arbitrary number of additions. This may used instead of Paillier's encryption scheme. One can then use private information retrieval on encrypted data.

Furthermore, recently Gentry discovered fully homomorphic encryption [12]. Fully homomorphic encryption allows an arbitrary number of additions and multiplications. Nevertheless it is not yet practical in terms of performance [13], but this is an ongoing very active research area and should be monitored for future results.

A fundamental difference between homomorphic encryption and the other encryption schemes presented in this section is that in homomorphic encryption the database remains oblivious to the result. Therefore implementations of database

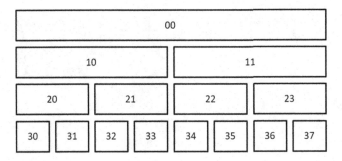

Fig. 5.7 Tree of ranges

queries based on homomorphic encryption cannot make use of any optimizations dependent on (intermediate) results. Instead an algorithm that is oblivious to the result must be executed. While this brings a security advantage – the result is kept confidential – , this may also bring a performance disadvantage.

5.3.3 Secure Range Queries

Apart from join and aggregation operations, range queries are a further essential class of operators for queries and, therefore, require also an efficient implementation for encrypted databases.

Disjunctive Queries

Neither homomorphic nor searchable encryption so far support the queries with an inequality (greater than or lower than) operator. Nevertheless such queries are common for database engines. We have shown an example in the introduction to this section. The protection goal is to conceal the value of the range operands sent by the user.

The first proposal by Shi et al. is an extension of searchable encryption [22]. The basic idea is to divide the domain into a tree of ranges. At the top layer the range spans the entire domain. At each lower layer the above ranges are split into half. At the bottom layer each element is assigned to its own range. Each range is assigned a unique identifier. Figure 5.7 shows such a tree with identifiers for four layers.

An element can be represented as its path from the root to the top. Each range along the path is marked. Not that there is exactly one such range per layer. Let m be the size of the domain. Then there are $O(\log m)$ ranges per entry. Figure 5.8 shows an example starting from range "34". Let s_i be the range at layer i for value v. The ciphertexts of the range identifiers are stored in the database (using IND-CPA secure encryption).

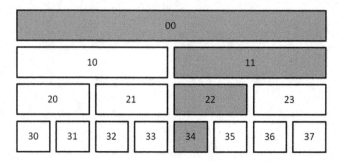

Fig. 5.8 A value as the set of ranges along its path from top to bottom

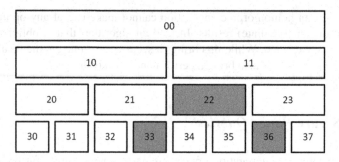

Fig. 5.9 A range query as the set of ranges in the tree

A range query can now also be represented as a set of ranges. There is a bottom delimiter a and a top delimiter b. Each bottom range representing elements between these delimiters is included in the query. Each range that is completely represented by its upper layer range is recursively replaced by that upper layer range. Note that, since ranges are necessarily consecutive, there are not at most two ranges per layer in the query, i.e. there are at most $O(\log m)$ ranges in the query. Let $t_{0,i}$ and $t_{1,i}$ be the two ranges at layer i. If there is no such range $t_{j,i}$ it is replaced by a dummy value that matches no range identifier. Figure 5.9 shows an example for the query from "33" to "36".

The key insight of Shi et al. [22] now is that the query can be performed as a disjunctive query: $q = \bigvee_i t_{0,i} = s_i \vee t_{1,i} = s_i$. If $a \leq v \leq b$, then and only then q evaluates to true, i.e. there is exactly one range in common between query and value. Furthermore, the expression has only $O(\log m)$ terms that need to be evaluated, i.e. the evaluation is fast. The encryption system now has to implement disjunctive queries and they even extend it to multiple ranges which is of limited interest in case of flexible queries. For details we refer the reader to [22].

Order-Preserving Encryption

An even more efficient implementation of range queries than searchable encryption is possible. The equivalent to deterministic encryption for ranges is order-preserving encryption. In order-preserving encryption the range query can be performed directly on the ciphertexts by the database. Let $E(x)$ denote the order-preserving encryption (ciphertext) of plaintext x. Then the following property holds:

$$x < y \Longleftrightarrow E(x) < E(y)$$

The order of the plaintexts is preserved under encryption. This property already prevents the encryption scheme from being secure against chosen plaintext attacks. Such an order-preserving encryption does not fulfill the expectations for an encryption scheme in many respect. For example an order-preserving encryption scheme can never be public-key. The holder of the public key could perform a binary search on the ciphertext thereby breaking the encryption in time linear to the security parameter. Consequently all order-preserving encryption scheme have to be symmetric. It is therefore a debate among security professionals whether such an encryption should be used at all. No serious attempts at cryptanalysis have been performed yet.

Boldyreva et al. nevertheless present a scheme with an interesting property [5]. It is provably the most secure order-preserving encryption scheme, i.e. if the order-preserving property should hold, then an encryption scheme cannot be more secure. It is then up to the judgment of the user about his trust into the database service provider whether he intends to use such a scheme.

The basic idea of the scheme is as follows: Let $x \in \mathbb{X}$ denote the elements of the plaintext domain and $y \in \mathbb{Y}$ denote the elements of the ciphertext domain. For an order-preserving encryption scheme to work, the domain of the ciphertexts needs to be much larger than the domain of the plaintexts: $|\mathbb{Y}| > |\mathbb{X}|$. The mapping between plaintexts and ciphertexts is now computed as follows:

Based on a chosen seed (i.e. the key) random numbers are drawn. First, for the median element $\bar{x}$ of $\mathbb{X}$ a random element is drawn uniformly from $\mathbb{Y}$. Let $\bar{y}$ be that elements. Now, we establish that $E(\bar{x}) = \bar{y}$. Then, this is recursively repeated for both "halves" of the domain. Let $\underline{x}$ be the median element of $[0, \bar{x} - 1]$ and $\bar{\bar{x}}$ be the median element of $[\bar{x} + 1, |\mathbb{X}| - 1]$. Now, $\underline{x}$ is assigned a uniform random element from $[0, \bar{y} - 1]$ as ciphertext and $\bar{\bar{x}}$ a uniform random element from $[\bar{y} + 1, |\mathbb{Y}| - 1]$. In such a way both halves are again divided until recursively each element has been assigned a ciphertext. In [5] a method to compute encryption and decryption more efficiently than using this procedure is described.

Order-preserving encryption leaks significantly more information than disjunctive searchable encryption. In order-preserving encryption the order relation between any pair of ciphertexts is revealed whereas in disjunctive searchable encryption only the matching rows are revealed. In the equality comparison of deterministic encryption and searchable encryption this may be acceptable, but the security impact incase of inequality comparison is still somewhat unclear.

5.4 Summary

Data management in the Cloud is typically supported by additional services which go beyond traditional database technologies. First of all, outsourcing services to external providers requires to guarantee certain levels of quality. We have discussed the notion of service level agreements to describe such service qualities and responsibilities. Furthermore, we have described techniques to implement guarantees, particularly workload management as a classic database technique and cloud-oriented resource provisioning. We have shown models to predict system performance of given system configurations and approaches to allocate resources. This task of finding the optimal configuration to meet the SLAs while minimizing the cost is a highly relevant and still challenging problem in cloud computing, both at customer and provider side. Thus, there are several other approaches tackling this problem, e.g. [27] and [18] propose dynamic resource adjustment strategies for virtual machines in cloud environments. [25] takes additionally green power management into account. A dynamic resource allocation scheme particularly for auction-based pricing models such as Amazon's spot instances is for instance presented in [26].

A second issue of outsourcing database services is billing. The pay-per-use pricing model of cloud computing has proven as an attractive approach for many customers. We have shown the different cost types contributing to the pricing and presents subscription types which are supported by current cloud services.

Finally, we have presented techniques to address the challenge of keeping data in the cloud securely and confidentially by exploiting encryption. We have summarized how to implement the most common database operations, such as joins, aggregation and range queries, securely on an encrypted database. We were able to achieve the most important goal of managing the key of the encryption at the client, i.e. the database service provider will not be able to decrypt, but needs to operate on ciphertexts. This provides the opportunity to outsource sensitive, privacy relevant data to the cloud.

In terms of security the encryption schemes can be broadly classified as follows: In homomorphic encryption the service provider remains entirely oblivious. It does not know either the input to the query (i.e. the operands) or the result. The result is computed as a ciphertext. In (disjunctive) searchable encryption the service provider does not learn the input to the query, but learns which tuples match the query, i.e. the result, although the tuples may be encrypted. In deterministic and order-preserving encryption the service provider may choose the tuples as input to the query itself and learns the result. It knows the result for any pair of (encrypted) values, be it for equality or inequality comparison.

Usually the less security is provided, the better the performance, but, of course this is a trade-off the client has to choose. It remains difficult to judge the security of a combined system that approaches the full functionality of SQL. In terms of security there is a challenge: What can be inferred from homomorphic encryption can also be inferred from searchable encryption and what can be inferred from searchable encryption can also be inferred from deterministic or order-preserving encryption (depending on the comparison type). Therefore a system that, e.g., implements order-preserving encryption in order to implement range queries is at most as secure as order-preserving encryption. What happens when one combines different types of comparison (equality and inequality) is yet unclear.

It remains to be shown whether and how all these encryption schemes can be integrated into one system. It then remains to be shown that this system can implement the full functionality of SQL. A first system of this kind has been shown by Ada Popa et al. [2]. It uses all the encryption techniques presented in Sect. 5.3. They report that they can support 99.5% of the columns seen in traces of real SQL queries. Furthermore, they report a decrease in throughput of only 14.5–26% compared to unmodified SQL. They uses a special technique in order to limit the leakage from combining the different encryptions. Not all columns require all ciphertexts, since not all columns need to support all operations. Therefore the weaker encryption schemes' ciphertexts are encrypted using a strong IND-CPA encryption. This technique is called *onion encryption*. On demand, i.e. when a query arrives that requires this operation, the weaker ciphertext is decrypted using user-defined functions. Once decrypted, the ciphertexts are left in the database. The results are promising for real-world applications, since only most semi-sensitive fields, such as timestamps, need the order-preserving ciphertext. For many columns an IND-CPA secure encryption is best.

References

1. Abdalla, M., Bellare, M., Catalano, D., Kiltz, E., Kohno, T., Lange, T., Malone-Lee, J., Neven, G., Paillier, P., Shi, H.: Searchable encryption revisited: Consistency properties, relation to anonymous ibe, and extensions. Journal of Cryptology 21(3), 350–391 (2008)
2. Ada Popa, R., Redfield, C.M.S., Zeldovich, N., Balakrishnan, H.: Cryptdb: Protecting confidentiality with encrypted query processing. In: SOSP (2011)
3. Armbrust, M., Fox, A., Griffith, R., Joseph, A.D., Katz, R.H., Konwinski, A., Lee, G., Patterson, D.A., Rabkin, A., Stoica, I., Zaharia, M.: Above the clouds: A berkeley view of cloud computing. Tech. Rep. UCB/EECS-2009-28, EECS Department, University of California, Berkeley (2009). URL http://www.eecs.berkeley.edu/Pubs/TechRpts/2009/EECS-2009-28.html
4. Bellare, M., Boldyreva, A., O'Neill, A.: Deterministic and efficiently searchable encryption. In: CRYPTO (2007)
5. Boldyreva, A., Chenette, N., Lee, Y., O'Neill, A.: Order-preserving symmetric encryption. In: EUROCRYPT (2009)
6. Boneh, D., Franklin, M.K.: Identity-based encryption from the weil pairing. SIAM Journal of Computing 32(3), 586–615 (2003)
7. Boneh, D., Goh, E.J., Nissim, K.: Evaluating 2-dnf formulas on ciphertexts. In: TCC (2005)
8. Cassier, P., Defendi, A., Fischer, D., Hutchinson, J., Maneville, A., Membrini, G., Ong, C., Rowley, A.: System Programmer's Guide to Workload Manager. No. SG24-6472-03 in Redbooks. IBM (2008)
9. Damgård, I., Jurik, M.: A generalisation, a simplification and some applications of paillier's probabilistic public-key system. In: Public Key Cryptography (2001)

10. Dolev, D., Dwork, C., Naor, M.: Nonmalleable cryptography. SIAM Journal of Computing **30**(2), 391–437 (2000)

11. Ganapathi, A., Kuno, H.A., Dayal, U., Wiener, J.L., Fox, A., Jordan, M.I., Patterson, D.A.: Predicting multiple metrics for queries: Better decisions enabled by machine learning. In: ICDE, pp. 592–603 (2009)

12. Gentry, C.: Fully homomorphic encryption using ideal lattices. In: STOC (2009)

13. Gentry, C., Halevi, S.: Implementing gentry's fully-homomorphic encryption scheme. Cryptology ePrint Archive, Report 2010/520 (2010)

14. Goldwasser, S., Micali, S.: Probabilistic encryption. Journal of Computer and Systems Sciences **28**(2), 270–299 (1984)

15. Hacigümüs, H., Iyer, B.R., Li, C., Mehrotra, S.: Executing sql over encrypted data in the database-service-provider model. In: SIGMOD (2002)

16. Kephart, J.O., Das, R.: Achieving self-management via utility functions. IEEE Internet Computing **11**(1), 40–48 (2007)

17. Kushilevitz, E., Ostrovsky, R.: Replication is not needed: Single database, computationally-private information retrieval. In: FOCS (1997)

18. Lee, L.T., Lee, S.T., Chang, J.C.: An extenics-based dynamic resource adjustment for the virtual machine in cloud computing environment. In: , 2011 4th International Conference on Ubi-Media Computing (U-Media), pp. 65–70 (2011)

19. Ostrovsky, R., III, W.E.S.: A survey of single-database private information retrieval: Techniques and applications. In: Public Key Cryptography (2007)

20. Paillier, P.: Public-key cryptosystems based on composite degree residuosity classes. In: EUROCRYPT (1999)

21. Ramamritham, K.: Real-time databases. Distributed and Parallel Databases **1**(2), 199–226 (1993)

22. Shi, E., Bethencourt, J., Chan, H.T.H., Song, D.X., Perrig, A.: Multi-dimensional range query over encrypted data. In: IEEE Symposium on Security and Privacy (2007)

23. Soror, A.A., Minhas, U.F., Aboulnaga, A., Salem, K., Kokosielis, P., Kamath, S.: Automatic Virtual Machine Configuration for Database Workloads. ACM Transactions on Database Systems **35**(1), 1–47 (2010)

24. Xiong, P., Chi, Y., Zhu, S., Moon, H.J., Pu, C., Hacigümüs, H.: Intelligent management of virtualized resources for database systems in cloud environment. In: ICDE, pp. 87–98 (2011)

25. Yang, C.T., Wang, K.C., Cheng, H.Y., Kuo, C.T., Chu, W.: Green power management with dynamic resource allocation for cloud virtual machines. In: 2011 IEEE 13th International Conference on High Performance Computing and Communications (HPCC), pp. 726 –733 (2011)

26. Zhang, Q., Zhu, Q., Boutaba, R.: Dynamic resource allocation for spot markets in cloud computing environments. In: 2011 Fourth IEEE International Conference on Utility and Cloud Computing (UCC), pp. 178–185 (2011)

27. Zhu, Q., Agrawal, G.: Resource provisioning with budget constraints for adaptive applications in cloud environments. In: Proceedings of the 19th ACM International Symposium on High Performance Distributed Computing, pp. 304–307 (2010)

Chapter 6
Overview and Comparison of Current Database-as-a-Service Systems

As described in Chap. 1 the different services that can be obtained from a cloud are typically classified by the categories Infrastructure-as-a-Service (IaaS), Platform-as-a-Service (PaaS), and Software-as-a-Service (SaaS). The three different layers are often displayed as a stack, indicating that the services of one cloud layer can be built based on the services offered by the lower layers. For example, a Software-as-a-Service application can exploit the scalability and robustness offered by the services on the Platform-as-a-Service layer. That way the Software-as-a-Service application is in the position to achieve good scalability and availability properties by itself.

Recently, a fourth category for cloud services has emerged, named Data-as-a-Service which is highly related to the Software-as-a-Service layer. The new category refers to services which center around cleansing and enriching data in a centralized place and then offering this enriched data to customers on demand.

In the following, this chapter will highlight the most prominent representatives of those cloud layers. Particularly, we will give an overview on services offered by Amazon, Rackspace, and Microsoft and discuss each system with regard to the categories: offered service, service-level agreements, interoperability issues, and pricing model as well as performance evaluation from recent papers.

6.1 Infrastructure-as-a-Service

The services offered on the Infrastructure-as-a-Service layer of the cloud service stack focus on the on-demand provisioning of IT infrastructure components like compute power, storage, and network interconnects.

W. Lehner and K.-U. Sattler, *Web-Scale Data Management for the Cloud*,
DOI 10.1007/978-1-4614-6856-1_6, © Springer Science+Business Media New York 2013

6.1.1   Amazon Elastic Compute Cloud

The Amazon Elastic Compute Cloud (EC2) is a central component of Amazon's overall cloud product portfolio and currently one of the most dominant players in the "Infrastructure-as-a-Service" domain. Amazon EC2 offers its customers to acquire access to potentially large amounts of compute power which is hosted inside one of their managed cloud data centers. Currently, Amazon runs their EC2 service in five different data centers spread across North America, Europa, and Asia.

Service Offered

The compute power of Amazon EC2 is made accessible to the customers in the form of virtual machines. Customers can use a web service interface to create, manage, and terminate those virtual machines without significant deployment times. Recent evaluations of Amazon EC2 have quantified the deployment time for a new virtual machine, i.e. the time from issuing the create request until the machine is reported to be available, between 1 and 3 min [5, 10, 14].

Before a new virtual machine can be instantiated, the EC2 customer has to select a so called Amazon Machine Image (AMI) which acts as a template for the virtual machine's initial file system content. Customers can either choose from a set of preconfigured machine images or provide custom images which fit their particular requirements. Depending on their accessibility, Amazon currently distinguishes between three different classes of AMIs. The first class, the so called public AMIs can be used by any EC2 customer. Public AMIs usually include free software whose license agreements permit an unrestricted distribution, for example GNU/Linux. In contrast to that, the so-called paid AMIs, the second class of images, allow companies to provide preconfigured EC2 images including proprietary software which can then be used by other EC2 customers according to different billing models. Finally, private AMIs, the third class of images, can only be used by their respective creators.

Besides the machine image, the second important parameter for creating a new virtual machine on Amazon EC2 is the type of the virtual machine. The virtual machine type, also referred to as the instance type according to Amazon's own terminology, describes the hardware characteristics of the virtual machine to be instantiated. Each virtual machine type defines a distinct combination of CPU power, amount of main memory, and disk space. As of August 2012, Amazon offered a fixed set of virtual machine types their customers can choose from. Fig. 6.1 shows an excerpt of this set.

Amazon expresses the compute power of each virtual machine type in so-called Amazon EC2 Compute Units (ECUs), a custom unit the company has introduced to improve the consistency and predictability of a virtual machine's compute capacity across different generations of hardware. According to Amazon's website, an EC2 Compute Unit equals the CPU capacity of a 1.0–1.2 GHz 2007 Opteron or 2007

Name	Computing Power	Main Memory	Storage	Platform
Micro	up to 2 Compute Units	613 MB	—	32/64 bit
Small	1 Compute Unit	1.7 GB	160 GB	32/64 bit
Medium	2 Compute Units	3.75 GB	410 GB	32/64 bit
Large	4 Compute Units	7.5 GB	850 GB	64 bit
Extra Large	8 Compute Units	15 GB	1690 GB	64 bit
High-Memory Extra Large	6.5 Compute Units	17.1 GB	420 GB	64 bit
High-Memory Double Extra Large	13 Compute Units	34.2 GB	850 GB	64 bit
High-Memory Quadruple Extra Large	26 Compute Units	68.4 GB	1690 GB	64 bit
High-CPU Medium	5 Compute Units	1.7 GB	350 GB	32 bit
High-CPU Extra Large	20 Compute Units	7 GB	1690 GB	64 bit

Fig. 6.1 Excerpt of virtual machine types available at Amazon EC2

Xeon Processor. Recently, Amazon has also added more domain-specific virtual machine types, like virtual machines with very fast network interconnects or special graphic adapters for high performance computing applications.

Pricing Model

The term "Elastic" in the name Elastic Compute Cloud makes reference to Amazon's primary pricing model, according to which customers are charged per virtual machine on a per-hour basis. Partial hours are billed as full hours, however, after the customer has terminated his virtual machine, no further payment obligations exist.

The concrete per-hour price of a virtual machine depends on two major factors: The virtual machine type, i.e. the machine's hardware characteristics, and the Amazon Machine Image the customer has chosen to instantiate his virtual machine from.

The fees for the different virtual machine types grow according to their hardware properties and also vary slightly across the different Amazon data centers. While virtual machines of the least powerful machine type (instance type Micro) can be rented starting at 0.02 USD per hour, the high-end virtual machines with special graphic hardware cost up to 3.00 USD per hour (as of August 2012).

In addition to the virtual machine type, the Amazon Machine Image (AMI) influences the per-hour price of a virtual machine. In general, Amazon EC2 offers to run virtual machines with Linux/UNIX-based operating systems or Microsoft Windows. Compared to Linux/UNIX-based virtual machines, Windows-based machines have a slightly higher per-hour cost to cover up for the additional Windows license cost.

Recently, Amazon introduced two extensions to its pure per-hour pricing model, referred to as so-called Reserved Instances and Spot Instances.

Reserved Instances have been introduced to meet the concern that the initial per-hour pricing does not provide any resource guarantee, so a customer's request for new or additional compute nodes could potentially be rejected by the EC2 system. With Reserved Instances, an EC2 customer can make a one-time payment and reserve the resource required to run a virtual machine of a certain type for a particular time span, for example one year. The one-time payment only covers the reservation of the resources, not the cost for actually running the virtual machine. However, Amazon allows a discount on the per-hour price of Reserved Instances.

The second extension to the per-hour pricing model, the Spot Instances model, is used by Amazon to sell temporary excess capacity in their data centers. As a result, the per-hour price of Spot Instances is not fixed, but determined by the current demand for compute resources inside the respective EC2 data center. An EC2 customer can bid a price he is willing to pay for a particular virtual machine type per hour. Depending on the current data center utilization, Amazon launches the requested type of virtual machine at the bidden price. As a consequence, it is often significantly cheaper to acquire access to Spot Instances in comparison to regular virtual machines on EC2 [22]. However, in case the other customers agree to pay a higher hourly fee, Amazon reserves the right to terminate running Spot Instances without further notice to reclaim physical resources.

Performance Characteristics

The prospect of using 1,000 virtual machines for 1 h at the same cost as running one virtual machines for 1,000 h has made Amazon EC2 a promising platform for large-scale distributed applications. As a result, several research projects have recently evaluated Amazon's compute service and compared its performance characteristics against those of traditional compute clusters. While their have been no negative remarks with regard to the scalability of the platform, some of the system characteristics received mixed reviews.

Walker [19] and Ostermann et al. [14] examined Amazon EC2 in terms of its suitability for compute-intensive scientific applications. Ostermann et al. conclude that the CPUs which run the Amazon virtual machines in general provide excellent addition but only poor multiplication capabilities. MPI-based applications, which have to exchange messages among the involved virtual machines, run significantly slower on Amazon EC2 in comparison to native cluster setups, according to both Walker and Ostermann et al. Besides the CPU performance, Ostermann et al. also examined the disk performance of EC2-based virtual machines. According to their results [14], all types of virtual machines generally provide better performance for sequential operations in comparison to commodity systems with the same hardware characteristics.

The work of Wand and Ng [20] focused on Amazon EC2's scheduling strategies for virtual machines and their impact on the virtual machines' network performance. Through a serious of microbenchmarks the authors were able to show that in particular the inexpensive virtual machines types on Amazon EC2 often share one physical processor. This processor sharing can lead to frequent interruptions of individual virtual machines which, in turn, can have detrimental effects on the machine's network performance. Wang et al. also found this to be the reason for the very unstable TCP and UDP throughput of particular virtual machine types on EC2.

According to their paper, the TCP/UDP throughput experienced by applications can fluctuate between 1 GB/s and 0, even at a timescale of tens of milliseconds. Moreover, the authors describe abnormally large packet delay variations which can be 100 times larger than the propagation delay between two end hosts [20].

In [16] Schad et al. evaluated Amazon EC2 as a platform for scientific experiments. During their evaluation, the authors put special emphasis on performance variations that would limit the repeatability of scientific experiments on the cloud platform. Their paper highlighted that virtual machines of the same type (with the same declared hardware properties) may run on different generations of host systems. This can result in significant performance discrepancies for different runs of the same experiment across different instantiations of the same virtual machine type. These discrepancies pertain to both the virtual machines' compute capabilities as well as their I/O characteristics. Therefore, the authors conclude that performance predictability on Amazon EC2 is currently hard to achieve.

Interoperability

From a technical point of view, an Amazon Machine Image (AMI), which represents the basis for running any type of application on Amazon EC2, is a regular file system image. Therefore, an AMI can in principle be manipulated and used outside of Amazon EC2, for example with a XEN hypervisor [1]. However, the accessibility of the AMI depends on the way the AMI was originally created.

Basically, there are two ways of creating an AMI. The first way is to set up the entire content of the image from scratch on a local computer, to bundle the image, and then to upload it to EC2. The second way consists of booting a public AMI on EC2, modifying the file system content inside the virtual machine, and finally to create a snapshot of the running machine. For customers pursuing the first way, Amazon offers a set of client tools to convert the created file system image into a so-called AMI bundle and to manage the following upload. Although the conversion from the original file system image into the AMI bundle involves steps like compression, splitting and cryptographic signing, it is always possible to regain the original data from the bundle. In contrast to that, regaining the file system image when the AMI was created from a snapshot is more difficult because the image resides inside the EC2 cloud only. Amazon provides no direct methods to download a virtual machine snapshot, however, several descriptions on how to work around this limitation can be found in EC2-related discussion bulletin boards.

6.1.2 Further IaaS Solutions

Rackspace is another cloud platform provider in the market offering various services. This includes Cloud Servers for renting virtual machines running Linux or Windows similar to EC2, Cloud Files as a cloud-based storage comparable to

Amazon S3 (Sect. 6.2.1) as well as Cloud Tools which is a catalog of applications and software stacks such as PHP or MySQL database services. For these services Rackspace has a similar per-hour pricing model as Amazon ranging from $0.022 per hour for a small 1 core/512 MB Linux instance to $1.56 per hour for a 8 core/30 GB Windows instance.

The Rackspace platform is running on OpenStack,[1] an open-source "cloud operating system" for controlling pools of compute, storage, and network resources. Rackspace has founded the OpenStack project together with NASA and the project is now supported by companies like Intel, AMD, IBM, HP, Cisco and others. OpenStack provides APIs which are compatible with Amazon's AWS services and thus allows to port client applications with minimal effort.

Another open source cloud platform is the Eucalyptus project [12] launched in 2008 by a research group at the University of California, Santa Barbara. Targeted at private cloud computing on compute clusters, Eucalyptus provides programming interfaces which are compatible to the one of Amazon EC2, but is built completely upon open source software components. In addition, Eucalyptus also offers to deploy AMI bundles originally created for the Amazon cloud and run them on top of the open source software stack. Eucalyptus provides several features known from Amazon EC2, for example support for Linux and Windows-based virtual machines, elastic IPs, and security groups. Today, Eucalyptus is available in two versions: The open source version which is still free of charge as well as a so-called enterprise edition which provides additional features and support for commercial settings.

6.2 Platform-as-a-Service

Platform-as-a-Service combines infrastructure services with higher-level functionalities for developing and deploying applications such as data management solutions and middleware. In the following we will describe some data management related PaaS solutions currently offered from Amazon and Microsoft.

6.2.1 Amazon S3, DynamoDB, and RDS

As part of its cloud-based Amazon Web Service (AWS) infrastructure, Amazon offers several different data management services ranging from simple, scalable storage services such as S3 over NoSQL solutions like SimpleDB and DynamoDB to full-fledged SQL systems as part of Amazon RDS.

---

[1]http://www.openstack.org

Primary Key	Attributes ...		
CustId = 1	Name = Fred	Emails = { fred@mail.com, me@fred.com }	
CustId = 2	Name = Bert	City = Dresden	Street = Main St.
CustId = 3	Name = Peter	Email = peter@freemail.org	Address = SF,CA

Fig. 6.2 A table in DynamoDB

Service Offered

Amazon Simple Storage Service (S3) is a distributed storage for objects of sizes between 1 Byte and 5 TB of data. Objects are handled as binary large objects (BLOBs) and are not further structured by the service. S3 provides a REST-based interface to read, write, and delete objects. Objects are organized into buckets which are owned by an AWS user and are uniquely identified within a bucket by a user-defined key. Buckets and object keys are addressable by simple URLs such as http://s3.amazonaws.com/bucket/key, requests to buckets and objects are authorized using access control lists. From a data management point of view, S3 has to be seen more as a file system than a real data management solution. The service only provides atomic single-key updates and does not support locking. The offered data consistency model is eventual consistency. For some geographical regions read-after-write consistency is provided for inserting new objects. According to Amazon, S3 stores more than one trillion objects in 2012. Some of the most well-known services built on top of S3 are probably Dropbox and Ubuntu One.

DynamoDB is Amazon's scalable, distributed NoSQL system which is the successor of SimpleDB. DynamoDB is based on technologies developed in the Dynamo project and described in [4]. It removes some limitations of its predecessor: there are no more limits on the amount of data to be stored and it allows to grow the request capacity by spreading data and traffic for a table automatically over a sufficient number of servers to handle the load.

In DynamoDB, data entries are stored on solid state disks and organized in tables consisting of so-called "items" (Fig. 6.2). Items are collections of attributes which are name-value pairs. Each item is identified by its primary key, which is used internally for an unordered hash index. An item may not exceed 64 KB in size including all attributes and attribute values. In contrast to the relational data model, a table in DynamoDB has no schema: all attributes apart from the primary key are optional and each item could have in principle its own set of items. For supporting range queries two attributes can form a composite key, where one attribute serves as a hash attribute for partitioning the workload across multiple servers and the second one is used as a range attribute. Two kinds of data types are supported for attribute values: scalar data types to represent strings and numbers as well as multi-valued types (sets) of scalar values.

Amazon offers a Web-based management console as well as a Web Service API using HTTP/HTTPS and JSON for creating tables and manipulating data. In addition, SDKs for Java, .NET, and PHP are provided. The API allows to create, update, delete, and retrieve a single item based on a given primary key. For update and delete operations also a condition can be specified to perform the operation only if the item's attributes match the condition. Furthermore, atomic counters are supported which allow to atomically increment or decrement numerical attributes with a single call. In addition to these single-item operations, batch operations are supported which allow to insert, update or delete up to 25 items within a single request. However, this is not a transaction, because atomicity is guaranteed only for single-item access. DynamoDB offers different ways to retrieve data stored in tables:

- The most basic approach is the GetItem operation for retrieving all attributes of an item with a given primary key.
- A more advanced solution is the Query operation which allows to retrieve multiple items by their primary key *and* a given condition on the range key. Obviously, this is a case for composite keys mentioned above: the condition is evaluated only on an attribute which is part of the primary key. This range key is also used for determining the order of returned results.
- The Scan operation is used to scan an entire table and allows to specify filters to refine results. However, it is not as efficient as the Query operation.
- Finally, DynamoDB can be used also together with Amazon Elastic MapReduce (see below), i.e. MapReduce jobs as well Hive can directly access DynamoDB tables.

In addition to these specific data management solutions, AWS offers also access to full-fledged SQL systems like MySQL, Oracle, and SQL Server. This service is called Amazon Relational Database Services (RDS) and provides a Web Service to set up and operate a MySQL (Oracle, SQL Server) database. In case of MySQL, a full-featured version of MySQL 5.1 or 5.5 is offered together with Java-based command line tools and Web Service API for instance administration. In addition, features such as automatic host replacement in case of hardware failures, automated database backups, and replication are supported. Replication allows to create a standby replica in a different availability zone as well as to maintain read replicas to scale out for read-intensive workloads. Apart from these features, RDS provides native database access using the standard APIs of the system. As the hardware basis, customers can choose between different instance classes ranging from Micro DB with 630 MB memory and 3 ECU up to Extra Large with 68 GB memory and 26 ECU.

Pricing Model

Pricing[2] of S3 consists of three components: storage, request and data transfer. Storage prices start at $0.125 per GB for 1 TB of data per month, uploads are free of charge, downloads cost $0.120 per GB for up to 10 TB per month (where the first GB is free of charge). Prices for performing requests depend on the kind of request: write request (PUT, COPY) as well as LIST requests cost $0.01 per 1,000 requests, read requests (GET) are $0.01 per 10,000 requests.

Billing in DynamoDB is different from S3: customers pay for a provisioned throughput capacity on a hourly basis. This describes how much capacity for read and write operations are reserved by Amazon. Prices are $0.01 per hour for every 10 units of writes and $0.01 per hour for every 50 units of reads, where a unit represents a read/write operation per second on an item of up to 1 KB size. Accordingly, larger items require more capacity. This means for instance, that an application that performs 100 writes and 1,000 reads per second on items of 5 KB size needs a capacity of 500 units write capacity and 5,000 units read capacity and a hourly rate of $0.01 \cdot 500/10 + $0.01 \cdot 5,000/50 = $1.5. Additional costs are billed for data storage and data transfer. The required storage space is calculated from the raw data plus 100 Byte for each item which is used for indexing. Storage costs in DynamoDB are $1.00 per GB and hour.

The billing of RDS instances follows the pricing model of EC2. Customers have to pay for each instance by the hour, depending on the type of instance. For example, the price for a micro DB instance (1 ECU, 630 MB memory, MySQL) is $0.025 per hour, for the largest DB instance running Oracle (26 ECU, 68 GB memory) it is $2.340 per hour. Additional fees are charged for the occupied storage ($0.10 per GB and month) as well as data transfer.

Performance Characteristics

Due to its simple BLOB storage model the performance of S3 is mainly affected by the speed of the upload/download network link. For RDS the performance is determined by the chosen machine type as in case of EC2 instances. However, evaluations such as [16] have shown a high variance of EC2 performance which might be the case for RDS, too. In contrast, DynamoDB follows a differentiating approach by providing performance reservation in terms of throughput capacity for which customers are billed.

In addition to performance (e.g. in terms of query response time), further service guarantees are important, too. Amazon S3 guarantees availability of 99.9 %, otherwise customers are credited back. Regarding consistency, read-after-write consistency for PUTs of new objects and eventual consistency for overwrite PUTs and DELETEs are provided for several regions (US West, EU, Asia pacific); the US Standard Region provides eventual consistency.

---

[2]All prices are from the Amazon Website, Summer 2012, for the US East region.

Because RDS runs conventional SQL DBMS, the standard ACID properties are guaranteed. For performing system maintenance tasks such as backups, software patching, and cluster scaling operations, a weekly maintenance window of up to 30 min is required by Amazon, but the customer is allowed to state preferences with respect to the maintenance window.

DynamoDB does not require a maintenance window – the no-maintenance operation was one of the design goals of the system. High availability is achieved by storing three geographically distributed replicas of each table. Furthermore, the system supports both eventual consistent and consistent reads. However, consistent reads are more expensive and cost twice the price of eventual consistent reads, i.e. for consistent reads the number of reserved read capacity units has to be twice of the number for eventual consistent reads.

Interoperability

Amazon RDS supports the standard interfaces of the chosen DBMS instance. Therefore, the available tool sets and APIs can be used without any modification or restriction. As a consequence, a database applications can be migrated to RDS with minimal effort. In addition, Amazon Management Console as well as Amazon CloudWatch are provided for system management and monitoring tasks.

S3 and DynamoDB provide a RESTful API and can be accessed using standard web technologies as well as the SDKs provided by Amazon. Whereas S3 handles the data only as non-interpreted binary data, DynamoDB uses JSON for reading and writing data. Using the provided SDKs simplifies the access and the development of applications but introduces some dependencies on Amazon's services.

6.2.2   Amazon Elastic MapReduce

Following the popularity of the MapReduce data processing pattern, Amazon Web Services extended the Platform-as-a-Service offerings with the introduction of their product Elastic MapReduce in 2009. Elastic MapReduce is targeted to provide a scalable and elastic framework for large-scale data analysis without the need to configure and manage the underlying compute nodes. Technically, Elastic MapReduce is built upon a preconfigured version of Apache Hadoop running on Amazon's cloud infrastructure service Amazon EC2 and the storage service Amazon S3.

Service Offered

With Elastic MapReduce, customers of Amazon Web Services can take advantage of Amazon's web scale compute and storage infrastructure to process large amounts of data using the Apache Hadoop framework. Although the service is based on the same infrastructure components that are also accessible as part of Amazon's Infrastructure-as-a-Service offerings, namely Amazon EC2 and their storage service S3, Elastic MapReduce provides a higher programming abstraction. Instead of having to worry about the setup of the individual worker nodes and the correct Hadoop configuration, customers of Elastic MapReduce can simply define a so-called job flow, specify the location of the job flow's input and output data, and submit the job flow to Elastic MapReduce service. Elastic MapReduce then takes care of allocating the required compute nodes from the EC2 cloud, setting up the Hadoop cluster as well as keeping track of the job flow's progress.

Currently, Elastic MapReduce offers five different ways to specify such a job flow. Each way implies a different level of programming abstraction that the customer must use to express his data analysis problem:

- **Custom JAR file:** Specifying a job flow as a custom JAR file is the most low-level programming abstraction offered by Elastic MapReduce. The data analysis program must be expressed as a map and a reduce function and implemented in Java.
- **Hadoop streaming:** Hadoop streaming is a feature of the Hadoop framework. Data analysis programs must still obey the semantics of the second-order functions map and reduce. However, they do not necessarily have to be implemented in Java, but, for example, in a scripting language like Python or Ruby. Technically, Hadoop streaming launches each map and reduce task as an external operating system process which consumes its input data line by line from its standard input pipe. Similarly, the external process simply writes its output data to the standard output pipe and feeds it back to the Hadoop framework.
- **Cascading:** Cascading [21] is light-weight programming library which builds upon the Hadoop processing framework. It provides a higher-level programming abstraction which lets developers express their data analysis problems as self-contained, reusable workflows rather than a sequence of individual MapReduce jobs. At runtime, however, Cascading disassembles the workflow into individual MapReduce jobs and sends them to the Hadoop cluster for the actual execution. The Cascading API is written in Java, so the data analysis workflows must be implemented in Java as well.
- **Pig:** Pig (Sect. 4.3.1) is another higher-level programming abstraction on top of Apache Hadoop. Unlike Cascading, Pig comes with a custom query language called Pig Latin [13] which must be used to express the data analysis problem. Although Pig Latin allows developers to extend the capabilities of the language by user-defined Java functions, it is significantly more declarative compared to the previous three ways of defining a Elastic MapReduce job flow. Therefore, Pig Latin queries are translated into a sequence of MapReduce jobs by a special compiler and then executed on the Hadoop cluster. Moreover, Pig also implicitly supports schemas and types.
- **Hive:** Similar to Pig, Hive [18] is another declarative query language which uses Hadoop as its execution engine. The Hive query language (Sect. 4.3.3) is heavily

influenced by traditional SQL-style languages. Therefore, in comparison to Pig, it relies heavily on schema information and types. Hive also supports user-defined functions written in Java, however, this feature is not as prominent in the language specification as in Pig Latin. At runtime, Hive queries are also compiled into a sequence of MapReduce jobs which are then executed on the Hadoop cluster.

Independent of the way the Elastic MapReduce job flow is specified, its execution always entails three mandatory steps:

First, the input data, i.e. the data the Elastic MapReduce job flow is supposed to work on, must be uploaded to Amazon's storage service S3. Second, after having uploaded the job flow's input data to S3, the customer submits his actual job flow to the Elastic MapReduce service. Amazon offers to submit the job flow using the management website, their command line tools, or the web service API. As part of the submission process, the customer must also specify the parameters for the Hadoop cluster which is booted on EC2 in order to process the job. These parameters include the virtual machine type and the initial number of virtual machines to start. Since Hadoop has not been designed to run in heterogeneous setups, all virtual machines must be of the same type. Moreover, each job flow always runs on a separate set of virtual machines. Following the guidelines of the EC2 compute services, the number of virtual machines each customer can acquire at a time is initially limited to 20. However, the customer can apply for an increase of his virtual machine limit.

Amazon Elastic MapReduce supports resizing of the set of virtual machines the customer's Hadoop cluster runs. That way the customer can respond to unexpected changes in the workload during the execution of his job flow. However, in order to guard against unintended loss of intermediate data, Amazon puts some restrictions on the possible resize operations.

As illustrated in Fig. 6.3, Amazon Elastic MapReduce separates the set of virtual machines a customer's Hadoop cluster consists of three distinct groups, the so-called instance groups. The master instance group only contains one virtual machine. This virtual machine runs the Hadoop JobTracker which coordinates the execution of the job's individual map and reduce tasks. The second group is the so-called core instance group. The core instance group contains one or more virtual machines which act as worker nodes for the Hadoop cluster. These machines run a so-called Hadoop TaskTracker which actually executes the work packages assigned by the JobTracker as well as a so-called HDFS DataNode. When running an HDFS DataNode, the virtual machine takes part in the Hadoop Distributed File System (HDFS) and contributes parts of its local storage to the overall file system capacity. Hadoop relies heavily on HDFS in order to store intermediate results between two consecutive MapReduce jobs. Although the data stored in HDFS is replicated across different virtual machines, removing virtual machines from the core instance group increases the risk of losing this intermediate data. For this reason, Elastic MapReduce allows customers to add additional virtual machines to the core instance group during the runtime of a job flow, but not to remove them.

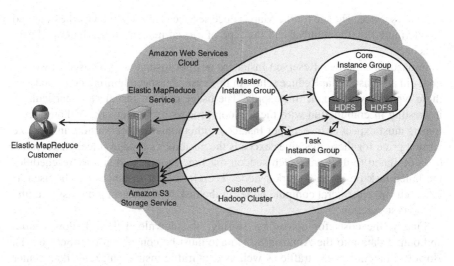

Fig. 6.3 Architectural overview of Elastic MapReduce

In contrast to the core instance group, virtual machines from the third group, the so-called task instance group, only run a Hadoop TaskTracker and do not participate in the HDFS. As a result, these nodes do not store intermediate results. Instead, each MapReduce job executed on these virtual machines either reads its input data remotely from the S3 storage or from a virtual machine of the core instance group. Elastic MapReduce allows customers to add and remove virtual machines from this group at any time. In case a virtual machine is terminated while processing a task, Hadoop's regular fault tolerance mechanisms take effect to compensate the hardware outage.

Finally, after a job flow has been successfully executed, its output data is written back to Amazon S3. The set of virtual machines which was used to run the Hadoop cluster is automatically shut down unless the customer explicitly specifies not to do so.

Pricing Model

The pricing model of Elastic MapReduce is tightly interwoven with the infrastructure components it builds upon. In general, the cost for executing a job flow depends on the amount of input and output data, the number and type of virtual machines used to setup the Hadoop cluster and execute the flow as well as the duration of the flow execution.

The billing of the virtual machines for the Hadoop cluster follows the same pricing model as the underlying EC2 compute cloud. A customer has to pay for each virtual machine by the hour, depending on the virtual machine type. Moreover, Amazon charges an additional fee for the Elastic MapReduce running on top their compute service. The fee for the MapReduce service is also charged by the hour and is determined by the number and the type of virtual machines the Hadoop cluster runs on.

Amazon also allows Reserved Instances or Spot Instances to be used as worker nodes in an Elastic MapReduce setup. In this case, the special billing conditions for these types of virtual machines apply. The usage of Spot Instances is particularly interesting in conjunction with the Hadoop processing framework. Although customers must expect to lose a Spot Instance without any further warning in case the current price for these machines exceeds the customer's bidden price, Hadoop has been designed to deal with such sudden machine failures and simply reschedules the failed task on another worker node. Therefore Spot Instances can be used as rather cheap, ephemeral compute nodes in the task instance group discussed in the previous subsection.

Finally, the costs for uploading, storing, and download the job flow's input and output data into the Amazon S3 storage must be considered (see Sect. 6.2.1). However, incoming data traffic as well as data traffic inside Amazon's data center (for example when data is transferred to virtual machines on EC2) is free of charge. In order to avoid excessive data transfer time and costs, Amazon also offers a service called AWS Import/Export. Customers using this service can send in physical storage devices like hard drives to Amazon's data centers. Amazon then either copies the devices' data to the S3 storage, or vice versa, creates a backup of the S3 data on the device and mails it back to be customer. As of August 2012, the cost for using this service was $80.00 per physical storage device plus an additional fee of $2.49 for each hour of data loading. Moreover, Amazon's regular fees for accessing objects on S3 add to the overall cost.

Performance Characteristics

The performance of Elastic MapReduce is largely influenced by the performance of the underlying compute and storage services EC2 and S3. Since we have already discussed the performance characteristics of Amazon EC2 in the previous subsection, this section will focus on the performance characteristics of Amazon S3.

Elastic MapReduce relies on S3 for storing a job flow's input and output data. Therefore, depending on the computational complexity of the processing job, the rate with which data can be read from and written to the service can be critical for the efficiency of the overall job execution. The authors Palankar et al. have evaluated Amazon S3 with respect to its suitability for scientific applications [15]. According to their results, S3's read performance for small objects (less than 1 MB in size) suffers significantly from the HTTP overhead that occurs with each object request. For larger objects, however, the authors found the HTTP overhead to become negligible, resulting in rates of approximately 20–30 MB/s per object and virtual machine, depending on the concrete experiment.

Interoperability

All the software components the Elastic MapReduce builds upon are available as open source software. As a result, any processing job which has been developed for the Elastic MapReduce service can in principle also be deployed on a local cluster or within an Infrastructure-as-a-Service environment.

In order to access the data on their S3 storage, Amazon has developed a set of lightweight protocols based on the popular web technologies REST and SOAP. As a consequence, a plethora of tools to simplify the data management has evolved around Amazon's storage service in recent years.

6.2.3 Microsoft Windows Azure

Microsoft announced to enter the cloud market in 2008 with their Platform-as-a-Service stack named the Windows Azure platform. In comparison to other PaaS offerings, which often rely on third-party software as building blocks for their actual services, the Windows Azure platform is entirely built on Microsoft's own software components, ranging from the data center software to the development tools for the customers. The Windows Azure platform is available to commercial customers since February 2010.

Service Offered

According to Microsoft, the Windows Azure platform is targeted to offer a reliable, scalable, and maintenance-free platform for Windows applications. Technically, Microsoft's cloud offering is centered around three major components:

- **Windows Azure:** Windows Azure builds the technological foundation to run Windows applications and store their data in the cloud. It provides a variety of programming interfaces which allow developers to write scalable and fault-tolerant applications. Windows Azure itself is divided into three core services, a compute service, a storage service, and a Content Distribution Network (CDN). While the compute service provides a framework for developing and executing Windows-based applications in the cloud, the storage service is responsible for providing persistent and durable storage. This includes a Binary Large Object (BLOB) service for storing text or binary data as well as a so-called Queue service for reliable message passing between services. Finally, the CDN is targeted to offer low-latency delivery of static data to end users worldwide.
- **SQL Azure:** With SQL Azure, Microsoft announced to offer an Internet scale relational database service providing full SQL language support. Building upon Microsoft SQL server technology [3], SQL Azure uses a partitioned database model over a large set of shared-nothing servers. It supports local transactions

through its so-called read committed snapshot isolation (RCSI) model, i.e. transactions that do not span multiple SQL Azure databases.

- **Windows Azure AppFabric:** Windows Azure AppFabric refers to a set of services designed to bridge the gap between local on-premise and cloud-hosted applications. The two most important services are probably Access Control and Service Bus. Access Control provides a federated identity management system that integrates enterprise directories such as Active Directory with web identity providers such as Windows LiveID, Google, Yahoo and Facebook. In contrast to that, Service Bus offers simplified inter-application communication across organizational boundaries.

Recently, Microsoft added a fourth major component to their Windows Azure platform. Formerly code-named Dallas and now marketed under the name Windows Azure Marketplace, this forth component enables customers to acquire access to large body of both commercial and public domain data sets. However, since this component does not fall into the "Platform-as-a-Service"-category, it is discussed in Sect. 6.3 in more detail.

Similar to the MapReduce pattern, applications for Windows Azure must obey a particular structure in order to take full advantage of the platform's scalability and fault tolerance capabilities. Microsoft refers to this structure as so-called roles in which the individual components of a Windows Azure application are expected to be split into. The so-called Web role is designed for those components which represent the application's visible surface, i.e. either the user interface or Web Service interfaces. In contrast to that, components which implement the actual application logic are supposed to inherit a so-called Worker role.

In order to implement the individual components according to their respective roles, Microsoft offers Software Development Kits for a variety of programming languages including the .NET language family such as Visual Basic and C#, but also supports third-party languages like Java or PHP. Web role components can also be implemented using Mircosoft's web-related technologies such as ASP.NET or, more general, the Windows Communication Foundation (WCF).

After the developer has finished implementing the application, each of its component, no matter if of Web or Worker role, runs inside its own virtual machine, which is controlled by the Azure Platform. This strict separation of the application components is pivotal for exploiting the Windows Azure's scalability and fault tolerance features. For example, in order to respond to changing workloads, Windows Azure allows to create multiple instances of each application component. Load balancing mechanisms built into the Web role then attempt to balance the incoming requests among the available instances. Moreover, if one instance of an application component fails, its virtual machine is simply terminated and restarted on another machine.

As a consequence of this application model, communication among the individual application components (or instances thereof) is only possible through predefined mechanisms such as the previously mentioned Windows Azure Queue service or the Windows Communication Foundation (WCF). In addition, the

Size	CPU	Memory	Storage	I/O Performance	Cost per Hour
Extra Small	1.0 GHz	768 MB	20 GB	Low	0.05 USD
Small	1.6 GHz	1.75 GB	225 GB	Moderate	0.12 USD
Medium	2 × 1.6 GHz	3.5 GB	490 GB	High	0.24 USD
Large	4 × 1.6 GHz	7 GB	1,000 GB	High	0.48 USD
Extra Large	8 × 1.6 GHz	14 GB	2,040 GB	High	0.96 USD

Fig. 6.4 Overview of virtual machines types available at the Windows Azure platform

application components themselves are expected to be stateless. Any application state must either be written to one of Azure storage facilities, for example SQL Azure, or pushed back to the client in the form of a web cookie.

In order to support legacy applications, which do not follow this novel Azure application model, Microsoft recently introduced a third role, the so-called virtual machine role. Instead of writing distinct application components, the virtual machine role lets customers create custom Windows Server 2008 virtual machine images and, by that means, deploy classic server applications on Microsoft's cloud platform. However, since the applications running inside those virtual machine roles cannot take advantage of Azure's scalability and fault tolerance features, Microsoft considers the this role mainly as a interim solution to support their customers in porting their existing applications to the new application model.

Pricing Model

Similar to other cloud providers, Microsoft also follows a pay-as-you-go pricing model with their Windows Azure platform; customers are therefore charged only for the data center resources they really use. The concrete pricing model depends on the Azure service being used. In the following, we will provide a short overview of the compute, storage, and database pricing model.

The compute capacity that a customer consumes on the Windows Azure platform is charged by the hour, starting at the moment the Windows Azure application is deployed. Partial compute hours are also billed as full hours. As described in the previous subsection, the Windows Azure application model requires each instance of an application component to run in a separate virtual machine. The hourly fee for running the entire application on the Windows Azure platform is therefore determined by the number of deployed virtual machines as well as their type. Figure 6.4 illustrates the cost per hour for each virtual machine type and their hardware characteristics as of August 2012.

The costs for storage on Windows Azure is calculated by averaging by daily amount of data stored (in gigabyte) over a monthly period. As of August 2012, the monthly fee for storing 1 GB of data on Microsoft's cloud was $0.15. In addition, Microsoft charged $0.01 per 10,000 storage transactions. Similar to Amazon's storage offerings, customers of Windows Azure must also take the cost for the data traffic into account which occurs when the data is accessed from outside the respective Azure data center. While inbound data transfers are generally free of charge, outbound traffic is billed at approximately $0.15–$0.20 per GB (as of August 2012), depending on the geographic region the data center is located in.

The database SQL Azure is available in two different versions, the web and the business edition. The choice of the version also affects the billing of the service. As their names imply, the web edition of SQL Azure is targeted to support small web-based applications while the business edition aims at offering a foundation for commercial Software-as-a-Service applications of independent software vendors. In general, the usage of SQL Azure is charged on a monthly basis, depending on the size of relational database instances. Databases of the web edition can grow up to 5 GB in size, as of August 2012, cost between $10 and $50 per month. In contrast to that, databases of the business edition provide up to 150 GB of storage ranged between $100 and $500 per month.

Performance Characteristics

Due to the relatively recent launch of the Windows Azure platform, only few independent evaluations are available so far.

Early performance observations of Windows Azure have been presented by Hill et al. [8]. The researchers conducted several performance experiments on Microsoft's cloud platform from October 2009 to February 2010. According to their conclusion, Windows Azure generally offers good performance compared to commodity hardware within in the enterprise. However, the authors also report relatively long instantiation times for new virtual machines (about 10 min on the average). In addition, they found the average transaction time for TPC-E queries on SQL Azure to be almost twice as high compared to an on-premise setup using the traditional Microsoft SQL Server 2008.

The survey of Kossmann et al. [9] focuses on the comparison of different cloud-based databases systems for transaction processing. The authors describe the different system architectures the respective databases build upon and illustrate the performance characteristics of the systems using the TPC-W benchmark. According to their results, SQL Azure offers good scalability and performance properties for the tested workloads in comparison to competitors like Amazon RDS and SimpleDB. Moreover, the authors highlight the good cost properties of SQL Azure for medium to large workloads.

Interoperability

According to a Microsoft website [11], interoperability has been a major goal in the design of the Windows Azure Platform. Indeed, Microsoft decided to support several open protocols which simplify the data portability between their cloud platform and third-party components. For example, the Azure storage service typically can be accessed using open Internet protocols like SOAP or REST, the database service SQL Azure offers a traditional ODBC interface.

However, while the risk of a data lock-in on the Windows Azure platform is relatively low, as for every "Platform-as-a-Service"-offering, the platform dependence must be carefully considered in the development process of new applications.

The technical foundation for any Windows Azure application is Windows Server 2008, so in principle Windows Azure can run any existing Windows application. However, in order to take full advantage of the platform features, namely the scalability and fault tolerance, it is necessary to modify the application structure to a certain extent. This involves the decoupling of application parts in independent components according to the different roles described in the previous subsections. Moreover, the internal state as well as the communication between these components must be transferred to the more reliable and persistent platform services such as SQL Azure or the Azure message queue service. In general, the tighter the application becomes interwoven with the Azure-specific services, the better its robustness and scalability will be on the one hand. However, one the other hand, the harder it will be to port the application back to a traditional Windows environment.

For customers who cannot store their data off-premise, Microsoft also offers Windows Azure Platform Appliances. Following the notion of a private cloud, it enables a customer to deploy the Azure cloud platform in his own data center while maintaining compatibility with the interfaces of the public cloud.

6.3 Software- and Data-as-a-Service

In the same spirit as the other members of the "as-a-Service"-family, Software-as-a-Service (SaaS) and Data-as-a-Service (DaaS) describe an approach to provide software services and commonly used data respectively at a central place and make them available to users in a timely and cost efficient manner. The SaaS offers range from productivity tools like email (e.g. Google Mail, Hotmail) and calendar (Google Calendar) over office applications (e.g. Google Drive, Office 365) to typical enterprise applications such as CRM or ERP systems. Most prominent examples of the latter are for example Salesforce.com offering CRM solutions and SAP Business ByDesign for ERP and CRM. SaaS solutions rely either on PaaS solutions to achieve robustness and scalability or at least use techniques described in the previous chapters to support virtualization and multi-tenancy [6]. Therefore, we will not discuss them here but focus in the following on the DaaS layer.

By using already matured web technologies such as the service-oriented architecture based on Web services with SOAP or REST APIs as well as new protocols for reading and writing data, such as the Open Data Protocol (ODATA) from Microsoft and the Google Data Protocol (GDATA), the place where the data resides has been become almost irrelevant. These standardized APIs allow users to build their applications in an on-demand fashion by integrating and mashing up third-party data with minimal implementation effort. On the other side, data providers are able to concentrate on their business which includes cleaning, integrating and refining data. Since one data provider is usually responsible for one specific data set this also improves the data quality because there is a single point for updates.

The whole Data-as-a-Service topic is mainly driven by the Open Data community which should be highlighted in the following. Additionally, we will classify open data platforms especially in terms of data reusability. Furthermore, we will sketch the status quo of commercial DaaS platforms, list the main players and discuss their business models. We conclude this section with an outlook beyond Data-as-a-Service and briefly illustrate the software ecosystem around DaaS.

6.3.1   The Open Data Trend

The concept of "Open Data" describes data that is freely available and can be used as well as republished by everyone without restrictions from copyright or patents. The goal of the Open Data movement is to open all non-personal and non-commercial data, especially (but not exclusively) all data collected and processed by government organizations. It is very similar in spirit to the open source or open access movements. Of course, there exist general limits in terms of data openness which should not be exceeded, e.g. the publication of diplomatic cables at Wikileaks. However, for a vast majority of data there are genuine reasons for being open. This applies to all data which have an infrastructural role essential for the civil use or the scientific endeavor, e.g. maps, public transport schedules, human genome, medical science, spending's or environmental pollution data. OpenStreetMap is a good example where the respective infrastructure information (the geographic data) was not open, which led to the well-known crowdsource initiative. The Open Data paradigm further applies to factual data (e.g. results of scientific experiments) which is not copyrightable or data that was generated with the help of public money or by a government institution. Opening up all this data to the public promises many advantages: ensuring transparency and accountability, improving efficiency of the government and their institutions, encouraging innovation and economic growth as well as educating and influencing people [17].

In the course of this trend, public agencies have started making governmental data available using web portals, web services or REST interfaces. Famous examples in this context are data.gov, data.gov.uk or offenedaten.de. The data published on these platforms covers a wide range of domains, from environmental data over employment statistics to the budgets of municipalities. Publishers can be individual government agencies or providers of larger repositories that collect public data sets and make them available in a centralized and possibly standardized way. Ideally, making this data available on the web would lead to more transparency, participation and innovation throughout society. However, publishing Open Data in the right way is a challenging task. In the following we want to illustrate a typical Open Data use case and discuss the data divide problem, which distinguishes between users who have access and the respective skills to make effective use of data those who do not. To conclude this chapter we will briefly discuss the properties an Open Data platform should have in order to maximize data reusability.

Use Case

Let us imagine university professors who are interested in research funding, e.g. where is which amount of money going? Which are the most subsidized projects and topics? Which institution is financed by which research funding organization? Have their been changes over time? In the first step, they need to get a detailed overview which funding organization provides open data sets, how this data is structured and how it can be interpreted. The most crucial part within this first step is the ability to find open data sets relevant for the specific problem, i.e. to have a central and responsive entry point where users can search for terms such as "NSF", "EU FP7" or "DFG". Given that some data sets have been found, this loosely coupled information has little value at this point and needs to be aligned on a technical and semantical level first. This can be very time consuming and hard work, since the data can be very heterogeneous. First of all, the file formats can be different, because, for example, one agency uses Open Office while another one prefers to publish everything as PDFs. Furthermore, the schema of the data can have significant differences such as one data set representing a name and address as a composite string whereas in another data set this information is normalized. Heterogeneity can also be found in data types (e.g. by using different currencies for subsidies) as well as the data (e.g. by using acronyms instead of the complete spelling). Ideally, all available open data sets are already aligned and described in a homogeneous manner. In practice, however, this is rarely the case, since for example each funding institution has it's own publishing policies. Nevertheless, in order to unburden the user from the data integration workload we need automatic tools (format converters, schema matchers, etc.) that already preprocess the data as far as possible. To extract knowledge from the integrated data sets, e.g. funding opportunities for a professors group, we have to empower the users to explore the data in a do-it-yourself manner and to visualize the results. In this regard, we need again a chain of tools that can be easily applied to the open data sets. What we can see from this example is that both, the integration and the exploitation part, requires machine-readable data (discoverable, standardized, explorable, etc.) in order to support the user in reusing this information.

The Data Divide

Government data could be a valuable resource of information if published in a proper manner. However, most end-users are not able to access the right data or to make use of it. Figure 6.5 illustrates this problem, which is sometimes called the *data divide*. As shown in the picture, there is no direct path from the data to the user. However, there are two approaches depicted, which can make the raw data more comprehensible for end-users. The first approach, depicted on the right, aims at providing the public with human-readable information instead of raw data. This usually means that existing raw data is transformed into documents, containing, for example, aggregated values, visualization or, more generally, simplifications

Fig. 6.5 The data divide, and
the two paths crossing it

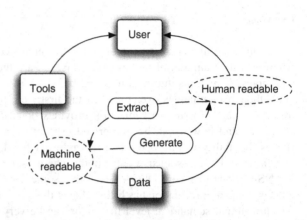

Fig. 6.5 The data divide, and the two paths crossing it

to make data comprehensible. A good human-readable report on research funding might solve our described use case if it contains the desired information. But it might also miss some important detail or not contain the required information, since it only contains the information that the report's author intended it to contain. Which means that, in our use case, the professors can only hope that someone created a report containing exactly the information they want. Such a manufactured report does not allow users to gain other insights than the ones provided by the author. It does also not allow reuse of the underlying raw data for other use cases. The process of regaining data from human-readable documents, i.e. data extraction, is very challenging and forms its own branch of research in computer science.

The second approach is publishing the raw data in a machine-readable format to enable software tools to process it. As the raw data is not useful for end-users, this approach requires experts who know how to use these tools, to sift through the available data, to understand it and to transform it into useful information. Not every user has the required expertise. But similar arguments have been made concerning another *open* movement: open source. Most people will not be able to make any use of a given piece of source code. Still, if one in thousand users has the skills to fix a critical security bug, all will profit. The same is possible for open data. If the raw data is available in a machine-readable format, it enables automatic processing and thus, makes the development of analysis tools a bit easier. In the end, all users can benefit from end user friendly tools. The professors in our use case may not have the skills or the time to process the raw, machine-readable data, but with adequate tools, they can find and analyze the datasets they need. And since the data is freely available in this machine-readable format, it can be reused for another use case without extra processing.

We argue in favor of the second approach, since it does not limit the number of possible use cases, but instead supports reusability. However, to be suited for reuse of the data, an ideal open data platform should be optimized towards technical users and programmatic reuse.

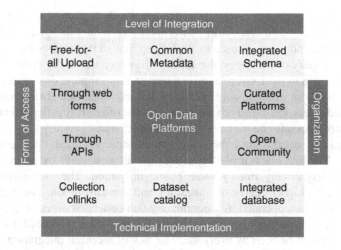

Fig. 6.6 Classification of open data platforms

Classification of Open Data Platforms

Open data platforms can be classified according several dimensions, which include the form of access, the technical implementation, the organization and the level of integration, illustrated in Fig. 6.6. While an API seems like a mandatory part of an open data portal a previous study [2] showed that 43 % of 50 open data platforms do not feature an API, but instead allow only manual download through listings of data sets. Without an API, a platform specific crawler would be required to access the data sets in order to allow an automatic processing. An API that offers access to standardized package metadata is a good first step. If a platform allows direct access to the data sets through the API, instead of providing file download links, users could automatically access that part of the data that is of interest, without the need to download the entire data set. This usually requires that the raw data is stored in a database management system.

Concerning the technical implementation, Braunschweig et al. [2] showed that the most common variant is a *collection of links*, which accounts for 55 % of the surveyed open data platforms. These platforms host only metadata, and store URLs as the only way of accessing data. This class is not only the largest, but also generally the least useful one. According to [2] of the provided links do not resolve to a working file download. Due to the distribution of the data over many different "spheres of influence", these platforms also have a lower level of standardization and integration between data sets. In contrast to link collections, data set catalogs materialize the provided information. Interestingly, platforms implementing this simple concept have a much higher level of standardization which directly improves their reusability [2]. *Integrated databases* represent the smallest class within the technical implementation. These platforms do not operate on the level of individual data sets or files, but offer integrated data sets using a database management system.

This difference in storage manifests in the actual web platform through the ability to filter and query data sets. Most platforms use relational data, but Linked Data (e.g. SPARQL endpoints) is used as well. Even though these repositories offer the highest reusability of data, they also achieve the poorest diversity of available data sets. This is due to the fixed relational schemata they employ: data.worldbank.org and data.un.org for example only offer statistical values that are always relative to a country and a year. On the other side, platforms that offer many different completely uncorrelated data sets can not resort to a unified schema.

In terms of organization there are curated and so-called open community platforms. The first class of platforms does not allow uploads by users. They are moderated and usually run by some public institution. The moderation allows them to have a higher degree of integration and standardization. The non-curated platforms are often operated by a community that collects sources of open data or raw data sets. In contrast to curated repositories, they offer facilities for uploading data sets that can be used by everyone. The lack of a central integration authority usually leads to less structured repositories. However, in countries that do not have an open data legislation, these are often the only platforms that exist.

The integration dimension is concerned with the establishment of uniformity across multiple data sets, which makes it easier for users to recombine different data sets. *Free-for-all Upload* repositories have no regulations concerning data sets that are published. Platforms in this category do not have standardization features such as standardized file format, domain categories as well as no spatial nor temporal metadata. The next category (*Common Metadata*) contains repositories which apply restrictions to the data sets or metadata that can be attached to them. Examples would be restricting the possible file types allowed for upload, or defining the date format for validity intervals of data sets. *Integrated Schema* platforms offers the highest degree of integration. These type of repositories may use one global schema for all data sets or map all data sets to a global domain ontology. Platforms that we categorized as centralized databases usually have an underlying relational schema, even it is not explicitly stated. As discussed above, platforms like data.worldbank.org and data.un.org use the same combination of attributes for a large number of datasets, usually mapping from a country and a year to an attribute value. Still, the schema is not being made explicit, and the integration of more complex relations remains an open problem.

6.3.2   Data Markets and Pricing models

Beside the non-commercial Open Data platforms that are mainly driven by government agencies or communities, there is also a rising interest for commercial DaaS, so-called data markets. Just like Open Data platforms, data markets provide a central entry point to discover, explore and analyze data. However, commercial platforms have a concrete business model which allows them to invest a lot of effort into cleaning, integrating, and refining the data. Data market customers are charged according different pricing models, based on data volume or the type of the requested data. The volume-base model distinguishes between quantity-based pricing where vendors are charged regarding the size of the data and the pay-per-call model, where each API call is taken into account e.g. customers pay for a specific number of transactions per month. Other platforms use a type-based model and offer different prices for different data domains as well for different data representations (tables, blobs, visualizations, etc.) Some vendors also allow data reselling, provided that the customer pays a commission (e.g. 20 % on non-free datasets at the Windows Azure Marketplace).

During the last year dozens of DaaS providers appeared in the market from which the most established should be highlighted in the following. Microsoft's Windows Azure Marketplace DataMarket[3] (former codename Dallas) was launched in 2010. The provided data sets include, among others, those from the Environmental Systems Research Institute (GIS data), Wolfram Alpha (which has high quality curated dataset in their backend systems) and the World Bank. Azure DataMarket is using the OData protocol which is already supported by most of the Microsoft's office tools such as Excel or PowerPivot, allowing direct access to the marketplace data. Factual[4] was one of the first vendors within the DaaS market and is specialized in geodata, e.g. 60 million entities in about 50 countries. To improve the overall quality the company offers discounts to their customers when they share edited and curated data back. In contrast to Factual, Infochimps[5] provides broad range of different data domains which includes 15,000 data sets from about 200 providers, e.g. Wikipedia articles, Twitter sentiment metrics for websites, census demographics and so on. Additionally Infochimps offers a set of cloud-based tools that simplifies the development of scale-out database environments. Another company, DataMarket,[6] offers more than 23,000 data sets of various topics but with a focus on country and industry statistics, e.g. data from the UN, the World Bank, Eurostat, Gapminder and others. DataMarket states that they hold more than 100 million time series. The platform also provides a wide range of tools to refine and visualize their data sets. In addition to these major players, there is a huge variety of small data suppliers not worth mentioning in the context of this book.

6.3.3   Beyond "Data-as-a-Service"

To make DaaS easily accessible novel exploitation tools for enriching, integrating, analyzing, and visualizing data are being developed. Most of them are implemented as web services which allows to build a whole data analytics stack by doing some

---

[3]http://datamarket.azure.com.

[4]http://www.factual.com.

[5]http://www.infochimps.com/.

[6]http://www.datamarket.com/.

simple service calls. For example, WolframAlpha, which is based on the software Mathematica, offers services to calculate mathematical expressions and to represent information. The service OpenCalais, developed by Thomsen Reuters, receives unstructured documents and extracts entities (people, organizations, products, etc.), facts, and events and then adds them as metadata to documents. In addition, a knowledge base is used to create associations to other documents. By doing so, documents can be transferred into a structured form and used for further data analyses. Google Fusion Tables [7], as a very popular example, provides tools for users to upload tabular data files, join, filter, and aggregate the data and visualize the results. The interface is a standard, menu-based point and click interface, no steps of the process are assisted or automated. Similar tools are GeoCommons[7] and to some extend ManyEyes,[8] which focus on the visualization and do not offer analytical functions. One of the more successful platforms focusing on end-user data mashup's is Yahoo Pipes.[9] It uses a visual data flow language to merge and filter feeds and to model user input. Executing a pipe (a data flow) results in a new feed, which can include parameters that the user specifies on execution. Resulting feed data can be displayed as a list, or on a map if the items contain spatial data. The system offers many operators and thus a high degree of flexibility, but lacks visualization or data other data exploration features, instead focusing on merging and processing of data. Furthermore, to use the system, the user has to understand the concept of data flow graphs, as well as many specific mashup problems, for example how web services are called with URL parameters.

6.4 Summary

Today, various cloud-based services for data management are available. These services range from renting virtual machine instances over storage space, different database solutions including SQL and NoSQL systems, data analytics platforms to software and data services and, in this way, address all of the levels of cloud computing. This situation allows customers to choose services fulfilling their requirements in terms of level of abstraction, performance and scalability as well as billing model. Furthermore, recent developments and initiatives such as OpenStack aim to avoid vendor lock-ins.

In this chapter, we have presented some selected representative examples of commercially available cloud services for data management. These examples shall both demonstrate the variety of available services and give the reader an overview on features, pricing models, and interoperability issues. The presentation reflects the

---

[7]http://geocommons.com/.

[8]http://www-958.ibm.com/software/data/cognos/manyeyes/.

[9]http://pipes.yahoo.com/pipes/.

current[10] market situation but is not intended to give a complete market overview. Furthermore, it should be noted that the area of cloud-based services is a fast-paced and vibrant business where constantly newly developed features are added, prices and pricing models may change and new offerings may appear on the market.

References

1. Barham, P., Dragovic, B., Fraser, K., Hand, S., Harris, T., Ho, A., Neugebauer, R., Pratt, I., Warfield, A.: Xen and the art of virtualization. SIGOPS **37**, 164–177 (2003)
2. Braunschweig, K., Eberius, J., Thiele, M., Lehner, W.: The state of open data - limits of current open data platforms. In: WWW conference (2012)
3. Campbell, D.G., Kakivaya, G., Ellis, N.: Extreme scale with full sql language support in microsoft sql azure. In: SIGMOD, pp. 1021–1024 (2010)
4. DeCandia, G., Hastorun, D., Jampani, M., Kakulapati, G., Lakshman, A., Pilchin, A., Sivasubramanian, S., Vosshall, P., Vogels, W.: Dynamo: amazon's highly available key-value store. In: SOSP, pp. 205–220 (2007)
5. Dornemann, T., Juhnke, E., Freisleben, B.: On-demand resource provisioning for BPEL workflows using Amazon's Elastic Compute Cloud. In: CCGRID, pp. 140–147 (2009)
6. The force.com multitenant architecture – understanding the design of salesforce.com's internet application development platform. White Paper. http://www.developerforce.com/media/ForcedotcomBookLibrary/Force.com_Multitenancy_WP_101508.pdf
7. Gonzalez, H., Halevy, A.Y., Jensen, C.S., Langen, A., Madhavan, J., Shapley, R., Shen, W., Goldberg-Kidon, J.: Google fusion tables: web-centered data management and collaboration. In: SIGMOD conference (2010)
8. Hill, Z., Li, J., Mao, M., Ruiz-Alvarez, A., Humphrey, M.: Early observations on the performance of windows azure. In: HPDC, pp. 367–376 (2010)
9. Kossmann, D., Kraska, T., Loesing, S.: An evaluation of alternative architectures for transaction processing in the cloud. In: SIGMOD, pp. 579–590 (2010)
10. Marshall, P., Keahey, K., Freeman, T.: Elastic site: Using clouds to elastically extend site resources. In: CCGRID, pp. 43–52 (2010)
11. Microsoft Corp.: Windows azure platform and interoperability. http://www.microsoft.com/windowsazure/interop/
12. Nurmi, D., Wolski, R., Grzegorczyk, C., Obertelli, G., Soman, S., Youseff, L., Zagorodnov, D.: The eucalyptus open-source cloud-computing system. In: CCGRID, pp. 124–131 (2009)
13. Olston, C., Reed, B., Srivastava, U., Kumar, R., Tomkins, A.: Pig latin: a not-so-foreign language for data processing. In: Proceedings of the ACM International Conference on Management of Data (SIGMOD), pp. 1099–1110 (2008)
14. Ostermann, S., Iosup, A., Yigitbasi, N., Prodan, R., Fahringer, T., Epema, D.: A performance analysis of EC2 cloud computing services for scientific computing. In: Lecture Notes of the Institute for Computer Sciences, Social Informatics and Telecommunications Engineering, vol. 34, pp. 115–131. Springer-Verlag GmbH (2010)
15. Palankar, M.R., Iamnitchi, A., Ripeanu, M., Garfinkel, S.: Amazon s3 for science grids: a viable solution? In: DADC, pp. 55–64 (2008)
16. Schad, J., Dittrich, J., Quiané-Ruiz, J.A.: Runtime measurements in the cloud: Observing, analyzing, and reducing variance. PVLDB **3**, 460–471 (2010)

---

[10]Summer 2012.

17. Schellong, A., Stepanets, E.: Unchartered waters - the state of open data in europe. CSC Deutschland Solutions GmbH (2011)
18. Thusoo, A., Sarma, J.S., Jain, N., Shao, Z., Chakka, P., Anthony, S., Liu, H., Wyckoff, P., Murthy, R.: Hive: a warehousing solution over a map-reduce framework. VLDB Journal 2(2), 1626–1629 (2009)
19. Walker, E.: Benchmarking Amazon EC2 for high-performance scientific computing. USENIX; login: magazine 33(5), 18–23 (2008)
20. Wang, G., Ng, T.S.E.: The impact of virtualization on network performance of Amazon EC2 data center. In: INFOCOM, pp. 1163–1171 (2010)
21. Wensel, C.K.: Cascading: Defining and executing complex and fault tolerant data processing workflows on a hadoop cluster (2008). http://www.cascading.org
22. Yi, S., Kondo, D., Andrzejak, A.: Reducing costs of spot instances via checkpointing in the Amazon Elastic Compute Cloud. In: CLOUD, pp. 236–243 (2010)

Chapter 7
Summary and Outlook

The overall goal of this book is to give an in-depth introduction into the context of data management services running in the cloud. Since the "as-a-Service"-philosophy is considered one of the extremely relevant developments in computer and information technology and a huge number of different variants of services – ranging from infrastructural services to services providing access to complex software components – is already existing, it is time to provide a comprehensive overview and list of challenges for "Data-as-a-Service" (DaaS). The DaaS approach is not only relevant because data management is one of the ubiquitous core tasks in many service and application stacks and the market for database technologies is a very big and growing market. We also believe that this kind of service will change the way of how we will work with data and databases in the near future: in terms of data access, data volumes we can process, and building data-centric applications.

The basic idea of this book was to paint the big picture and bridge the gap between existing academic and "researchy" work on core database principles required for service-based data management offerings and the wealth of existing commercial and open-source systems.

In addition to providing the unified view on academic concepts and existing systems, the book also tries to structure the area of data management as a service in multiple directions. On the one hand, we intentionally position the concept of virtualization as the core of an efficient and flexible service offering. We have shown that software stacks for data management show at least four different opportunities to introduce a decoupling between provided and offered resources. Virtualization may start at the physical layer and abstract from specific CPU, main memory, and storage system; it may also be used to bundle multiple database scenarios on a database server, database or database schema level. The different opportunities may not only combined with each other, they may also show different variants at different levels. As shown, schema virtualization may be achieved using different methods providing different degree of isolation or sharing of data and metadata.

A further classification scheme, which was deployed within the book, comprises the differentiation of transactional and analytical workloads which pose very different challenges to data management, e.g. in terms of query support, data access,

W. Lehner and K.-U. Sattler, *Web-Scale Data Management for the Cloud*, DOI 10.1007/978-1-4614-6856-1_7, © Springer Science+Business Media New York 2013

and data consistency. Different database techniques are positioned suitable to cope with these specific requirements. For example, the CAP theorem and the notion of BASE consistency reflect the corner stones for transactional behavior in large-scale systems. We also presented techniques to manage large volumes of data while preserving consistency to a certain degree. For example, we discussed different alternatives of data fragmentation and types of data replication. Both topics are of fundamental importance to build reliable web-scale data management systems. In the context of analytical workloads, we outlined the core principles of parallel query processing using the MapReduce paradigm with some extensions especially in the context of declarative query languages.

As a third component, we presented different aspects of non-functional requirements and solutions of hosted data management services. For example, service-level agreements (SLAs) are not known in an on-premise setup, where the provided service only depends on the local infrastructure. In a web-scale and hosted environment, SLAs may be used to trade monetary efforts against a guaranteed quality of service. SLAs are also used within the DMaaS software stack to establish contracts with underlying software layers. A further, non-functional aspect addresses security concerns and techniques. We outlined different methods to implement joins or aggregation queries within a secured database environment.

As already mentioned, the book aims at providing conceptual foundations and insight into current systems and approaches in the wider context of data management in the cloud. We therefore provide a compact overview of systems in different "as-a-Service"-classes. Covering service offerings for "Infrastructure-", "Platform-", and "Software-as-a-Service", we intentionally added a comprehensive overview of existing and future services for data management as a service. In addition to commercial services like Microsoft Azure and Amazon AWS, we compiled information about the new trend of the Open Data initiative into the presentation.

7.1 Outlook, Current Trends, and Some Challenges

The general crux (and joy) of data management research and development is the permanent pressure from real-world scenarios. Applications are generating data and applications demand a comprehensive and efficient access to data. Perfect solutions provided for the yesterday's challenges are already questioned and usually no longer feasible for today's challenges. Research and development for data management solutions is therefore permanently reinventing itself. From that perspective, working in this context is extremely challenging, demanding, but also interesting to steadily push the envelope for novel methods and techniques.

Within the context of web-scale data management, we clearly see some major trends and challenges beyond fine-tuning and extending currently existing techniques.

- **Service planning and management:** Currently available data services provide a very good foundation for DaaS applications. However, we think there is significant research opportunity in providing support to "size" a hosted data management service in an optimal way. We would envision to have capacity management solutions available for the consumer and provider side. On the consumer side, capacity management may help to estimate the right number of nodes or database size depending on workload samples etc. Similarly, the same mechanisms may help the provider side to provision the infrastructure avoiding to violate SLAs or operating idle resources.

- **Service configuration:** As of now, a consumer of a data management service is tied to the functionality provided by the underlying infrastructure. For example, if the underlying system is providing full ACID semantics, the consumer has to take all the accompanying side-effects, if required for the application or not. In the other extreme, if the application is running BASE consistency but an application requires strict consistency to support some core application routines, either a switch to a different system or a compensation at the application layer is necessary. It would be therefore very applicable to have a configurable service layer where the application is able to sign a contract on the specific non-functional properties, i.e. agree on certain isolation/consistency or durability properties.

- **From batch processing to interactive analytics:** All techniques associated with the "Big Data" discussion are still centered around the notion of batch processing. However, since the "Big Data" move makes it more and more into supporting operational decisions, we clearly see the requirement to move to interactive analytical capabilities even over very large datasets. The Dremel project [2] may certainly be considered a first step into that direction.

- **Comprehensive solutions:** "Big Data"-platforms are reflecting a master-piece on a core database system level. However, in order to provide solutions for data management problems, those systems have to be enriched to provide a comprehensive platform for data management applications. On the one side, systems have to by extended with infrastructural service, like HIVE to provide tools for extracting and loading data into the platform. On the other side, there is a significant need to already provide pre-integrated data sources. For example in the context of biomolecular research, publicly available and de-facto standard databases (for genes, proteins etc.) can be provided in a pre-integrated way. Similar scenarios can be envisioned for commercial scenarios as well.

- **Crowd enablement:** Exploiting the crowd is an extremely interesting and relevant development, which should be incorporated into serviced data management scenarios. For example, crowd computing may alleviate data integration problems: data and schema integration algorithms may generate integration and mapping proposals which can be validated by members of the crowd if the problem is split into many small and easy to answer crowd queries. In the same way, task in data analytics may be outsourced to the anonymous members of a crowd seamlessly if a conceptual and technical integration exists.

In addition to requirements and challenges from a more service-oriented and infrastructural perspective, we also see a huge number of interesting research and development areas from a core database technology perspective:

- **Tight integration of application code and data management platform:** Good old user-defined functions (UDFs) provide a mean to push down any arbitrary application code into the database engine. In the context of data-intensive statistical processing, this mechanism is gaining more and more attention. However, the next-generation UDFs are required to provide an abstract and easy-to-use model to run application code in parallel. Similarly to the MapReduce programming model, parallel programming model frameworks are required to cope with the need for massive parallelization not only of the core database operators but also of the application code. Parallel programming and parallel database technology have to go together.

- **Fault tolerant query processing:** As massive parallelism is the name of the game, errors in a huge variety will be omnipresent. The database technology therefore has to move away from the "graceful degradation", i.e. stop a transaction as soon as an error occurs, to a "graceful progress"-principle. The Hadoop implementation taught that lesson to the database community, where it has to be picked up, generalized, and transferred to the more database engines.

- **Flexible schema support:** Considering the "variety" property of the "Big Data" characteristics, demanding a flexible mechanism to store different types of data is essential for future data management solutions. However, structural consistency, e.g. normal forms, referential integrity etc., is one of the main success factors of database systems. What is needed is a comprehensive support of flexible schemas on the conceptual as well as the implementation layer. The challenge on the conceptual layer is to bridge the gap from the extremely static classical database design principle to a "Big Table" approach [1], where adding a column is not controlled by any design guideline. On the implementation level, different storage formats should be automatically deployed by the record manager to provide the best performance for the current workload.

- **Secure query processing:** As already outlined in the book, secure query processing is an elegant way to support the demand for security in the context of cloud computing. However, we are convinced that many different scenarios enable different configurations of secure query processing or query answer validation. We see a significant demand of research in that direction.

- **Para-virtualization:** As intensively discussed in the book, virtualization represents the key concept for providing a scalable data management solution. However, we also see the drawback of virtualization if control over some components of the software stack gets lost. Pushing the notion of para-virtualization, the data management software would be able to "see" some details of the underlying stack and could ask for some specific characteristics of the provided environment. For example, the database system might request memory which is replicated within a node, within a cluster, within or beyond a computing center to provide a certain level of resilience.

7.2   ... the End

In summary, the book provides a comprehensive and detailed presentation of the current trends in the context of "Data-as-a-Service". We clearly consider – in addition the well-known three types of "as-a-Service"-types (IaaS, PaaS, and SaaS) – the "Data-as-a-Service"-philosophy a building block of large scale future applications serving both, transactional and analytical workloads for large data volumes on a per-use basis. To be able to lower TCO providing an efficient and flexible data management layer is the key of the success. In this book, we identified some problems and challenges and showed some solutions. More will definitely come in the very near future!

References

1. Chang, F., Dean, J., Ghemawat, S., Hsieh, W.C., Wallach, D.A., Burrows, M., Chandra, T., Fikes, A., Gruber, R.: Bigtable: A distributed storage system for structured data. In: OSDI, pp. 205–218 (2006)
2. Melnik, S., Gubarev, A., Long, J.J., Romer, G., Shivakumar, S., Tolton, M., Vassilakis, T.: Dremel: Interactive analysis of web-scale datasets. In: VLDB, pp. 330–339 (2010)

Printed in the United States
By Bookmasters

Printed in the United States
By Bookmasters